Archaeology

Under Fire

D1739374

Archaeology Under Fire is a ground-breaking collection which addresses the Middle East and Eastern Mediterranean as one of the most politically-charged regions in which archaeology is implicated. Historically, this area played a formative role in the emergence of archaeology as a discipline. However, until now, study of the sociopolitical implications of archaeology has focused on Western Europe rather than the region explored here, where the materiality and practice of archaeology is inextricably linked to the political and cultural realities faced by their respective peoples.

Leading academics present chapters on Cyprus, Greece, the former Yugoslavia, Bulgaria, Turkey, Lebanon, Iraq, Israel, the Gulf and Egypt, addressing the role of archaeology in current political issues, from ethnic cleansing in the Balkans to the division of Cyprus. Globalism, postcolonialism and the positive role of the past as a means of reconciliation are some of the themes explored in this volume. The contributors interweave theory and practice and demonstrate how this area of the world can provide a relevant model for understanding archaeological praxis.

Archaeology Under Fire will be essential reading for archaeology students and professionals and all those interested in the impact of the past on current political debate.

Lynn Meskell is Research Fellow at New College, Oxford. She has written extensively on Egyptian and Mediterranean archaeologies and the application of feminist theory and sociopolitics to archaeology.

Archaeology Under Fire

Nationalism, politics and heritage in the Eastern Mediterranean and Middle East

Edited by

Lynn Meskell

London and New York

First published 1998
by Routledge
11 New Fetter Lane, London EC4P 4EE

Simultaneously published
in the USA and Canada
by Routledge
29 West 35th Street, New York, NY 10001

Typeset in Perpetua and Bell Gothic by
RefineCatch Limited, Bungay, Suffolk
Printed and bound in Great Britain by
TJ International Ltd, Padstow, Cornwall

British Library Cataloguing in Publication Data
A catalogue record for this book is available
from the British Library

Library of Congress Cataloging in Publication Data
A catalog record for this book has been
requested

ISBN 0–415–16470–2 (hbk)
ISBN 0–415–19655–8 (pbk)

Contents

Contents

Illustrations

Contributors

Sophia Antoniadou is currently pursuing her PhD in archaeology at the University of Edinburgh studying trade and changes in social organisation in Late Bronze Age Cyprus. Her main interests are the later prehistory of Cyprus and the Western Mediterranean, the application of social theory to archaeology and the impact of politics in archaeological interpretation and practice. Her research is funded by an award from the A. G. Leventis Foundation.

Zainab Bahrani is a Lecturer in Art History and Critical Theory at the State University of New York, at Stony Brook. Her research and publications have focused on postcoloniality, cultural difference and the construction of Mesopotamia in Western discourse. She is currently working on a book, *Writing Presence: Assyrian Art, Colonialism and the Discourse of Oriental Antiquity*.

Douglass W. Bailey is Lecturer in European Prehistory in the School of History and Archaeology at the University of Wales at Cardiff. He is an expert on the later prehistory of southeastern Europe. His main publications focus on settlement, architecture and art of the late Neolithic (or Copper) Ages. Important publications include: Bailey *et al.* (forthcoming) 'Expanding the dimensions of early agricultural tells: the Podgoritsa Project, Bulgaria', *Journal of Field Archaeology*; and Bailey and Panayotov (eds) *Prehistoric Bulgaria*. He is currently directing fieldwork in southern Romania.

K. S. Brown is a lecturer in anthropology at the University of Wales, Lampeter. As well as work on the role of the past in the present, he has published chapters and articles on the relations between nationalism and expressive culture. He has conducted field and archive research in Macedonia on both sides of the former

Yugoslav–Greek border, and in the USA, and is now working on a project tracing the importance of migration in modern Balkan history.

Fekri A. Hassan is Flinders Petrie Professor of Archaeology at University College, London. He has excavated extensively in North Africa and the Middle East and is currently editor of the *African Archaeological Review*. His research interests include the origins of agriculture and civilisation, geoarchaeology, demographic and ecological archaeology, philosophy and cultural heritage management. He has written extensively on these areas, including *The Archaeology of the Dishna Plain* (1974) and *Demographic Archaeology* (1981).

Ian Hodder is Professor of Archaeology in the University of Cambridge and Director of the Çatalhöyük Research Project. His main interests are in archaeological theory and European prehistory and he excavated mainly in Britain before undertaking fieldwork in Turkey. His main publications include *Symbols in action* (1982); *Reading the past* (1986 and 1991); *The Domestication of Europe* (1990); *Theory and Practice in Acheaeology* (1992); and *The Archaeological Process* (1998).

A. Bernard Knapp is Reader in Archaeology in the Department of Archaeology, University of Glasgow. He received his PhD in Mediterranean Archaeology in 1979 from the University of California, Berkeley. He has held research appointments at the University of Sydney, the Cyprus American Archaeological Research Institute, Cambridge University, and Macquarie University (Sydney). Research interests include archaeological theory, archaeological survey, the archaeology and anthropology of mining, and Bronze Age Mediterranean prehistory. He edits the *Journal of Mediterranean Archaeology* (with John F. Cherry) and the series *Monographs in Mediterranean Archaeology*.

Kostas Kotsakis is Associate Professor in the Department of Archaeology, University of Thessaloniki. His main research involves the Neolithic of South Eastern Europe, as well as material culture and theory. His publications include *The Middle Neolithic Pottery of Sesklo* (1983); 'The Powerful Past' in I. Hodder (ed.) *Archaeological Theory in Europe* (1991); Review of Aegean Prehistory: The Neolithic and Bronze Age of Northern Greece, *American Journal of Archaeology* 100 (1996).

Lynn Meskell is Research Fellow at New College, Oxford University. Her PhD from Cambridge University focused on social dynamics in New Kingdom Egypt. Her interests include Egyptian and Mediterranean archaeologies, feminist theory, the body in antiquity and sociopolitics. She has published in *World Archaeology*, *Cambridge Journal of Archaeology*, *Antiquity, Gender and History*, *Norwegian Archaeological Review* and the *American Journal of Archaeology*. She has forthcoming volumes with Blackwell and Princeton University.

Albert Farid Henry Naccache is a Professor in the Department of Archaeology at the Lebanese University. He received his PhD, on the long-term history of the Mashriq, from the University of California at Berkeley in 1985. In 1969 he received the Diplôme de l'Institut d'Études Politiques de Paris in Sociology, and in 1972 an MSc in Neurophysiology from the American University at Beirut. He is primarily interested in applying theoretical approaches to the conception and representation of history of the Mashriq (Near or Middle East), from the emergence of hominids to the present.

Mehmet Özdoğan is Professor of Prehistoric Archaeology at Istanbul University. He has directed surveys in the regions of Marmata and the Euphrates and excavations including Çayönü, Yarımburgaz, Hoca Çeşme, and Toptepe. He is currently excavating at Aşağı Pınar and Kanlıgeçit in collaboration with the DAI in Berlin. His main areas of interest are the development of Neolithic economies, environmental archaeology and the history of the discipline and he has written widely on these topics.

D. T. Potts is Edwin Cuthbert Hall Professor of Middle Eastern Archaeology at the University of Sydney. He has excavated extensively in the United Arab Emirates, most notably at Tell Abraq, Al Sufouh, Jabal Emalah, Awhala and Sharm, and he is the author of a two-volume synthesis of Gulf archaeology entitled *The Arabian Gulf in Antiquity* (1990) and *Mesopotamian Civilisation: The Material Foundations* (1997). He has recently completed a new work on Elam which is to be published by Cambridge University Press.

Ann Macy Roth is an Assistant Professor of Egyptology at Howard University in Washington, DC. She received her PhD from the University of Chicago, in 1985, with a dissertation on the evolution of the system of Egyptian phyle organisation in the Archaic Period and Old Kingdom. Her primary research interests are Egyptian archaeology, particularly cemetery archaeology of the Old Kingdom, and religion. Her most recent book is the sixth volume of the Giza Mastabas series, *A Cemetery of Palace Attendants* (1995).

Neil Asher Silberman is an author and historian with a special interest in the history, archaeology and politics of the Near East. A former Guggenheim Fellow, he is a graduate of Wesleyan University and was trained in Near Eastern Archaeology at the Hebrew University of Jerusalem. He is a contributing editor for *Archaeology Magazine* and a frequent contributor to other archaeological and general interest periodicals. His books include *Inheriting the Kingdom* (with Richard A. Horsley, 1997); *Invisible America* (with Mark P. Leone, 1995); *The Hidden Scrolls* (1994); *A Prophet from Amongst You: The Life of Yigael Yadin* (1993); *Between Past and Present* (1989); and *Digging for God and Country* (1982).

Archaeology matters

Lynn Meskell

When the British Army of Occupation marched into Egypt in 1882, that country most unexpectedly became the object of thought of every intelligent thinker in Europe and of every English-speaking nation throughout the world. The diplomat, the soldier and the politician each looked upon Egypt with a practical eye, and meditated what advantage could be got from it for the country which he represented . . . But others besides the practical men were interested in the opening up of Egypt by the British – we mean the student of general history and the archaeologist, not to mention the expert Egyptologist . . . who flocked to Egypt demanded with no uncertain voice that all the available information on the subject should be given to them.

> (Illustrated London News, 7 March 1896, accompanying
> coverage of de Morgan's discoveries at Dahshur)

We know the civilisation of Egypt better than we know the civilisation of any other country. We know it further back; we know it more intimately; we know more about it. It goes far beyond the petty span of the history of our race, which is lost in the prehistoric period at a time when the Egyptian civilisation had already passed its prime.

> (Arthur James Balfour, addressing the House of Commons
> on the necessity for England being in Egypt)

During the 1990s a burgeoning corpus of literature has arisen devoted specifically to ethnicity, nationalism, cultural identity and politics, as they impact on our own field of archaeology. The majority of these volumes deal with issues of nationalism and constructions of identity in times past (Díaz-Andreu and Champion 1996;

Layton 1989; Shennan 1989) — many situated in the nineteenth century. Many are also confined to Europe, particularly Western Europe (Atkinson, Banks and O'Sullivan 1996; Díaz-Andreu and Champion 1996, Graves-Brown, Jones and Gamble 1996), although there have been limited discussions of African and Asian regional archaeologies in a handful of volumes (Chakrabarti 1997; Kohl and Fawcett 1995; Ucko 1995). Nationalism has been the key issue in these works, and whilst it may have been the dominant paradigm of the nineteenth century (Nederveen Pieterse 1995: 52), globalism now takes its place in the twentieth century.

To date, one major area of the globe has been overlooked by archaeologists — one which played a formative role in the birth of archaeology as a discipline — namely the Eastern Mediterranean and Middle East. This omission seems inexplicable not only on these grounds, but also given that the *materiality* and *practice* of archaeology in this region is inextricably linked to the political and cultural realities faced by their respective peoples. Anthropologists and historians have certainly seized upon the importance and potential of this region for its own sake and for its reflexive role in the construction of their own disciplines.

Given the ongoing relevance of archaeological pasts to this region, one has to question why this vast region is erased from contemporary theorising in archaeology, which is currently concerned with issues of heritage, contested identities, nationalism and politics. Some might posit a racist, Orientalist agenda, others may cite ignorance. Perhaps a more realistic explanation lies somewhere between the two. It is no coincidence that most influential archaeological theorising stems from Anglo-American institutions and, as such, its focus sits squarely within the continental geographies of Europe and the Americas. In this schema other regional archaeologies such as Mediterranean, Near Eastern and Egyptian are marginalised fields whose practitioners are considered still trapped in the throes of culture history (see Bailey, Chapter 4; Kotsakis, Chapter 2 and Silberman, Chapter 9) and thus reticent to engage in contemporary issues of politics or praxis. Given this view, contributions from such peripheral fields have been deemed irrelevant on a global scale and significant events involving archaeology have had negligible impact beyond that *koine* (see Nacacche, Chapter 7). This volume represents an initial engagement with the archaeologies of the Eastern Mediterranean and Middle East with special reference to the cultural and national politics in which it is intertwined and the social impact of antiquity for the people involved. For many of us, archaeology represents a luxury or an intellectual enterprise and its repercussions rarely have life or death consequences: this is not the case in the former Yugoslavia (see Brown, Chapter 3), Cyprus (see Knapp and Antoniadou, Chapter 1) or Israel (see Silberman, Chapter 9). Archaeological and historical narratives are deeply imbricated within sociopolitical realities. In this region archaeology matters in very tangible, as well as ideological, ways.

The past has been deployed by Western archaeologists to construct the non-West, to forge ourselves a cultural lineage and to carve out opposing identities. It has never been a neutral field of discourse. We should be aware that modern cartographies and mappings are recent inscriptions that did not have contiguous parallels in antiquity: these national constructions can also be the result of colonialist or imperialist imperatives. The grammar of colonial power centred on three key institutional concepts – the census, map and museum (Anderson 1991: 163), in which archaeological pasts are deeply embedded. As Said (1978: 4–5) and Bahrani (Chapter 8) remind us, these territories are not simply there to be discovered, analysed, and taxonomised as culturally- and geographically-bounded entities: they are *man* made and indeed *men* make their own history.

This is particularly true of Western constructions of 'Mesopotamia' as an entity, characterised by despotism and decay (Bahrani, Chapter 8; Hodder, Chapter 6; Pollock and Lutz 1994). Such narratives continue to this day. Consider Larsen's (1996: 3–4) description of Mosul: 'like most Near Eastern towns of the time it was a sleepy and shabby place, and in spite of its glorious past it was reduced to rubble and decay . . . not a nice place to spend the summer, or for that matter any other time of the year.' Perhaps academic disciplines, like archaeology, still remain the stepchildren of imperialism.

Quite rightly, sociopolitics has become a viable and important subfield within archaeology (Moser 1995) and we are currently moving towards ethical notions of disciplinary responsibility on both local and global levels (Kotsakis, Chapter 2; Trigger 1989, 1995). However, such responsibilities can be inherently problematic enterprises which again have the potential to overspill into hegemonic proclamations of global knowledge and discourse. The discourses of Orientalism and colonialism are certainly guilty of implementing those power imbalances: consider the role of monuments and 'the past' throughout the Gulf War (Pollock and Lutz 1994). During the conflict, Saddam Hussein was portrayed as a modern Assyrian king (*read* despot) in the Western media whilst at the same time the monuments of his country were appropriated as part of a common Western lineage of civilisation. The media expressed greater concern for the loss of ancient ziggurats than the lives of modern people. Archaeology is not free from hegemonic flows, rather it has been indelibly entwined with their politics. It is a dilemma which we all unavoidably face. Despite the desire to engage with different voices and viewpoints, this book itself is still couched in Western discourse – yet such reflexivity at least provides a check on those flows.

Orientalism, postcolonialism, postprocessualism

Edward Said's monumental work, *Orientalism* (1978) is, by now, both well known and widely critiqued (Bhabha 1994; Clifford 1988; Turner 1994). Said himself was guilty of polarising East and West in a continuing and somewhat unhelpful duality, with West fulfilling the simplistic role of oppressor and East, the oppressed. He follows a rigid Foucauldian notion of discourse and, subsequently, power. In the process Said pacifies, feminises and depoliticises his Orient. His own discourse is somewhat monolithic and has been criticised for its Occidentalism. Indeed, the wider significance of postmodernism stems from an acknowledgement that there are epistemological limits to all ethnocentric ideas about dissonant histories – whether they concern women, the colonised, or minority groups (Bhabha 1994: 5). We need to critique all metanarratives, including those of Said, which seek to formulate people as *one* and move away from the singularities of class, sex, geopolitical locale, sexual orientation (ibid.: 1–2). However, Said's work is important in illustrating how discourses, values and patterns of knowledge actually construct the *facts* which scholars attempted to study *objectively* (Turner 1994: 4). This book is not an attempt to separate out an Orient – its aim is to redress the imbalance which has seen the archaeologies of Eastern Europe, the Eastern Mediterranean and the Middle East marginalised or ignored. These regions are not invoked *en masse*, but contextually analysed by writers who have actively participated in the archaeology and politics of those countries.

The familiar postmodern project of deconstructing master narratives, unsettling binaries and acknowledging marginalised knowledges is closely linked to the objectives of postcolonial scholarship. Like feminism, postcolonial politics cannot enjoy the luxury of poststructural engagements with decentred subjectivities (Jacobs 1996: 29). They cannot simply *play* postmodernism, with its focus on surface, spectacle and heteroglossia. The past as play undermines the real and material consequences for living individuals, especially in the region in question, as opposed to the relatively safe domains which Euro-Americans inhabit. The past is not a static, archaic residue, rather it is an inherited artefact which has an active influence in the present through the interplay of popular and officially inscribed meanings. Constructions of identity for colonised groups inevitably entail a complex interweaving of past and present, which in themselves rely on the discourses of alterity, authenticity and origins (ibid.: 155). Clear examples of these processes are found in the tourism industry – itself a form of neo-colonialism – in countries such as Egypt, Greece, Cyprus and Turkey. Alterity need not have a negative face. Rather it can have a positive impact on situating the self in a multicultural present. In our own society, difference can also be domesticated, embraced and steeped in nostalgia.

Few would argue against the view that the West has constituted itself as the subject of history. The postcolonial enterprise aims to challenge that position by highlighting other geographies, *geographies that struggle*. The archaeology of power – to name, classify and domesticate – doubles as the means to obliterate, silence and negate other histories and ways of dwelling in the same space (Brown, Chapter 3; Bahrani, Chapter 8; Chambers 1996: 48–9). There exists a multiplicity of cultural borders, historical temporalities and hybrid identities. Such multiple realities cannot be relegated simply to the political domain, as Chambers reminds us (1996: 51):

> In the ruins of previous anthropology, sociology, history and philosophy, in the interstices of these torn and wounded epistemes where the rules of disciplinary genres are blurred and betrayed, the object disappears to be replaced by intimations of a potential space in which all subjects emerge modified from encounters that are irreducible to a unique point of view. As authority slips from my hands into the hands of others, they, too, become the authors, the subjects, not simply the effects or objects of my ethnography.

Postcolonial criticism highlights the unequal and uneven forces of cultural presentation involved in the contest for sociopolitical authority within the current world order (Bhabha 1994: 171). These critical revisions arise from the colonial testimony of Third World countries and minority voices. Such a theory need not simply be a heuristic enterprise, it can offer potential avenues for reconciliation, as can archaeology itself (cf. Hodder, Chapter 6; Knapp and Antoniadou, Chapter 1; Naccache, Chapter 7). This aim is worth pursuing, rather than continuing the grim analogies of Hobsbawm (1993: 63) so widely cited in archaeology: history is linked to the raw material of poppies for opium, and our studies are likened to the potential of bomb factories. An aware, responsible and engaged global archaeology might be a relevant, positive force which recognises and celebrates difference, diversity and *real* multivocality. This has certainly been the intent of the present volume. Under these common skies and before divided horizons such exposure to global difference and alterity prompts us all to seek responses and responsibility. In the process, knowledge and culture can be reworked, and with them, power and politics (Curti and Chambers 1996: xii). Engagement is the first step and each of the contributors in this book is passionately dedicated to that aim, moving beyond models of oppressor versus oppressed to more nuanced analyses which recognise the specific historical context and national and local character of the areas in which they work and/or live. These new social topographies, in which our discipline is inextricably bound, could profitably be examined through the lens of *globalism* – a more holistic means of viewing our fundamental interconnectedness (cf. Hassan, Chapter 11; Potts, Chapter 10).

Lynn Meskell

Processualism and postprocessualism

Global developments are not separate to archaeology, but have been reflected in our own disciplinary interests and epistemological directions. We have moved from universal narratives, supposedly applicable across time and space, to more contextual studies which stress cultural difference, social diversity and the creation of multiple identities. This parallels the current decline in Western hegemony and decentralisation, coupled with the concomitant rise of cultural movements, new identities and national entities that clearly challenge cultural homogenisation on a global scale (Friedman 1994: 37). Archaeology might be in step with larger social forces, yet postprocessual archaeology has changed more than the epistemological field of discourse: it has opened up the discipline to more players, more voices and has made valid new subject matters. The whole idea of sociopolitics in archaeology would not have been possible within the constraints of the New Archaeology. Such pursuits would not have been deemed the arena of archaeology, and it is unlikely that feminist, postcolonial and indigenous archaeologies would have come to the fore. The 'neutral scientificism' and positivism of New Archaeology did not address these issues (Hamilakis and Yalouri 1996: 117; Bailey, Chapter 4). Trigger (1995: 277) goes as far as saying processualism 'played a role in devaluing local cultures and promot[ed] a universalistic outlook that has served the far from altruistic goals first of American and then of international capitalism.' However, I would not say that processual archaeologists are not *currently* engaged in sociopolitics, rather that the intellectual inheritance of 1980s postprocessual archaeology should be acknowledged.

Anthropology and, by extension, archaeology, was born out of the ideological relationships between exploration, mercantilism, colonialism, exoticism and primitivism. Subsequently it developed notions of a centre/periphery/margins structure of Western civilisation and established evolutionary relationships between the West and its 'less developed' forerunners: a mistranslation of space into time (Fabian 1983; Friedman 1994: 5). Evolutionary anthropologists organised the world into coherent taxonomic schemes, from bands to tribes to chiefdoms to states. Processualists still retain an interest in applying these constructions to archaeological data. In retrospect, anthropology and archaeology could be said to have shifted their emphasis from evolutionism to primitivism, from materialism to culturalism, and from collectivism to individualism (ibid.: 55). This parallels the movements of processualism and postprocessualism, although both can exist side by side – especially in North America. It is only when scholarship developed an interest in the connection between writing history and the establishment of social identity that cultural difference, fragmentation and the power of the past became viable avenues of research.

Postprocessual archaeology has an explicit interest in difference and identity politics, and has much in common with third-wave feminist and postcolonial temporalities. Both these theoretical movements force us to rethink the sign of history and its subjects (Bhabha 1994: 153). Developments in archaeological theory are now in keeping with developments in the humanities and social sciences, which position issues of social and cultural diversity as central. Systems of meaning and the processes by which cultural meanings change for individuals and groups lie at the heart of postprocessualism. Whatever the historical background, our project now would seem to revolve around issues on both local and global stages. For instance, after the collapse of the modernist project in the 1960s and 1970s, political fragmentation coupled with the assertion of new local and regional identities, implicated archaeology and archaeological pasts: the destruction of the Mostar bridge (Chapman 1994), Saddam Hussein's rebuilding of Babylon, the legal battle for the Kanakaria mosaics (Knapp and Antoniadou, Chapter 1), the rise of Afrocentrism (Roth, Chapter 12; Asar Jubal 1991; Crawford 1996; Sewell 1997), the importance of Vergina for Macedonia (Kotsakis, Chapter 2), and the assassination of Rabin for handing over the Bible lands.

As Potts reminds us in Chapter 10, the planet is now our field of enquiry. As such, our responsibilities must also extend further than ever before, to our colleagues across the globe, to their respective countries and the issues which concern them. Sadly, there are pressing contemporary issues in forgotten geographies of which we hear little: the looting of Iraqi museums after the Gulf war or the destruction of the cultural heritage of Afghanistan. These actions have been decried as 'crimes against civilisation' (Riedlmayer 1997). But archaeology can take an effective and politicised stance. The boycotting of South African archaeology (Ucko 1987) and the incidents surrounding Ayodhya mosque (Colley 1995) are key events which might mark our initial global engagement.

Global archaeology

Globalism refers to the symbolic compression of the world and the growing awareness of the globe as a single entity. Coupled with this recognition is a whole series of localising phenomena (ethnicity, indigenous movements, exoticism): they are, in fact, two sides of the same coin. As Gellner proposed, modern society is both more homogeneous and more diversified than those which preceded it (cited in Eriksen 1993: 147). We could also argue that global culture is not new – consider Alexander's Hellenisation of the Near East and Mediterranean world, drawing upon local motifs through the lens of Macedonian expression (Smith 1990: 177). The field of globalism has been the subject of anthropology and the social and political sciences (e.g. Eriksen 1993; Featherstone 1990; Featherstone *et al.* 1995; Friedman 1994; Turner 1994) but has yet made little impact on archaeology (but see Hodder 1997). In view of our present social, political and cultural global climate, it is an appropriate theoretical strategy for archaeological and heritage issues as the twentieth century draws to a close.

Globalism involves people and processes on a world stage. The last fifty years have witnessed movements of people on an unprecedented scale, the disintegration of empires, decolonisation, the destruction of old nations and the re-formation of new ones (Hall 1996: 65). Many of these struggles are based on claims revolving around national, racial or linguistic identities: Serbia, Croatia, Palestine, Rwanda, Azerbijan, Armenia, the Kurds (Zaretsky 1995: 244–5). These processes present us with the contradictory tendencies of globalism and localism existing side by side. Whilst a new internationalism unites us (e.g. tourism, communication systems, environmental issues), new nationalisms and ethnicities criss-cross these expanses, providing lines of boundedness. Globalisation might have been fuelled by tourism, world sport, world news, CocaColonisation and McDonaldisation, AIDS, human rights etc. (Turner 1994: 9), but it is not simply synonymous with Westernisation given, for example, the massive influence of Asian markets and the indigenisation of the West. Contradictory tensions and possibilities are juxtaposed at an ever-increasing periodicity. Globalisation seemingly produces homogeneity, whilst the trend toward localisation produces difference, transformation and new identities (Grossberg 1996: 170).

Future archaeological questions could be directed towards the ways in which meanings and identities are attributed and negotiated, rather than in the direction of origins. Benedict Anderson (1983) has discussed this under the rubric of imagined communities, whilst Arjun Appadurai (1990) has considered the parallel phenomenon of cultural flows: ethnoscapes, mediascapes, technoscapes, finanscapes and ideoscapes. These multiple worlds are constituted by the historically situated imaginations of individuals and groups spread across the globe (Appadurai 1990: 296–7). Yet, as the following chapters show, there are often disjunctures between these *imaginary* landscapes, whether they are in Krushevo (Brown, Chapter 3), Beirut (Naccache, Chapter 7), or Çatalhöyük (Hodder, Chapter 6). Together they form a mosaic of possible histories and a corresponding mélange of presents and potential futures.

Conclusions

This volume is not meant to document a 'litany of horrors' which some might say is specific to the region in question: if we are to learn anything from the last few years it is that historically-based tensions can affect all nations. More specifically, it suggests that the residues of empire and colonialism are still at the heart of many conflicts, as well as our own scholarly constructions. If this is the case, then many more countries should be mindful and learn the lessons of our time. Perhaps that acknowledgement can prevent future tensions, or at least make some sectors of the global community more aware. Archaeologists the world over must be aware of the *potentials* of the past. Here too, this book aims to outline the positive potentials of our field – where archaeology can impact in concrete and beneficial ways to bring about reconciliation and acceptance (Hodder, Chapter 6; Naccache, Chapter 7; Potts, Chapter 10), rather than simply being the raw material for hostility. This negative view prevails in several studies on nationalism in archaeology and stems from certain misplaced attacks on postprocessualism as being relativistic. Such a view conflates epistemic relativity (all beliefs are socially produced) and judgemental relativism (all beliefs are equally valid) (see Lampeter Archaeology Workshop 1997). Not only is this position incorrect, it is irresponsible and counter-productive to the discipline.

The contributions in this book aim to address a range of important issues which directly impact upon archaeological praxis. First, they aim to highlight situations where archaeology, and archaeologically substantiated pasts, matter in countries which have been previously ignored or marginalised. Second, the narratives deployed in various chapters (Chapters 3, 6, 7 and 11) detail the day-to-day negotiations between individuals working within complex frameworks where the interplay of archaeologies, ethnicities, nationalisms and identities intersect. Several chapters deal explicitly with issues of postcolonialism (Chapters 1 and 8) and with the residual effects of colonial intervention (Chapters 5, 10 and 11). Third, the book seeks to provide a forum for other voices and other positions on the value of archaeology, and archaeologists (Chapters 4, 6, 9 and 12). It illustrates that there are no monolithic notions of nationalism, as there are no coherent archaeological pasts (Chapters 2, 3, 7 and 10).

Neil Silberman (1995: 257) has claimed a symbolic link between countries such as Israel, the Gulf, Egypt, Cyprus, Turkey, Greece and the Balkan region. Many might claim a cultural unity throughout this vast region, both then and now. That shared past has often led to competing claims and the attribution of multiple meanings for monuments, places and histories: many overlapping pasts exist within this common framework. Archaeology also has an emotional power linking the present to a particular golden age (Shnirelman 1995: 12). Coupled with this is the theme of 'origins' and most often this has been co-opted into the metanarrative of European civilisation. There is likely to be a host of reasons for the emotional impact of archaeology in this area of the world, whether it be cultural contact, a great antiquity, golden ages, a colonial backlash or contemporary political issues.

The contributors demonstrate that this region can contribute to archaeological dialogues, and provide theoretical insights which lie beyond culture historical approaches. In future, such insights into contemporary discussions of heritage, constructions of the past and identity politics (Chapters 1, 6 and 11) should be incorporated into the mainstream given the aims of a postprocessual archaeology. Each chapter aims to go beyond historiography and to situate firmly its relevant themes in a contemporary context. Their views can only be personal, political and, at times, conflicting with other contributions in the book. Such is the nature of *real* pluralism. These are individual voices and there can be no one, uniform position. Whilst consensus is unlikely, we can be sure that in this significant sector of the globe archaeology matters in very real ways.

Acknowledgements

I would like to thank the contributors to the book for their dedication to the project and the larger goals expressed within. Special thanks to my colleagues who discussed these ideas with me and who read and commented on this section: Zainab Bahrani, Emma Blake, Yannis Hamilakis, Ian Hodder, Carol McDavid, Darrin Lee Long and Dominic Montserrat. For their patience and support, we all acknowledge the efforts of Victoria Peters and Nadia Jacobson.

Bibliography

Anderson, B. (1991) *Imagined Communities*, revised edition, London: Verso.
Appadurai, A. (1990) 'Disjuncture and difference in the global cultural economy', in M. Featherstone (ed.) *Global Culture: Nationalism, Globalization and Modernity*, London: Sage: 295–310.
Asar Jubal, J. (1991) *Black Truth*, Longbeach, CA.: Black Truth Enterprises.
Atkinson, J. A., Banks, I. and O'Sullivan, J. (eds) (1996) *Nationalism and Archaeology*, Glasgow: Cruithne Press.
Bhabha, H. K. (1994) *The Location of Culture*, London: Routledge.
Brown, K. S. (1994) 'Seeing stars: character and identity in the landscapes of modern Macedonia', *Antiquity* 68, 261: 784–96.
Chakrabarti, D. K. (1997) *Colonial Indology: Sociopolitics of the Ancient Indian Past*, New Delhi: Munshiram Manoharlal.
Chambers, I. (1996) 'Signs of silence, lines of listening', in L. Curti and I. Chambers (eds) *The Post-Colonial Question: Common Skies, Divided Horizons*, London: Routledge: 47–62.
Chapman, J. (1994) 'Destruction of a common heritage: the archaeology of war in Croatia, Bosnia and Hercegovina', *Antiquity* 68, 258: 120–6.
Clifford, J. (1988) *The Predicament of Culture: Twentieth Century Ethnography, Literature, and Art*, Cambridge, MA: Harvard University Press.

Colley, S. (1995) 'What happened at WAC-3', *Antiquity* 69, 252: 15–18.

Crawford, C. (ed.) (1996) *Recasting Ancient Egypt in the African Context*, Trenton, NJ: Africa World Press, Inc.

Curti, L. and Chambers, I. (1996) Preface, in L. Curti and I. Chambers (eds) *The Post-Colonial Question: Common Skies, Divided Horizons*, London: Routledge: xi–xii.

Díaz-Andreu, M. and Champion, T. (eds) (1996) *Nationalism and Archaeology in Europe*, London: University College London Press.

Eriksen, T. H. (1993) *Ethnicity and Nationalism*, London: Pluto Press.

Fabian, J. (1983) *Time and the Other: How Anthropology makes its Other*, New York: Columbia University Press.

Featherstone, M. (ed.) (1990) *Global Culture: Nationalism, Globalization and Modernity*, London: Sage.

Featherstone, M., Lash, S. and Robertson, R. (eds) (1995) *Global Modernities*, London: Sage.

Friedman, J. (1994) *Cultural Identity and Global Process*, London: Sage.

Graves-Brown, P., Jones, S. and Gamble, C. (1996) *Cultural Identity and Archaeology: The Construction of European Communities*, London: Routledge.

Grossberg, L. (1996) 'The space of culture, the power of space', in L. Curti and I. Chambers (eds) *The Post-Colonial Question: Common Skies, Divided Horizons*, London: Routledge: 169–88.

Hall, C. (1996) 'Histories, empires and the post-colonial momen', in L. Curti and I. Chambers (eds) *The Post-Colonial Question: Common Skies, Divided Horizons*, London: Routledge: 65–77.

Hamilakis, Y. and Yalouri, E. (1996) 'Antiquities as symbolic capital in modern Greek society', *Antiquity* 70, 267: 117–29.

Hobsbawm, E. J. (1993) 'The new threat to history', *New York Review* 15 December: 63.

Hodder, I. (1997) '"Always momentary, fluid and flexible": Towards a reflexive excavation methodology', *Antiquity* 71, 273: 691–700.

Jacobs, J. M. (1996) *Edge of Empire: Postcolonialism and the City*, London: Routledge.

Kohl, P. L. and Fawcett, C. (eds) (1995) *Nationalism, Politics and the Practice of Archaeology*, Cambridge: Cambridge University Press.

Lampeter Archaeology Workshop (1997) 'Relativism, objectivity and the politics of the past', *Archaeological Dialogues* 4, 2: 164–75.

Larsen, M. T. (1996) *The Conquest of Assyria: Excavations in an Antique Land 1840–1860*, London: Routledge.

Layton, R. (ed.) (1989) *Conflict in the Archaeology of Living Traditions*, One World Archaeology Series, London: Unwin Hyman.

Moser, S. (1995) *Archaeology and its Disciplinary Culture: The Professionalisation of Australian Prehistoric Archaeology*, PhD Dissertation. Department of Prehistoric and Historical Archaeology, University of Sydney.

Nederveen Pieterse, J. (1995) 'Globalization as hybridization', in M. Feather-stone, S. Lash and R. Robertson (eds) *Global Modernities*, London: Sage: 45–68.

Pollock, S. and Lutz, C. (1994) 'Archaeology deployed for the Gulf War', *Critique of Anthropology* 14, 3: 263–84.

Riedlmayer, A. (1997) 'War damage: Afghanistan's sites devastated', electronic message posted on ANE bulletin board, 21 January 1997.

Said, E. (1978) *Orientalism*, London: Routledge and Kegan Paul.

Sewell, R. L. (1997) '"Mother Africa": Afrocentrism, African-Americans and Africa's Past', paper presented at the 95th American Anthropological Association Conference, San Francisco.

Shennan, S. J. (ed.) (1989) *Archaeological Approaches to Cultural Identity*, One World Archaeology Series, London: Unwin Hyman.

Shnirelman, V. A. (1995) 'Alternative prehistory', *Journal of European Archaeology* 3, 2: 1–20.

Silberman, N. A. (1995) 'Promised lands and chosen peoples: the politics and poetics of archaeological narrative', in P. L. Kohl and C. Fawcett (eds) *Nationalism, Politics and the Practice of Archaeology*, Cambridge: Cambridge University Press: 249–62.

Smith, A. D. (1990) 'Towards a global culture', in M. Featherstone (ed.) *Global Culture: Nationalism, Globalization and Modernity*, London: Sage: 171–91.

Trigger, B. G. (1989) 'Hyperrelativism, responsibility, and the social sciences', *Canadian Review of Sociology and Anthropology* 26: 776–97.

—— (1995) 'Romanticism, nationalism, and archaeology', in P. L. Kohl and C. Fawcett (eds) *Nationalism, Politics and the Practice of Archaeology*, Cambridge: Cambridge University Press: 263–79.

Turner, B. S. (1994) *Orientalism, Postmodernism and Globalism*, London: Routledge.

Ucko, P. J. (1987) *Academic Freedom and Apartheid: The Story of the World Archaeological Congress*, London: Duckworth.

—— (ed.) (1995) *Theory in Archaeology: A World Perspective*, London: Routledge.

Zaretsky, E. (1995) 'The birth of identity politics in the 1960s: psychoanalysis and the public/private division', in M. Featherstone, S. Lash and R. Robertson (eds) *Global Modernities*, London: Sage: 244–59.

Chapter 1

Archaeology, politics and the cultural heritage of Cyprus

A. Bernard Knapp and
Sophia Antoniadou

Introduction

Across the spectrum of contemporary archaeology, few would deny that political realities impact powerfully and often negatively on both archaeological practice and archaeological interpretation. We hear more and more of archaeology's role in the construction and legitimisation of cultural or ethnic identity, and of the destruction, sale and obliteration of archaeological pasts from their modern cultural contexts. Such 'cultural cleansing' is nourished by the consequences of war, nationalistic fervour, inter-ethnic conflict, and the illicit and universally condemned trade in antiquities. In these situations, political neutrality is unachievable and can no longer be condoned by archaeologists (Pollock 1992: 301–4).

Nor can archaeology deny its overtly political role in informing us about our human past, disrupting long-held myths and prejudices, and impacting our current social constructions within the global village. The current literature is awash with articles treating ethnicity, cultural identity, politics and nationalism in archaeology (for example, Atkinson *et al.* 1996; Díaz-Andreu and Champion 1995; Graves-Brown *et al.* 1996; Jones 1997a; Kohl and Fawcett 1995a; Schmidt and

Patterson 1995; Trigger 1984; Whitelam 1996). Archaeologists tend to adopt current social concerns such as these, make them their own, and relate them – consciously or unconsciously – to the historic as well as the prehistoric past (Wilk 1985). However, it is not enough simply to be aware of the atrocities committed during the last decade as a result of ethnic or nationalistic turmoil throughout the world: we must also realise that archaeological information in these regions has been accessed, used and abused for unintended purposes by diverse special interest groups (Preucel 1995: 161).

Images and symbols from the past play conspicuous and powerful roles in the political present. Archaeological finds may become banners for newly-created ethnic groups or nations (see Brown 1994, Chapter 3). Mythical and historical evidence for ancient migrations may be cited to justify ethnic cleansing or to legitimise present-day territorial expansion. Renfrew (1994: 156) maintains that 'the perversion of ethnicity is the curse of our century.' As a direct result of national funding practices or even of individual archaeologists' personal interests, disproportionate emphasis is given to certain sites (for example, Great Zimbabwe) or classes of data (for example, Islamic pottery in Iron Age east Africa) that are seen to be politically useful. Such overt political bias in archaeological research and interpretation is neither new nor unusual: what has changed is the willingness of archaeologists to recognise such realities. By its nature archaeology has always had an obvious political dimension, and nationalism – like ethnic or cultural identity – makes manifest the character of archaeology as a social, historical and political enterprise (Silberman 1995: 249; see Hodder, Chapter 6).

Despite a long-standing archaeological tradition and the potential global impact implicit in any study of the Middle East, most studies of archaeology and ethnicity or nationalism have steered clear of the region's volatile states (cf. Elon 1994; Jones 1997b; Silberman 1987, 1989). Meskell in the introduction to this book maintains that this reality is linked inextricably to the construction of our field, which views archaeologies in the region as conservative and theoretically challenged (similarly Knapp 1996: 141–2); in this respect, world archaeology simply has shortchanged itself. However, in order to treat the politics of archaeology in this region, it is necessary to consider deeper currents in the unfolding of the modern world system – the spread of capitalism, and the eventual but inevitable reaction of postcolonial cultures.

Such a statement implies that we exist in a state of 'postcoloniality', but in fact the present is entirely bound up in colonial formations. Postcolonial means more than just *beyond* colonialism: it is also concerned with implementing sociopolitical action to resist and replace dominant imperial structures (Jacobs 1996: 161). Whereas people, cultures and nations may actively resist and deny colonialist tendencies and colonial constructs (Thomas 1994: 58–60), the past is always being reworked nostalgically and adapted creatively to the present. When contemporary European states began their economic and imperial expansion over the globe during the seventeenth to eighteenth centuries, empirical dogma began to replace religious beliefs, and the proponents of classical or biblical archaeology found themselves forced to counter historical doubts cast on the validity of scripture by Darwinian evolutionary theory and by European evolutionary archaeology (Silberman 1995: 255). The discovery and excavation of sites in ancient western Asia and the eastern Mediterranean positioned 'Western' scholars as the legitimate cultural (and imperial) heirs of a rich archaeological past (see Özdoğan, Chapter 5; Bahrani, Chapter 8 and Hassan, Chapter 11). Residual formations of colonialism like this are still very powerful in the eastern Mediterranean and the Middle East, despite postcolonial 'resistance'; moreover, the (formerly) colonised still engage in complicity, conciliation and even disregard for colonialism. It is mainly those who harbour nostalgic feelings for imperialism that see the formerly colonised as actively resisting the former 'core' (Jacobs 1996: 14–15). As long as assumptions of superiority and the right of force are galvanised in the rhetoric of contemporary research, part of what Said (1978: 12, 94–5) called the 'Orientalist discourse', constructions of the past will devalue indigenous cultures and histories, and propagate the dominant, Euro-American presentations of the past constantly repeated by the major figures in the field (Whitelam 1996).

The situation on the eastern Mediterranean island of Cyprus also involves a somewhat different, cultural translation of a far more distant colonial past (cf. van Dommelen 1997: 306). Silberman (1995: 259), for example, states:

> For a nation like the Republic of Cyprus, with its obvious political attach-ment to images of Greek antiquity, the extensive excavation and presentation of classical cities like Paphos, Kition, and Ammathus [*sic*] are clearly linked to a modern, national self-consciousness.

But what of those places that do not become part of the official heritage, or are denied a role in that heritage because they are inaccessible (i.e., in occupied territory)? Such sites take on powerful political roles and set the stage for struggles over cultural identity and political power. Heritage, then, imbues certain places with symbolic values and beliefs, and transforms them into a space where cultural identity is defined or contested, and where the social order is reproduced or challenged (Jacobs 1996: 35). Increasingly, heritage culture represents a strategy of response to global forces, centred on the preservation rather than the reinter-pretation of identities; the imperative is to salvage 'placed identities for placeless times' (Robins 1991: 41). Heritage involves a dynamic process where multiple pasts compete to become sanctified. The politics of archaeology on Cyprus are both multiple and ambiguous: dividing lines are sharply drawn on the land itself, and contrasting arguments and ideologies are precisely defined. Yet both sides, for entirely different reasons, follow political or economic agendas that affect the preservation of Cyprus' cultural heritage (see also Özdoğan, Chapter 5).

The 1974 Turkish invasion and subsequent occupation of the northern part of the island precipitated a blatantly ideological, cultural cleansing of the Greek Cypriote past; it also set in motion a train of events which continues to impact negatively on the practice and potential of archaeology on the island. The list of antiquities that have gone missing or been destroyed since 1974 continues to grow. Archaeologists no longer have any legal status to study or conduct any kind of research in the occupied northern part of the island. The status of Turkish Cypriote archaeologists in this regard can be debated, of course, but they have nonetheless a moral duty to control and protect the cultural heritage in the face of its large-scale destruction and looting. Whatever the situation may have been prior to 1974, the prevailing culture history of Cyprus has become quite biased, based as it is on excavations and surveys that have been limited for the past twenty three years to the southern sixty three per cent of the island. Since 1974, in other words, the cultural, archaeological, environmental and ideological conditions that prevail in the north have been inaccessible to most practising field archaeologists, to virtually all people who study Cypriot archaeology and to all Greek Cypriotes.[1]

In the attempt to treat all these diverse and volatile issues, this chapter presents first a general discussion of politics in archaeology, followed by a more focused treatment of imperialism, postcolonialism, globalism and the cultural identity of Cyprus. Two factors are then considered that have impacted the politics of archaeology within contemporary Cyprus. First, we outline the political and religious background to events that resulted in the Turkish invasion of Cyprus in 1974, and examine the pattern of destruction and desecration in the northern part of the island, citing data from public records. Second, we consider from a cultural and political perspective the negative impact of such developments on the practice and interpretation of archaeology in Cyprus today. We conclude with an overview of the politics of postcolonial place, and argue that Cypriot archaeologists will have to frame their own political agenda as contemporary political realities beyond their control shape and re-shape the cultural heritage of Cyprus.

The politics of archaeology

Shanks and Tilley (1987a, 1987b, 1989) have argued that only political goals are viable in archaeological research; archaeological discussion and interpretation thus should aim to disempower political and intellectual élites by affirming the validity of diverse explanations of the past (Trigger 1995: 263; cf. Holtorf *et al.*

1996). Other archaeologists who speak from gender, Third World, or rural perspectives maintain that archaeologists like Shanks and Tilley are élitist in their own right, and have done nothing to advance the position of the real archaeological underclasses (e.g., Andah 1995; Ferguson 1992; Handsman 1991; Spector 1993; Wylie 1991, 1993; Zimmerman 1995). Trigger (1995: 263–4) points out that archaeological data have been adopted to promote bigotry, violence and destruction just as much as they have been used to promote social justice. When archaeological enterprise is used to justify unpredictable or unacceptable political ends, archaeologists have to move beyond polemic, and attempt to redress the social or moral imbalance.

The way archaeologists interpret the past is conditioned by what they individually and collectively believe they know about the past, and by the techniques available for recovering, analysing and interpreting archaeological evidence (Trigger 1995: 265–6). Archaeologies influenced by nationalism are neither all bad nor all good, and the intricate relations between nationalistic archaeologies and political practice stem from the nature, tradition and relevance of archaeology to the political process (Trigger 1995: 270). For their part, archaeologists must recognise that their personal attitudes towards politics or nationalism are likely to stem from what they perceive to be in their own self-interest. Whatever such personal views or biases may be, there can be no justification for deliberately distorting the archaeological record, or for misinterpreting it with political ends in mind (Kohl and Fawcett 1995b: 9).

At one end of the spectrum, archaeological data have been misinterpreted for nationalistic or political purposes, and human history has been deliberately reconstructed. At the opposite end, nationalistic archaeology has generated questions about ethnicity or local cultural configurations that most processual and culture historical archaeologists would have eschewed. Viewed optimistically, then, the practice of a political archaeology can help to resist and overcome colonial and imperial residues. As Meskell emphasizes in the introduction to this book, postprocessual or interpretive archaeologies foreground social and political contexts; they work at the local level and are concerned with issues of meaning, symbolism, ethical and political responsibilities, and cultural or even individual identities. Postmodernist approaches to the study of the past (Knapp 1996; Preucel 1995) now extol the proliferation of competing narratives. Indeed, it is only within a theoretical milieu which encourages diverse viewpoints that archaeology can develop its social conscience and political stance. Ethnic cleansing and cultural fragmentation are not simply academic matters; they are human reactions that involve the creation of new polities, the assertion of re-worked cultural identities, the disempowerment of social groups and the destruction of past histories. Given such realities, the intrinsic power of the past challenges archaeology's engagement in the present and raises compelling questions about archaeological practice on a local level and archaeological responsibilities on a global level.

Postcolonialism, globalism and cultural identity

In order to consider the various political issues that impact on the archaeology of Cyprus, our perspective is necessarily local, historical and relativistic. However, because we believe these developments arose and persist primarily in the context of British imperialism and its local reflection, colonialism, this chapter is not intended as a retreat into 'nostalgic localism'. Nor is it an act of defiance against global capitalism: neither the transnational tendencies of colonialism nor the spread of multinational corporations have been able to obliterate the local or contain the national. Capitalism in both its imperial and postmodern forms operates through *difference*, through the 'specificity of the local' (Jacobs 1996: 6), and through a range of cultural processes that engage both Self and Other in constructing hierarchies of power. Indigenous groups living in colonial situations periodically seek to redefine their social position, thus articulating the local within a wider, global context (van Dommelen 1997: 309).

During the nineteenth and early twentieth centuries, those hierarchies that had produced and maintained colonial structures were progressively undermined as new nation states emerged and counter-colonial movements sought to reclaim or re-establish their cultural (or ethnic) identity, or even to revamp such identities as had been constructed under the colonial umbrella. It is precisely within such a framework that we must look at the 'Cyprus problem', the formation of Greek Cypriote and Turkish Cypriote identities, the illicit trade in antiquities, and the concomitant developments in Cypriot archaeology, in other words, at the processes by which Self (the imperial British) and Other (the colonial Cypriotes) were defined and articulated as a crucial part of the *cultural* dimensions of colonialism and postcolonialism. These processes delimited categories of difference that became inscribed as imperial/colonial structures, where the making and remaking of cultural identity was carried out in representational, material and ideological spheres (Jacobs 1996: 2). Our focus on the local, or colonial, then, makes it possible to engage the global, or imperial, as we consider the shaping of the Cypriot identity, the practice of Cypriot archaeology over the past century, and the postcolonial condition that envelops the 'Cyprus problem' and dictates the constitution of Cyprus' cultural heritage.

But before we celebrate prematurely the concept of postcolonialism as an ideal theoretical construct, we also need to be aware of its limits, of problems inherent in the application of dualities such as colonial/postcolonial, or Self/Other, when it is the presence of agency or intentionality that is critical to postcolonial

formations. Even if postcolonial theory challenges the notion of unilinear development and its associated binary ways of thinking, the very term paradoxically sets
up a binary orientation and perpetuates the logic of Western historicism. The
politics of agency must be incorporated into any analysis of the wide range
of postcolonial formations expressed in various ways and in diverse settings.
Negotiations of identity and the dynamics of agency are located within specific
hierarchies of power that permeate particular politico-economic frameworks
(Jacobs 1996: 28). Thus it is more effective to conceptualise postcolonialism as a
set of formations that seek to negotiate social, ideological and material power
structures established under colonialism. If the term postcolonialism necessarily
implies globalism, and thus generalises diverse histories and links them too tightly
to the imperial core, at the same time it provides the practices and experiences of
the Other with an agency, a strategic sensibility that reacts against the core. If this
notion appears to be driven by nostalgia, by a seduction with the primitive and
exoticness of the Other, at least it offers an alternative way of conceptualising
'otherness' and of distinguishing the independent place of divergent, local cultures (Stoler 1989). These are issues of postcolonial theory, not of postcoloniality
itself, and so must not infringe negatively upon the varied perspectives that can be
formulated, critiqued and revised. Most importantly, these diverse perspectives
can engage and contest the study of colonial cultural productions, and facilitate
the critical analysis of postcolonial peoples and nations who still speak from the
margins.

We turn now to consider how the imperial past and postcolonial present have
affected the cultural heritage of Cyprus. In order to do so, we present here a
narrative of events and issues (see Table 1.1) that led, first, to the establishment of
an independent Republic of Cyprus and, second, to the 1974 Turkish invasion and
occupation of the northern part of the island, which fractured that independence.

Cyprus – politico-religious background (1571–1997)

In 1571, Cyprus became a province of the Ottoman Empire, as had many other
southeastern Mediterranean countries throughout the sixteenth century.
Incorporating Cyprus into the Ottoman Empire entailed certain social and demographic developments which altered the ethnic composition of the island and
which survived in much the same form into the twentieth century. The Sultan,
for example, issued six *firmans* (edicts) ordering the emigration to Cyprus of
one-tenth of the population of several Anatolian provinces, ostensibly in order to
boost the depleted population of the island. And, in order to revive the rural
economy (Kyrris 1985: 259), grants of land were made to Turkish officials for
their military service; in time such lands passed largely into small-holding peasant

Table 1.1 Cyprus: historical outline, political and religious developments, 1571–1997

12th–16th centuries AD Frankish and Venetian rule of Cyprus
1571 Cyprus becomes a province of the Ottoman Empire
1878 Cyprus ceded to the British Empire, following Turkey's defeat in Russo-Turkish wars
1881 British census: the Greeks of Cyprus constitute 73.9% of population, the Turks 24.4%
1914 Turkey enters First World War as an ally of Germany, and Cyprus is annexed to the British Empire
1923 Treaty of Lausanne, by which Turkey renounces its claim to Cyprus
1925 Cyprus proclaimed a Crown Colony
1955 National struggle against colonial power/policy started by EOKA; Archbishop Makarios III leads EOKA's political wing and General Grivas its military wing
1955 'Tripartite Conference': in discussing the Cyprus situation, British, Turkish and Greek foreign ministers recognise Turkey's equal rights on Cyprus for first time since the Lausanne Treaty (1923)
1958 Zürich agreement (Turkey and Greece) gives constitutional status to Cyprus
1960 London agreement between Britain, Turkey, Greece, Greek Cypriotes and Turkish Cypriotes (1959) leads to foundation of the Republic of Cyprus on 21 August (Archbishop Makarios III elected President and Dr Fazil Küçük Vice-President)
1960 Cyprus joins British Commonwealth (March) and becomes a United Nations member (September)
1961 Cyprus gains membership in the Council of Europe
1963 Makarios puts forward to Küçük thirteen proposals for constitutional revisions, which spark intercommunal fighting between Greek and Turkish Cypriotes
1964 'Green Line' established, dividing the two communities in Nicosia and marking arrival of the United Nation Forces in Cyprus as 'peacekeepers'
1967 Grivas and Turkish Cypriotes clash, which prompts threat of Turkish invasion; Grivas banished
1971 Grivas returns to oppose independence of Cyprus and the rule of Makarios; with support of Greek military junta (ruling Greece, 1967 to 1974), Grivas sets up EOKA B', a para-state terrorist organisation committed to overthrowing the government
1974 Greek military coup on Cyprus (15 July) provokes the Turkish invasion (20 July); culminates on 14 August with Turkish military occupation of 37.2% of the island
1974 UN Security Council demands that all states respect sovereignty, independence and territorial integrity of the Republic of Cyprus (Resolution 353, adopted unanimously on 20 July, 1974)
1975 Turkey ignores UN conventions and establishes a 'Federal Turkish-Cypriote State'
1983 Turkey unilaterally declares independence and establishes the 'Turkish Republic of Northern Cyprus', an action condemned by the UN Security Council (Resolution 541/83 and subsequent)
1997 Cyprus problem remains unresolved

ownership. In this way, villages and village quarters of Turkish-speaking Moslem peasants came to be interspersed throughout the island within, or nearby, the villages of Greek-speaking peasants. It is generally agreed that the Turkish settlers numbered between sixteen and twenty thousand (Hadjidimitriou 1987: 229; Hunt 1990: 227).

For the first time in Cyprus there existed settled Moslem communities predominantly Turkish in origin. The dispersal throughout the landscape of both Greek-speaking and Turkish-speaking Cypriotes remained a firm and immutable geopolitical fact until the population uprootings of 1964 and the Turkish invasion of 1974. Relations between the Greek-speaking and Turkish-speaking Cypriotes in the countryside were reportedly amicable (Argyrou 1995: 199; Hunt 1990: 254); the reality was surely more complex, but at least there were relations, until the second half of the twentieth century.

After some three hundred years of Ottoman rule, in 1878 the island became part of the British Empire in the wake of Turkey's defeat in the Russo-Turkish wars. The cession of Cyprus to Britain was greeted enthusiastically not only by the British government (Tsalakos 1981: 139), but apparently also by the Cypriotes. In his welcoming address to the first High Commissioner in Larnaca, Archbishop Sophronios declared: 'We accept the change of the government inasmuch as we trust Great Britain will help Cyprus as it did the Ionian Islands to be united with Mother Greece with which it is naturally connected' (Alastos 1955: 308; Constantinides 1880: 116–17; Hill 1952: 297; Pantelis 1985: 71). Britain thus represented to the Greeks of Cyprus a 'philhellenic' power which in 1864 had ceded the Ionian islands to Greece. In reality, of course, other agendas were at work: British colonial policies meant domination over a people and its territories to ensure that raw materials were available for exploitation and that new markets were created for manufactured goods. Above all, Cyprus represented a strategic piece of land in an area where Britain still had limited influence.

The common origin and language, the shared myths, symbols and ideologies, and the strong historical bonds between the Greeks in Greece and on Cyprus, that is, the fundamental characteristics of their common *ethnos*, served to shape the Greek national identity. In Greek, the word *ethnos* means 'nation', yet ethnicity and nationalism operate in different ways: nations, for example, can be established and obliterated as political events take their course but ethnic identity is not so easily adopted or abandoned (Banks 1996: 2–3). Ethnicity, on the other hand, is expressed in the extent to which an individual feels connected to and acts within a particular social setting: it is an almost mythological arena of feelings and beliefs. Equally important are the notions of choice and self-perception (Banks 1995: 183–7). Ethnicity is a social construct which allows people to classify, locate and identify themselves within the world; it helps to inform and guide individual behaviour and, significantly, to distinguish it from another ethnic group's behaviour. The modern-day Greek *ethnos* was established as part of the widespread nineteenth century national awakenings throughout Europe (Díaz-Andreu 1995: 39–41; MacConnell 1989: 107–9; Trigger 1995: 266–72).

The Cypriotes accepted the change from an Ottoman to a British administration only as a temporary and transitional measure. The British administration, for its part, regarded the Greeks of Cyprus as having a well developed system of political representation through the Church and the Archbishop as political leader (*ethnarch*), as well as a degree of ethnic/nationalistic consciousness within their leading groups. This was especially so after the foundation of the Greek state (1830), and derived from the subordinate, if somewhat autonomous, position of Greek-speaking Cypriotes in the Ottoman Empire. By contrast, Moslems in general and Turkish Moslems in particular had been the dominant administrative unit (*millet*) of the Ottoman Empire and thus had little reason to develop nationalistic movements. As a consequence of their membership in the ruling class, the Turks in Cyprus developed few nationalistic sentiments. Moreover, because they were a minority, the Turks had no qualms about identifying with the colonial organisation established by the British administration, nor about giving their support to the new colonial power.

These conditions served as the basis for the development of relations between Greeks and Turks on Cyprus. Nationalism as a political emotion thus developed asynchronically amongst Greeks and Turks, whilst the relationship of the two ethnic groups to the British colonial power was decidedly asymmetrical (Attalides 1979: 2). Even after Turkey renounced its claim to Cyprus in favour of Britain (1923), indeed even after World War II, Turkish nationalism remained comparatively weak on Cyprus, at the same time that the Greek Cypriotes were escalating demands for unification with Greece. Britain, however, resisted any possibility of *enosis* (union) with Greece, which resulted in the national struggle started by EOKA [National Organisation of Cypriote Fighters] in 1955 against colonial policies. Once Turkey's equal rights on Cyprus were re-established by the Tripartite Conference (1955) (Pantelis 1985: 298), the involvement of Turkey and its opposition to Cyprus' unification with Greece contributed significantly to the negative reaction of the Turkish Cypriotes to this national demand.

The Republic of Cyprus was founded in August 1960, with Archbishop Makarios as President and Dr Fazil Küçük as Vice-President. The process of decolonisation as initiated by the establishment of an independent Cypriot republic is perhaps a poor indicator of 'postcoloniality', because the formal move to independence was permeated with imperialism. Decolonisation, in other words, set the stage for neo-colonialism rather than postcolonialism. The demographic restructuring that followed independence was in effect a neo-colonial formation, and the Cypriote people – Greek and Turkish – led lives still shaped by the ideologies of domination and imperialism. Turkish Cypriotes became marginalised culturally by the same rhetoric of exclusion – otherness and backwardness – that the British had formerly adopted against the Greek Cypriotes. Postcolonialism perhaps implies a level of liberation that is effectively beyond the capacity of existing power relations. And chauvinistic nationalism is nothing more than a form of neo-imperialism (Said 1993: 325–31). In Cyprus, independence might better be categorised as a sociopolitical formation that attempted to negotiate the ideological and material structures of power established under British imperialism.

According to its new constitution, Cyprus was forbidden to pursue either union or partition. Cyprus' territorial integrity, the basic articles of the constitution and its independence, were guaranteed by Britain, Greece and Turkey, each of which reserved the right to take separate action to restore the status quo in case of a breach. Although Greek Cypriotes made up eighty two per cent of the population (Crawshaw 1986: 1), the ratio of the administrative rights given to the Greek and Turkish communities was 70:30 respectively (Hunt 1990: 281; Koumoulides 1986). Accordingly, Archbishop Makarios put forward to Dr Küçük in November 1963 thirteen proposals intended to revise the constitution. These sparked intercommunal fighting and set in train Turkish threats of invasion. Subsequent discontent led to the establishment of the 'Green Line' in 1964, thus dividing the two communities in Nicosia and marking the arrival of the United Nation 'Peacekeeping' Forces (UNFICYP) in Cyprus.

General Grivas and the Turkish Cypriotes clashed during 1967 and Grivas was subsequently banished from the island; however, he returned secretly in 1971, opposing both independence and Makarios. With the support of the Greek military junta, Grivas set up EOKA B', a para-state terrorist organisation, whose primary target was Makarios and whose chief intention was to overthrow the government. The Greek military *coup d'état* in Cyprus on 15 July 1974 provoked the Turkish invasion five days later. The invasion culminated on 14 August 1974 with the military occupation of 37.2 per cent of the island, a situation that remains in force today.

This invasion and subsequent occupation of the northern part of Cyprus by Turkish troops eventually led to demographic upheavals which produced 200,000 refugees and over 1,600 missing persons, and led to the forced transferral of Greek Cypriotes to the south and of Turkish Cypriotes to the north, the widespread destruction of property, the colonisation of the northern part of the island by new Turkish settlers who now outnumber in many areas the Turkish Cypriote population (Jansen 1986: 321; Kapsos 1995: 185–6), and a number of atrocities which continue unabated. The Security Council of the United Nations has taken up the 'Cyprus problem' on frequent occasions since July 1974 and has also called repeatedly for an immediate end to foreign intervention and the withdrawal of all foreign troops. Turkey continues to ignore these decisions and appeals, and in 1983 unilaterally declared an independent 'Turkish Republic of Northern Cyprus'. This action was condemned by the UN Security Council (Resolution 541/83); the political entity thereby established is recognised by no other nation of the world, except Turkey.

Destruction and illicit trade of antiquities

The destruction of Cyprus' cultural heritage (see Figure 1.1) is a subject that concerns not only the people of Cyprus but also the entire international community, especially inasmuch as this is articulated through binding conventions and agreements amongst the nations of the world. A number of treaties, conventions and decisions aim to protect and preserve the international cultural heritage (see Table 1.2). Of these, the most basic is the Hague Convention (14 May 1954) which was designed to protect cultural property in the event of armed conflict and which was accompanied by an 'Execution' clause and a 'Protocol' aimed at its implementation. Article 18 sets the provisions for the application of the Convention, and Article 4 regulates this subject and stipulates the special obligations of the occupying forces toward cultural properties. These articles fully cover the case of occupied northern Cyprus.[2]

The destruction of archaeological sites (see Figure 1.2) and the illicit trade of antiquities in the northern part of Cyprus has had dramatic and likely irreversible consequences, both for Cyprus' cultural heritage and for archaeological research on the island. Documents from the Turkish Cypriot (Yasin 1982) and foreign press (Fielding 1976; Gallas 1990), scientific journals (Knapp 1994), and a UNESCO authorised report[3] provide specific references and information on the

Figure 1.1 Monastery at Tochni, Famagusta district: destroyed and used as a sheepfold (Courtesy: Director of the Department of Antiquities, Cyprus)

Table 1.2 Treaties protecting the international cultural heritage

The UNESCO General Conference (Paris, 19 November 1964):
   'the means prohibiting and preventing the illicit export, import and transfer of ownership of cultural property'

The European Convention (London, 6 May 1969):
   'for the protection of the archaeological heritage'

The UNESCO Convention (Paris, 14 November 1970):
   'the means of prohibiting and preventing the illicit export, import and transfer of ownership of cultural heritage'

International Convention (Paris, 16 November 1972):
   'the protection of world cultural and natural heritage'

Source: P. S. O'Keefe and L. V. Prott (1989) *Law and the Cultural Heritage*, Vol. 3, London: Butterworths.

Figure 1.2 Archaeological site at Soloi, classical period: pipeline (conduits) running through site
(Courtesy: Director of the Department of Antiquities, Cyprus)

systematic looting and cultural cleansing that has occurred on Cyprus since 1974 (see Tables 1.3–1.6, below).

The case of the sixth century AD Kanakaria mosaics, stolen in 1979 and actually returned to the Republic of Cyprus in 1991 after a notorious legal battle in the USA, is an exception to the fate of Cypriot antiquities looted and sold abroad

Table 1.3 Destruction of the cultural heritage of occupied Cyprus

Type of Monument	Present Condition	Number
Churches	used as mosques	55
Monasteries and Churches	diverted to alien uses (military purposes, art galleries, cinemas)	44
Historical Monuments, Churches	looted, damaged, or destroyed	40
Cemeteries	looted	26
Total		**106**

Source: Ministry of Foreign Affairs, Republic of Cyprus (1995) *Report on the Plundering of the Cultural Heritage in Occupied Cyprus*, 29 November.

Table 1.4 Individual cultural monuments

Monument	Date	Location	Present condition / use
Acheiropeitos Church	5th–10th, 12th–15th centuries AD	Karavas	military purposes
St Themonianos Church	13th–14th centuries AD	Lyssi	looted
Virgin Mary of Eleousa Church	15th century AD	Rizokarpaso	sheepfold
St Evlalios Church	Byzantine	Lambousa/Karavas	military purposes
St James Church	Byzantine	Trikomo	looted
St Panteleimon Monastery	18th century AD	Myrtou	looted/military purposes
St Spyridon Monastery	18th century AD	Tremetousia	military purposes
St Andronikos		Kythrea	destroyed
St Kassianos Church		Nicosia	destroyed
St Paul Church		Nicosia	looted
St George Church		Spatharico/Messoria	bombarded
St Mamas Church		Gaidouras	sheepfold

Source: Ministry of Foreign Affairs, Republic of Cyprus (1995) *Report on the Plundering of the Cultural Heritage in Occupied Cyprus*, 29 November; (1994) *Cyprus – The Plundering of a 9000-Year-Old Civilisation*, Athens: Cultural Centre, Municipality of Athens.

(*Annual Report of the Department of Antiquities for the Year 1990*, p. 6; Byrne-Sutton 1992; Hofstadter 1992a, 1992b, 1994). Immense efforts to repatriate stolen antiquities have been undertaken by the Department of Antiquities with the economic support and generosity of the Leventis Foundation (Jansen 1986: 322).

Table 1.5 Different types of material looted or destroyed

Item	Date	Location	Present condition
Mosaics	6th century AD	Virgin Mary of Kanakaria/ Lithrangomi	removed
Frescoes of the 'Elkomenos' and 'Descent from the Cross'	12th century AD	Virgin Mary of Apsinthiotissa/Synchari	removed and cut in pieces
Fresco of St Gregory of Agrigento	12th century AD	St John Chrysostomos Koutsoventis/Kyrenia	whitewashed
2 Icons	12th century AD	St John Chrysostomos Koutsoventis/Kyrenia	stolen
Icon of the Virgin Mary	12th–14th centuries AD	Virgin Mary of Apsinthiotissa/Synchari	stolen
Frescoes	13th–14th centuries AD	St Themonianos Church/ Lyssi	looted
Frescoes	12th–15th centuries AD	Antifonitis Church/Kyrenia	removed or destroyed
5 Icons	16th century AD	St John Chrysostomos Koutsoventis/Kyrenia	stolen
All icons	16th–17th centuries AD (Franco-Byzantine)	St Mamas/Morphou	stolen
150 icons and manuscripts	Byzantine	St Spyridon Monastery/ Tremetousia	looted
Ecclesiastic implements and icons	All periods	St Paul's Church/ Nicosia	stolen

Sources: Ministry of Foreign Affairs, Republic of Cyprus (1995) *Report on the Plundering of the Cultural Heritage in Occupied Cyprus*, 29 November; (1994) *Cyprus – The Plundering of a 9000-Year-Old Civilisation*, Athens: Cultural Centre, Municipality of Athens.

Although a full party to the 1954 Hague Convention, Turkey has failed to meet its contractual obligations and has repeatedly ignored the binding regulations of international agreements by tolerating or ignoring the theft, plunder and destruction of antiquities (Tenekides 1994: 55). Moreover, the demographic composition of the population in the occupied zone has been altered systematically by the immigration of Turkish settlers, whilst most Greek toponyms for villages have been changed to Turkish names (Stylianou 1987: 69–75). There is a disconcerting parallel here with the military origins of modern archaeology (e.g. Napoleon's campaigns in Egypt) and the imperially-controlled mapping of colonial territories (e.g. Kitchener in Cyprus and Palestine; Burckhardt in Syria-Palestine), which makes it possible to define, name and thus to control place, for commercial,

Table 1.6 Recovered and repatriated archaeological objects from the Hadjiprodromou Collection in Famagusta

Item	Material	Date	Number of items
Cruciform Figurines	picrolite	Chalcolithic, 3200–2500 BC	5
White-Painted VI Juglet	clay	Late Bronze I, 1700–1400 BC	1
Zoomorphic Rhyton	clay	Submycenean, 1100–1050 BC	1
Bird-Shaped Figurine	terracotta	Cypro-Archaic I, 750–600 BC	1
Wall-Bracket	clay	Cypro-Archaic I, 750–600 BC	1
'Flute-Player' Figurine	terracotta	Cypro-Archaic I, 750–600 BC	1
Zoomorphic Figurine	terracotta	Cypro-Archaic I, 750–600 BC	1
Bichrome IV Juglet	clay	Cypro-Archaic II, 600–475 BC	1
Head of Child	limestone	Hellenistic I, 325–150 BC	1
Total			13

Sources: (1994) *Cyprus – The Plundering of a 9000-Year-Old Civilisation*, Athens: Cultural Centre, Municipality of Athens.

Note
Only thirteen out of 2,000 objects have been recovered of the Hadjiprodromou Collection in Famagusta, which was entirely looted immediately after the Turkish invasion. These thirteen items, found in the possession of an antiques dealer in Dover, England, were confiscated by the authorities and returned to Cyprus.

politico-ideological and military reasons (Carter 1987; see also Bahrani, Chapter 8).

The Cyprus situation and the ongoing destruction of its cultural property cannot be viewed as an accidental incident and goes far beyond the unavoidable consequences of damages sustained during hostilities. As Chippindale (1994: 2) argues, destroying the visible evidence of one culture's presence in another culture's land does not happen by simple accident of war, nor by folly. If the relationship between a nation's ethnic/cultural identity, its historical past and its landscape is best preserved over time through its material culture, and is best symbolised by its monuments, then this sort of 'cultural cleansing' is usually an integral part and an early stage of ethnic cleansing. That is precisely why the Cyprus case and the rescue of its cultural property is not simply a case of limited significance or the defiance of international agreements (Tenekides 1994). In such situations do we judge the credibility and the effectiveness of international organisations such as UNESCO, which have undertaken the responsibility to set in motion the indispensable mechanisms of safeguarding cultural property, wherever it may be found. The Hague Convention accurately declares that 'damage to cultural property belonging to any people whatsoever means damage to the cultural heritage of all mankind.' To what extent do such sociopolitical agendas impact on the practice of Cypriot archaeology and the interpretation of archaeological data?

The politics of Cypriot archaeology

The relationship between Cypriot archaeology and political reality must be considered within the wider historical, cultural and political processes that unfolded over the last two centuries in Europe, the Middle East and the Mediterranean basin, when nationalistic rumblings led to the foundation of independent nation-states (Kohl and Fawcett 1995b: 12; MacConnell 1989: 107). The development of archaeology as an independent discipline can only be understood in the context of national history and global identity, that is, a history directed at legitimising a nation's existence and therefore its right to constitute an independent state (Díaz-Andreu 1995: 54).

Antiquarianism

The case of Cyprus is rather different, inasmuch as Cyprus' independence lay so far in the future (1960). Be that as it may, the archaeology of nineteenth century Cyprus was an archaeology of antiquarianism, imperialism, and the looting of antiquities (Goring 1988). Around the middle of the nineteenth century Cyprus, still part of the Ottoman Empire, was a land densely packed with antiquities that were both collected and exported by foreign officials resident on Cyprus. The Ottoman Antiquities Law declared that finds were to be divided three ways: between the excavators, the owner of the land and the government (Dikaios 1961b: x). Sir Robert Hamilton Lang, one of the first foreign consuls to show interest in Cypriot antiquities, became a well-known collector (Lang 1878: 330–7). In 1870 he loaned a large collection to the Glasgow Museum and Art Gallery (Goring 1988: 9), a collection that remains almost entirely unpublished. Of all the foreign consuls the most active and consequently the most devastating for Cyprus' cultural heritage was the American, General Luigi Palma di Cesnola (Cesnola 1877; Myres 1914: xiii–xxv; Swiny 1991). His large scale plundering expeditions netted more than 10,000 items, most of which were exported from the island after 1870 and purchased by the Metropolitan Museum in New York, at least partly in exchange for Cesnola's appointment as director of the Museum (Casson 1937: 9; Myres 1914).

Colonial archaeology

In 1878, when Cyprus came under direct British administration, a ban was imposed on unauthorised excavations and, by 1887, excavation permits were given only to professional archaeologists represented by public and scientific bodies. Beginning in 1879, Max Ohnefalsch-Richter carried out extensive excavations at numerous sites on behalf of the British Museum, which ultimately received a considerable share of the finds (Myres and Ohnefalsch-Richter 1899). In 1883 the British government founded the Cyprus Museum to house its share of finds from excavations. In the same year, under the guise of philhellenism and with the support of the British School at Athens, the Society for the Promotion of Hellenic Studies, and Cambridge University, the Cyprus Exploration Fund was established to support legitimate field enterprises. The most profitable and professional work carried out under the Fund's aegis was that of J. L. Myres (Myres 1914; Myres and Ohnefalsch-Richter 1899).

With Cyprus' recognition as a Crown Colony in 1925, the archaeological scene changed once again. The fieldwork of the Swedish Cyprus Expedition (1927–31) established a new approach to the recording and analysis of archaeological data, based on stratified sequences and chronological associations (Åström *et al.* 1994: 7). The generous share of finds allocated to the Swedish mission was exported from the island and is now stored and exhibited in the Medelhavsmuseet (Museum of Mediterranean Archaeology) in Stockholm. It is worth noting that, with or without government sanctioning, a substantial stockpile of Cypriot archaeological material had been swept off to foreign museums in Glasgow, New York, London, Cambridge, Stockholm and elsewhere between about 1870 and 1940; such are the consequences of a colonial archaeology.

The international character which Cypriot archaeology gained as a result of the Swedish Cyprus Expedition's fundamental work mobilised the British colonial government to take a deeper interest in the island's antiquities. This led to the enactment of an Antiquities Law in 1935, and the creation of the Department of Antiquities, the latter responsible for all archaeological activity and associated publications on the island. A. H. S. Megaw, a Dubliner educated at the University of Cambridge, was appointed director of the Department, whilst Porphyrios Dikaios, a Greek Cypriote, became Curator of the Cyprus Museum (Dikaios 1961b: ix–xvi).

The culture historical approach to archaeology, introduced to the island by Gjerstad (1926), shaped post-1930 fieldwork and research, including that of Gjerstad's Swedish successors (Åström and Åström 1972; L. Åström 1967; P. Åström 1957, 1966; Sjöqvist 1940) and that of various Cypriote (Dikaios 1953, 1961a, 1969–71; Karageorghis 1965, 1983), French (Schaeffer 1952), British

(Du Plat Taylor 1952, 1957), Australian (Hennessy 1964; Stewart and Stewart 1950) and American (Benson 1972; McFadden 1946) teams. The period between 1935–60, that is, up to the time of Cyprus' independence, proved to be very productive, both for archaeological fieldwork and for various museums round the world (Brown and Catling 1980: 85–86; Peltenburg 1981; Tsielepi and Bienkowski 1988: 2; Webb 1986), which acquired material chiefly from excavations organised and financed by educational institutions. Despite the fact that native Cypriote archaeologists maintained an active and impressive role in the fieldwork of their island (Knapp 1994: 398), colonial attitudes meant that most excavations were still directed by foreigners (Åström 1971; Webb and Frankel 1995: 97, figure 4).

Postcolonial archaeology

In 1960 Cyprus gained its independence and P. Dikaios became the first Cypriote Director of the Department of Antiquities (Åström 1971: 27). Following Dikaios' retirement, Vassos Karageorghis became Director in 1963 and in 1964 the Antiquities Law changed in a critically important way: 'All antiquities which the holder of a licence . . . may discover throughout the duration of the excavations shall vest in the Cyprus Museum without any payment whatsoever' (Karageorghis 1985: 7). The increase of archaeological activity, the encouragement of international expeditions and Karageorghis' personal devotion and immense effort resulted in an international awareness of Cypriot archaeology. Although the culture historical approach was and remains (to a lesser extent) dominant in post-1970 Cypriot archaeology, new directions and eco-environmental approaches were introduced by Australian (Frankel 1974a, 1974b), British (Croft 1985, 1988, 1989; Peltenburg 1983, 1985; Stanley Price 1977, 1979; Todd 1987) and French (Le Brun 1981; Le Brun *et al.* 1987) prehistorians working on Cyprus. This culture historical bias is still prominent in Cypriot archaeology, but no more so than elsewhere in world archaeology, and no less than is essential for a viable programme of archaeological study and research. Several archaeologists working in Cyprus engage in both processual and postprocessual approaches to the study of the past (Hadjisavvas 1992; Held 1990; Karageorghis and Michaelides 1996; Keswani 1989, 1993, 1994; Knapp 1997; Knapp and Meskell 1997; Manning 1993; Peltenburg 1991a, 1991b, 1993; Rupp 1988; Webb 1992, 1995; Webb and Frankel 1994; cf. Merrillees 1994).

The 1974 Turkish invasion and occupation of more than one-third of the island has had a devastating impact on archaeological research. This was the real turning point in archaeological attitudes and political awareness, particularly because all archaeological fieldwork in the north came to an end in July 1974 and all archaeological sites became inaccessible. Moreover, the destruction of ancient and modern monuments and the illicit trade in antiquities began in earnest. Since that time no legal archaeological project or research has been conducted in the north because the only internationally recognised political authority, the government of the Republic of Cyprus, has had no practical control of the occupied area. In the south, however, new sites were made available to several foreign missions that had been working in the north by the Department of Antiquities; at the same time, new excavations and survey projects were encouraged (Karageorghis 1995: 857, Knapp 1994: 435). All current fieldwork and survey is concentrated in the southern part of the island, which has created a different kind of archaeological bias (Knapp 1994: 434). If the culture history of Cyprus was once based largely on the evidence of non-purposive survey and pottery from tombs in the north (Merrillees 1985: 16), interpretations of Cypriot material culture prevalent today are based almost entirely on the results of much more intensive survey and the extensive excavation of settlement sites in the south.

Conclusion

The dichotomy between the authenticity of the local and the appropriative nature of the global has produced its own nostalgia, whether the hope of resistance or the inevitability of the global. If one focuses only on the global appropriation of the local, one loses sight of the complex and contradictory ways in which the past envelops the complex strains of capital and power that constitute place. In fact, these oppositions may contain one another, and our current preoccupation with the sense of place may localise it artificially and contain it within boundaries that never actually existed. Such dichotomies between local histories and global appropriations of place should be reconstituted with a more dynamic concept in which one always and already inhabits the other (Jacobs 1996: 36). If local sites may be linked into global processes, and sanctioned heritage sites can be instilled into nationalistic imagery, then a politics of place becomes the politics of cultural identity.

This is a social geography of difference, of contested cultural reality, and nowhere is it better exemplified than on the island of Cyprus. Despite the pressures of contemporary politics and the limits on archaeological fieldwork, post-1974 developments in Cypriot archaeology have never looked back. The practice of archaeology has been redefined as a means of political expression and cultural representation. Imperial policies and attitudes no longer dictate the direction of Cypriot archaeology, and archaeologists working on the island need to write their own political agenda: the archaeology of Cyprus will never function outside its contemporary sociopolitical context and will never be politically innocent.

Cyprus' national cultural heritage is struggling with an overburden of popular memory and the reality of living in a sharply divided political space. Archaeological research and practice has a direct relevance here and is being shaped by politico-economic forces that demand a nationalistic perspective. However, in order to promote cooperation and to re-establish amicable relations amongst all ethnic groups on the island, it is essential to safeguard and preserve the cultural heritage of every community. The presentation of archaeological sites as cultural attractions in the Mediterranean world offers a nation the opportunity to surmount its colonial past and to reconstruct its archaeological narratives in a politically viable manner. As heritage constructs, such sites actively influence popular meanings or official sanctions imposed on them. The enterprise of heritage, in other words, is very much a political process in which certain places (for example, classical temples) are incorporated into the prescribed, nationalistic point of view, whilst others (for example, Moslem cemeteries) are denied or ignored because they are seen as a threat to nationalistic images.

If we wish to consider how grandiose imperial schemes became unstable, or even unethical, trajectories of power extending across time and space, it is essential to attend to the local, for there one can see how the past actively and influentially inheres in space (Jacobs 1996: 35, 158). The politics of (postcolonial) place involve arenas in which people or polities may express their sense of self and their concept of 'home' – whether that may be a village, an archaeological site, a region, or a nation, an indigenous home or one recently adopted. The politics that emerge from places being remade or reconstructed in a postcolonial image become politics of identity through which notions of culture, class, community or gender are formed (Jacobs 1996: 2; Read 1996). The politics of place and identity is neither decidedly local nor invariably global; rather it is framed around power structures constituted by broader geohistorical, colonial residues, imperialist presents and postcolonial opportunities.

Further issues continue to demand consideration: for example, as younger Greek Cypriotes become involved as participants, collaborators and leaders in the archaeology of their island, how will their contested view of the past be received? How may divergent viewpoints (Greek Cypriote and Turkish Cypriote) be reconciled, or at least debated, in the context of nationalist and ethnic extremism, where archaeology can play such a highly charged and politicised role? As long as personal identity remains inextricably linked to ethnicity and politics, and as long as overtly political acts continue to dictate the course of daily life for 750,000 people living in both the free and the occupied regions of the island, answers to these questions will be a long time coming. In the meantime, the cultural heritage of Cyprus will continue to be reformed in the face of changing and divergent nationalistic trends.

A. Bernard Knapp and Sophia Antoniadou

Acknowledgements

We both thank Lynn Meskell for asking us to contribute to this publication; it has been a challenge to do so. We sincerely thank the following people: Patroklos Stavrou, ex-Under Secretary of the President of the Republic of Cyprus, for providing several offprints and other helpful information, Dr Demos Christou, former Director of the Cypriot Department of Antiquities, for giving us permission to publish the photographs and Michael Mavros, for providing key references on 'antiquarianism' and 'colonial archaeology'. We are also grateful to several people, in addition to the editor, who read and commented upon earlier drafts of this study, and/or suggested further relevant sources: Theodora Alexopoulou, Eleni Antoniadou, David Frankel, Michael Given, Sophocles Hadjisavvas, Vassos Karageorghis, Demetra Papaconstantinou, Panayiotis Voilas, Kylie Seretis, and Stuart Swiny. For their enthusiasm, reaction, and comments, Bernard Knapp wishes to thank members of the honours course in Cypriot Prehistoric Archaeology at the University of Glasgow, and participants in a seminar organised by the School of History and Archaeology at the University of Glasgow.

Notes

1 Some would argue that Greek Cypriotes have specific political agendas, just as the Turks and Turkish Cypriotes do; all political entities are highly selective in their choice of an appropriate past. Others observe that Greek Cypriotes are engaged in the commodification of the past in the race for the tourist dollar. The reality is that the Cypriot Department of Antiquities has very little power, or personnel, to stop such destruction. The situation in the north is palpably worse, however much the relevant 'authorities' there may seek to control illegal looting and export. There is, moreover, little doubt that Turkish Cypriotes have been denied a voice in the archaeology of their island. However, given the current political situation, there is little we can say about northern Cyprus or about Turkish Cypriotes because we do not have access to information held by the Turkish authorities. Nor do we have the permission to cite anything because there is no legal authority to give permission. Under the present circumstances, we could never support or substantiate any details emerging from northern Cyprus. This article, in sum, represents our own personal and political views.

2 Article 18 states: (1) Apart from the provisions which shall take effect in time of peace, the present Convention shall apply in the event of declared war, or any other armed conflict which may arise between two or more of the High

Contracting Parties, even if the state of war is not recognised by one or more of them. (2) The Convention shall also apply to all cases of partial or total occupation of the territory of a High Contracting Party, even if the said occupation meets with no resistance. Article 4 states: (1) The High Contracting Parties undertake to respect the cultural property situated within their own territory as well as within the territory of other High Contracting parties, by refraining from any use of the property and its immediate surroundings or of the appliances in use for its protection for purposes which are likely to expose it to destruction or damage in the event of armed conflict and by refraining from any act of hostility directed against such property. (3) The High Contracting parties further undertake to prohibit, prevent and, if necessary, put a stop to any form of theft, pillage, or misappropriation of any acts of vandalism directed against cultural property.

3 The original one hundred page UNESCO report by Jacques Dalibard, a Canadian expert on religious art, was rejected by UNESCO, who published a 'bowdlerized version' in April 1976 with a UNESCO disclaimer detaching itself from the author's views. UNESCO thus effectively dropped the issue instead of using the report to apply pressure on Turkey, as well as on looters and smugglers (Fielding 1976; Jansen 1986: 315). Note that Tables 3 to 6 simply exemplify the type of theft, destruction, replacement etc. that has occurred – the actual numbers are much higher in each case.

Bibliography

Åström, L. (1967) *Studies on the Arts and Crafts of the Late Cypriot Bronze Age*, Lund: Berlingska.

Åström, L. and Åström, P. (1972) *The Swedish Cyprus Expedition* IV: ID, *The Late Cypriote Bronze Age. Other Arts and Crafts*, Lund: Swedish Cyprus Expedition.

Åström, P. (1957) *The Swedish Cyprus Expedition*, IV: IB, *The Middle Cypriote Bronze Age*, Lund: Swedish Cyprus Expedition.

—— (1966) *Excavations at Kalopsidha and Ayios Iakovos in Cyprus*, Studies in Mediterranean Archaeology 2, Lund: P. Åström's Förlag.

—— (1971) *Who's Who in Cypriote Archaeology*, Studies in Mediterranean Archaeology 23, Göteborg: P. Åström's Förlag.

Åström, P., Gjerstad, E., Merrillees, R. S. and Westholm, A. (1994) *The Fantastic Years on Cyprus: The Swedish Cyprus Expedition and Its Members*, Studies in Mediterranean Archaeology and Literature 79, Jonsered: P. Åström's Förlag.

Alastos, D. (1955) *Cyprus in History: A Survey of 5,000 Years*, London: Zeno.

Andah, B. W. (1995) 'Studying African societies in cultural context', in P. R.

Schmidt and T. C. Patterson (eds) *Making Alternative Histories. The Practice of Archaeology and History in Non-Western Settings*, Santa Fe: School of American Research Press, pp. 149–81.

Argyrou, V. (1995) 'Greek Cypriot nationalism and the poverty of imagination', in P. W. Wallace (ed.) *Visitors, Immigrants and Invaders in Cyprus*, Albany: Institute of Cypriot Studies, SUNY Albany, pp. 196–201.

Atkinson, J. A., Banks, I. and O'Sullivan, J. (eds) (1996) *Nationalism and Archaeology*, Glasgow: Cruithne Press.

Attalides, M. (1979) *Cyprus: Nationalism and International Politics*, Edinburgh: Q Press.

Banks, I. (1996) 'Archaeology, nationalism and ethnicity', in J. A. Atkinson, I. Banks and J. O'Sullivan (eds) *Nationalism and Archaeology*, Glasgow: Cruithne Press, pp. 1–11.

Banks, M. (1995) *Ethnicity: Anthropological Constructions*, Routledge: London.

Benson, J. L. (1972) *Bamboula at Kourion: The Necropolis and the Finds*, University Museum Monograph, Philadelphia: University of Pennsylvania.

Brown, A. and Catling, H. W. (1980) 'Additions to the Cypriot collection in the Ashmolean Museum', *Opuscula Atheniensia* 13: 91–137.

Brown, K. S. (1994) 'Seeing stars: character and identity in the landscapes of modern Macedonia', *Antiquity* 68/261: 784–96.

Byrne-Sutton, Q. (1992) 'The Goldberg Case: a confirmation of the difficulty in acquiring good title to valuable stolen cultural objects', *International Journal of Cultural Property* 1: 151–68.

Carter, P. (1987) *The Road to Botany Bay*, London: Faber and Faber.

Casson, S. (1937) *Ancient Cyprus, its Art and Archaeology*, London: Methuen.

Cesnola, L. P. di (1877) *Cyprus: Its Ancient Cities, Tombs and Temples. A Narrative of Researches and Excavations during Ten Years' Residence as American Consul in that Island*, London: John Murray.

Chippindale, C. (1994) 'Editorial', *Antiquity* 68: 1–9.

Constantinides, T. (1880) *Historia tis Kyprou* (History of Cyprus), Larnaca.

Crawshaw, N. (1986) 'Cyprus: the political background', in J. T. A. Koumoulides (ed.) *Cyprus in Transition*, London: Trigraph.

Croft, P. (1985) 'The mammalian faunal remains: summary and conclusions', in E. J. Peltenburg, *Lemba Archaeological Project I: Excavations at Lemba Lakkous, 1976–1983*, Studies in Mediterranean Archaeology 70.1, Göteborg: P. Åström's Förlag, pp. 295–6.

—— (1988) 'Animal remains from Maa-Palaeokastro', in V. Karageorghis and M. Demas, *Excavations at Maa-Palaeokastro 1979–1986*, Nicosia: Department of Antiquities, Cyprus, pp. 449–57.

—— (1989) 'The Osteology of Neolithic and Chalcolithic Cyprus', unpublished PhD thesis, Dept of Archaeology, Cambridge University: Cambridge.

Díaz-Andreu, M. (1995) 'Archaeology and nationalism in Spain', in P. L. Kohl and C. Fawcett (eds) *Nationalism, Politics, and the Practice of Archaeology*, Cambridge: Cambridge University Press, pp. 39–56.

Díaz-Andreu, M. and Champion, T. (eds) (1995) *Nationalism and Archaeology in Europe*, London: University College London Press.

Dikaios, P. (1953) *Khirokitia. Monograph of the Department of Antiquities of the Government of Cyprus* 1, Oxford: Oxford University Press.

—— (1961a) *Sotira*, University Museum Monograph, Philadelphia: University Museum Press.

—— (1961b) *A Guide to the Cyprus Museum,* Nicosia: Department of Antiquities, Cyprus.

—— (1969–1971) *Enkomi. Excavations 1948–1958*, vols 1–3, Mainz-am-Rhein: von Zabern.

Du Plat Taylor, J. (1952) 'A Late Bronze Age settlement at Apliki, Cyprus', *Antiquaries Journal* 32: 133–67.

—— (1957) *Myrtou-Pigadhes: A Late Bronze Age Sanctuary in Cyprus*, Oxford: Ashmolean Museum.

Elon, A. (1994) 'Politics and Archaeology', *New York Review of Books*, 29 September, 14–18.

Ferguson, L. (1992) *Uncommon Ground: Archaeology and Early African America, 1650–1800*, Washington, DC: Smithsonian Institution Press.

Fielding, J. (1976) *The Guardian*, 6 May, 1976.

Frankel, D. (1974a) *Middle Cypriot White Painted Pottery: An Analytical Study of the Decoration*, Studies in Mediterranean Archaeology 42, Göteborg: P. Åström's Förlag.

—— (1974b) 'Inter-site relationships in the Middle Bronze Age of Cyprus', *World Archaeology* 6: 190–208.

Gallas, V.K. (1990) 'Wo der Himmel unter die Räuber fält (Where the Heavens Are Plundered)', *Frankfurter Allgemeine Magazin*, Nicosia: Republic of Cyprus, PIO.

Gjerstad, E. (1926) *Studies on Prehistoric Cyprus*, Uppsala: Uppsala Universitets Årsskrift.

Goring, E. (1988) *A Mischievous Pastime: Digging in Cyprus in the Nineteenth Century*, Edinburgh: National Museums of Scotland.

Graves-Brown, P., Jones, S. and Gamble, C. S. (eds) (1996) *Cultural Identity and Archaeology: The Construction of European Communities*, London: Routledge.

Hadjidimitriou, K. (1987) *Istoria tis Kyprou*, Nicosia: Synergatiko.

Hadjisavvas, S. (1992) *Olive Oil Processing in Cyprus. From the Bronze Age to the Byzantine Period*, Studies in Mediterranean Archaeology 99, Jonsered: Paul Åström's Förlag.

Handsman, R. G. (1991) 'Whose art was found at Lipinski Vir? Gender relations and power in archaeology', in J. M. Gero and M. W. Conkey (eds) *Engendering Archaeology: Women and Prehistory*, Oxford: Basil Blackwell, pp. 329–65.

Held, S. O. (1990) 'Back to what future? New directions for Cypriot Early Prehistoric research in the 1990s', *Report of the Department of Antiquities of Cyprus*: 1–43.

Hennessy, J. B. (1964) *Stephania: A Middle and Late Bronze Age Cemetery in Cyprus*, London: Bernard Quaritch.

Hill, G. (1952) *A History of Cyprus*, volume 4, Cambridge: Cambridge University Press.

Hofstadter, D. (1992a) 'Annals of the antiquities trade 1: the angel on her shoulder', *The New Yorker* (13 July 1992): 36–65.

—— (1992b) 'Annals of the antiquities trade 2: the angel on her shoulder', *The New Yorker* (20 July 1992): 38–65.

—— (1994) *Goldberg's Angel: An Adventure in the Antiquities Trade*, New York: Farrar, Straus, Giroux.

Holtorf, C., Pluciennik, M. and Shanks, M. (1996) 'Review of P. L. Kohl and C. Fawcett (eds) *Archaeology, Nationalism, and the Practice of Archaeology* (Cambridge: Cambridge University Press, 1995)', *Arch-Theory* bulletin board (15 March 1996).

Hunt, D. (1990) *Footprints in Cyprus: An Illustrated History*, London: Trigraph.

Jacobs, J. M. (1996) *Edge of Empire: Postcolonialism and the City*, London: Routledge.

Jansen, M. (1986) 'Cyprus: the loss of a cultural heritage', *Modern Greek Studies Yearbook* 2: 314–23.

Jones, S. (1997a) *The Archaeology of Ethnicity: Reconstructing Identities in the Past and the Present*, London: Routledge.

—— (1997b) 'Whose Past? Archaeology and the Search for Origins in Ancient Palestine', seminar presented in the Dept of Archaeology, University of Glasgow (28 January 1997).

Kapsos, C. (1995) 'Modern invaders in Cyprus', in P. W. Wallace (ed.) *Visitors, Immigrants and Invaders in Cyprus*, Albany: Institute of Cypriot Studies, SUNY Albany, pp. 184–9.

Karageorghis, V. (1965) *Nouveaux documents pour l'étude du bronze récent à Chypre*, Études chypriotes 3, Paris: E. de Boccard.

—— (1983) *Palaepaphos-Skales: An Iron Age Cemetery in Cyprus*, Alt-Paphos 3, Constanz: Universitätsverlag.

—— (ed.) (1985) *Archaeology in Cyprus 1960–1985*, Nicosia: Leventis Foundation.

—— (1995) 'Archaeology in Cyprus: the last sixty years', *Modern Greek Studies Yearbook* 11: 849–95.

Karageorghis, V. and Michaelides, D. (eds) (1996) *The Development of the Cypriot Economy*, Nicosia: University of Cyprus and the Bank of Cyprus.

Keswani, P. S. (1989) 'Dimensions of social hierarchy in Late Bronze Age Cyprus:

an analysis of the mortuary data from Enkomi', *Journal of Mediterranean Archaeology* 2: 46–89.

—— (1993) 'Models of local exchange in Late Bronze Age Cyprus', *Bulletin of the American Schools of Oriental Research* 292: 73–83.

—— (1994) 'The social context of animal husbandry in early agricultural societies: ethnographic insights and an archaeological example from Cyprus', *Journal of Anthropological Archaeology* 13: 255–77.

Knapp, A. B. (1996) 'Archaeology without gravity? Postmodernism and the past', *Journal of Archaeological Method and Theory* 3: 127–58.

—— (1997) *The Archaeology of Late Bronze Age Cypriot Society: The Study of Settlement, Survey and Landscape*, Glasgow: Dept of Archaeology, University of Glasgow, Occasional Paper 4.

Knapp, A. B. (with Held, S. O. and Manning, S. W.) (1994) 'The Prehistory of Cyprus: Problems and Prospects', *Journal of World Prehistory* 8: 377–453.

Knapp, A. B. and Meskell, L. M. (1997) 'Bodies of evidence on prehistoric Cyprus', *Cambridge Archaeological Journal* 7: 183–204.

Kohl, P. L. and Fawcett, C. (1995a) (eds) *Nationalism, Politics, and the Practice of Archaeology*, Cambridge: Cambridge University Press.

—— (1995b) 'Archaeology in the service of the state: theoretical considerations', in P. L. Kohl and C. Fawcett (eds) *Nationalism, Politics, and the Practice of Archaeology*, Cambridge: Cambridge University Press, pp. 3–18.

Koumoulides, J. T. A. (ed.) (1986) *Cyprus in Transition*, London: Trigraph.

Kyrris, C. P. (1985) *History of Cyprus – With an Introduction to the Geography of Cyprus*, Nicosia: Nicocles Publishing House.

Lang, R. H. (1878) *Cyprus: Its History, Its Present Resources, and Future Prospects*, London: Macmillan and Co.

Le Brun, A. (1981) *Un Site néolithique précéramique en Chypre: Cap Andreas Kastros*, Recherches sur les Grandes Civilisations Mémoire 5 (Études néolithiques), Paris: ADPF.

Le Brun, A., Cluzan, S., Davis, S. J. M., Hansen, J. and Renault-Miskovsky, J. (1987) 'Le Néolithique préceramique de Chypre,' *L'Anthropologie* (Paris) 91(1): 283–316.

MacConnell, B. E. (1989) 'Mediterranean archaeology and modern nationalism: a preface', *Revue des Archaeologues et Historiens d'Art de Louvain* 22: 107–13.

McFadden, G. H. (1946) 'A tomb of the necropolis of Ayios Ermoyenis at Kourion', *American Journal of Archaeology* 50: 449–89.

Manning, S. W. (1993) 'Prestige, distinction and competition: the anatomy of socio-economic complexity in 4th–2nd millennium B.C.E. Cyprus', *Bulletin of the American Schools of Oriental Research* 292: 35–58.

Merrillees, R. S. (1985) 'Twenty-five years of Cypriot archaeology: the Stone Age and Early and Middle Bronze age', in V. Karageorghis (ed.) *Archaeology in Cyprus, 1960–1985*, Nicosia: Leventis Foundation, pp. 11–19.

—— (1994) 'Einar Gjerstad: Reflections on the past and the present', in *The Swedish Cyprus Expedition: The Living Past*, Medelhavsmuseet Memoir 9: 45–53, Stockholm: Medelhavsmuseet.

Myres, J. L. (1914) *Handbook of the Cesnola Collection of Antiquities from Cyprus*, New York: Metropolitan Museum of Art.

Myres, J. L. and Ohnefalsch-Richter, M. (1899) *A Catalogue of the Cyprus Museum*, Oxford: Clarendon Press.

O'Keefe, P. S. and Prott, L. V. (1989) *Law and the Cultural Heritage*, vol. 3, London: Butterworth.

Pantelis, S. (1985) *Nea Istoria tis Kyprou* (Modern History of Cyprus), Athens: I. Floros.

Peltenburg, E. J. (1981) *Cypriot Antiquities in the Birmingham Museum and Art Gallery*, Birmingham: Birmingham Museum and Art Gallery.

—— (1983) *Vrysi: A Subterranean Settlement in Cyprus*, Warminster: Aris and Phillips.

—— (1985) *Lemba Archaeological Project 1: Excavations 1976–1983*, Studies in Mediterranean Archaeology 70.1, Göteborg: P. Åström's Förlag.

—— (1991a) 'Kissonerga-*Mosphilia*: a major Chalcolithic site in Cyprus', *Bulletin of the American Schools of Oriental Research* 282–283: 17–35.

—— (1991b) *Lemba Archaeological Project 2:2. A Ceremonial Area at Kissonerga*, Studies in Mediterranean Archaeology 70.3, Göteborg: P. Åström's Förlag.

—— (1993) 'Settlement discontinuity and resistance to complexity in Cyprus, ca. 4500–2500 B.C.', *Bulletin of the American Schools of Oriental Research* 292: 9–23.

Pollock, S. (1992) 'Bureaucrats and managers, peasants and pastoralists, imperialists and traders: research in the Uruk and Jemdet Nasr periods in Mesopotamia', *Journal of World Prehistory* 6: 297–336.

Preucel, R. (1995) 'The postprocessual condition', *Journal of Archaeological Research* 3: 147–75.

Read, P. (1996) *Return to Nothing. The Meaning of Lost Places*, Cambridge: Cambridge University Press.

Renfrew, A. C. (1994) 'The identity of Europe in prehistoric archaeology', *Journal of European Archaeology* 2: 153–73.

Robins, K. (1991) 'Tradition and translation: national culture in its global context', in J. Corner and S. Harvey (eds) *Enterprise and Culture: Crosscurrents of National Culture*, London: Routledge, pp. 21–44.

Rupp, D. W. (1988) 'The Royal Tombs at Salamis, Cyprus: ideological messages of power and authority', *Journal of Mediterranean Archaeology* 1: 111–39.

Said, E. W. (1978) *Orientalism*, New York: Pantheon.

—— (1993) *Culture and Imperialism*, London: Vintage.

Schaeffer, C. F. A. (1952) *Enkomi-Alasia* I. *Nouvelles missions en Chypre 1946–1950*, Paris: Klincksieck.

Schmidt, P. R. and Patterson, T. C. (eds) (1995) *Making Alternative Histories. The Practice of Archaeology and History in Non-Western Settings*, Santa Fe: School of American Research Press.

Shanks, M. and Tilley, C. (1987a) *Re-Constructing Archaeology: Theory and Practice*, Cambridge: Cambridge University Press.

—— (1987b) *Social Theory and Archaeology*, Cambridge: Polity Press.

—— (1989) 'Archaeology into the 1990s', *Norwegian Archaeological Review* 22: 1–54.

Silberman, N. A. (1987) *Digging for God and Country: Exploration of the Holy Land 1799–1917*, New York: Anchor Books/Doubleday.

—— (1989) *Between Past and Present. Archaeology, Idealology, and Nationalism in the Modern Middle East*, New York: Doubleday.

—— (1995) 'Promised lands and chosen people: the politics and poetics of archaeological narrative', in P. L. Kohl and C. Fawcett (eds) *Nationalism, Politics, and the Practise of Archaeology*, Cambridge: Cambridge University Press, pp. 249–62.

Sjöqvist, E. (1940) *Problems of the Late Cypriote Bronze Age*, Stockholm: Swedish Cyprus Expedition.

Spector, J. (1993) *What This Awl Means. Feminist Archaeology at a Wahpeton Dakota Village*, St Paul: Minnesota Historical Society Press.

Stanley Price, N. P. (1977) 'Colonisation and continuity in the early prehistory of Cyprus', *World Archaeology* 9: 27–41.

—— (1979) *Early Prehistoric Settlement in Cyprus: A Review and Gazetteer of Sites, c. 6500–3000 BC*, British Archaeological Reports, International Series 65, Oxford: BAR.

Stewart, E. and Stewart, J. (1950) *Vounous 1937–1938*, Skrifter Utgivna av Svenska Institutet i Rom 14, Lund: Swedish Institute in Rome.

Stoler, A. (1989) 'Rethinking colonial categories: European communities and the boundaries of rule', *Comparative Studies in Society and History* 31: 134–61.

Stylianou, P. (1987) *The Plundering of the Cultural Heritage in Occupied Cyprus*, Nicosia: Kipriaki Basiki Bibliothiki.

Swiny, S. (1991) Foreward to reprinted edition of L. P. di Cesnola (1877) *Cyprus: Its Ancient Sites, Tombs and Temples. A Narrative of Researches and Excavations during Ten Years' Residence as American Consul in that Island* (London: John Murray), Limassol: James Bendon Ltd.

Tenekides, G. (1994) 'The rescue of the cultural heritage of occupied Cyprus.

The international dimensions', in *Cyprus: The Plundering of a 9000-year-old Civilization*, Athens: Committee for the Protection of the Cultural Heritage of Cyprus.

Thomas, N. (1994) *Colonialism's Culture: Anthropology, Travel and Government*, Cambridge: Polity Press.

Todd, I. (1987) *Excavations at Kalavassos-Tenta. Vasilikos Valley Project 6*, Studies in Mediterranean Archaeology 71.6, Göteborg: P. Åström's Förlag.

Trigger, B. G. (1984) 'Alternative archaeologies: nationalist, colonialist, imperialist', *Man* 19: 355–70.

—— (1995) 'Romanticism, nationalism, and archaeology', in P. L. Kohl and C. Fawcett (eds) *Nationalism, Politics, and the Practise of Archaeology*, Cambridge: Cambridge University Press, pp. 263–79.

Tsalakos, G. (1981) 'Suntome Episkopisi Orismenon Opseon tis Anglokratias stin Kypro' (Brief review of some aspects of the British rule in Cyprus), in E. Tenekides and Y. Kranidiotis (eds) *Kypros: Istoria, Problemata kai Agones tou Laou tis* (Cyprus: History, Problems and the Struggles of its People), Athens: Hestia.

Tsielepi, S. C. and Bienkowski, P. (1988) *Cypriot Pottery in the Liverpool Museum, An Interim List*, National Museums and Galleries on Merseyside, Occasional Papers 2, Liverpool: Liverpool Museum.

van Dommelen, P. (1997) 'Colonial constructs: colonialism and archaeology in the Mediterranean', *World Archaeology* 28: 305–23.

Webb, J. (1986) *Cypriote Antiquities in Abbey Museum, Queensland, Australia*, Corpus of Cypriote Antiquities 12, Studies in Mediterranean Archaeology 20(12), Göteborg: P. Åström's Förlag.

—— (1992) 'Funerary ideology in Bronze Age Cyprus – towards the recognition and analysis of Cypriote ritual data', in G. K. Ioannides (ed.) *Studies in Honour of Vassos Karageorghis*, Nicosia: Society of Cypriot Studies, pp. 87–99.

—— (1995) 'Abandonment processes and curate/discard strategies at Marki-Alonia, Cyprus', *The Artifact* 18: 64–70.

Webb, J. and Frankel, D. (1994) 'Making an impression: storage and surplus finance in Late Bronze Age Cyprus', *Journal of Mediterranean Archaeology* 7: 5–26.

—— (1995) 'Gender inequity and archaeological practise: a Cypriot case study', *Journal of Mediterranean Archaeology* 8: 93–112.

Whitelam, K. W. (1996) *The Invention of Ancient Israel: The Silencing of Palestinian History*, London: Routledge.

Wilk, R. R. (1985) 'The ancient Maya and the political present', *Journal of Anthropological Research* 41: 307–26.

Wylie, A. (1991) 'Feminist critiques and archaeological challenges', in D. Walde and N. D. Willows (eds) *The Archaeology of Gender. Proceedings of the 22nd Annual Conference of the Archaeological Association of the University of Calgary*, Calgary: Archaeological Association, University of Calgary, pp. 17–23.

——(1993) 'A proliferation of new archaeologies: beyond objectivism and relativism', in N. Yoffee and A. Sherratt (eds) *Archaeological Theory – Who Sets the Agenda?*, Cambridge: Cambridge University Press, pp. 20–6.

Yasin, M. (1982) 'Perishing Cyprus', *Olay* 26 April–17 May 1982.

Zimmerman, L. (1995) 'We do not need your past: politics, Indian time, and Plains archaeology', in P. Duke and M. C. Wilson (eds) *Beyond Subsistence: Plains Archaeology and the Postprocessual Critique*, Tuscaloosa: University Press of Alabama, pp. 28–45.

Chapter 2

The past is ours

Images of Greek Macedonia

Kostas Kotsakis

Introduction

In November 1977, in a packed auditorium at the University of Thessaloniki, the most spectacular archaeological find of the last decades was presented to the thrilled audience. Few of us realised at that time that the rich results of the excavations of the Great Tumulus at Vergina had opened a complete new chapter in Macedonia, and that this find would affect, directly or indirectly, the fate of all subsequent archaeology in this part of Greece. Still fewer, however, had imagined that these unlooted graves connected with King Philip II would bring to the fore aspects of the political use of the past, and be the focus of conflicting claims and interpretations on an international scale which would oblige the excavators, and the rest of archaeologists working in Macedonia for that matter, to defend the prerogative to consider their archaeological work as part of their cultural heritage.

In a sense, however, superficial similarities to the task of the nineteenth century, albeit only in form, did exist. According to the nationalist historiography of the new Macedonian state, which appeared as part of Yugoslavia in 1945 and as an independent state in 1991, the association between ancient Greeks and ancient Macedonians was a *post hoc* fabrication (Borza 1982; Danforth 1995: 167, esp. n. 22; Kofos 1994). During this process of conflicting interests and uses of the past latent characteristics of Greek archaeology emerged, which had so far remained in the background. However, whether perceived or not, they were not novel, but already existing even from the nineteenth century when archaeology was called to construct the images of the Hellenic past of the Greek state (Kokkou 1977; Petrakos 1987; Skopetea 1984). At that time, the international acceptance of this political construction, and the general ideological background of nineteenth-century romanticism, had helped to diminish the contradictions which this process entailed. Still, at the end of the twentieth century, in a multicultural political landscape of rapid political transformations on the one hand, and the emergence of new nations and states on the other, the situation was less favourable for the presentation of powerful collective myths, similar to those which had inspired the romantic passions of the last century.

In a sense, superficial similarities in form did exist. Once again, Greek scholars felt they had to deal with questions of ethnicity as they had done in the nineteenth century when Fallmereyer had challenged the continuity of Greek history (Skopetea 1997; Veloudis 1982). Equally, the relative eclipse of interest in the obscure Middle Ages was a well-described trait of that period (Dimaras 1985: 398–400) which was repeated now, in the case of Macedonia. But more than anything else, it was the thrust of collective memory into an arena of national political struggle that brought to the surface the character of this archaeological confrontation.

It would be naïve to underestimate the power of all nationalisms to direct the formation of collective memories, and to embody historical continuity (Miller 1995), be it part of a distinct homogeneous culture (Gellner 1983; 1987), or a 'necessary consequence of novelty . . . the expression of a radically changed form of consciousness' (Anderson 1991: xiv). From this point of view, the Greek experience is not different from similar cases described in various parts of the world and probably has no special interest as a historically documented process. What is perhaps different, is the particular place that Greek identity held for an international audience which consequently challenged the limits of self-ascription against the ascription by others, as perceived by Barth (1969). Over this ideo-logical tension, of which archaeology forms an integral part, the limits of our understanding of the discipline and of its role in a modern world are tried.

The constitution of Macedonia as a research object

Macedonia became part of the Greek state in 1913. As a distinct archaeological subject, however, it has only recently attracted some interest. With little excep-tion, until the 1970s no major archaeological projects comparable to those carried out in Southern Greece were launched in Macedonia, and the foreign missions, active in Greece since the nineteenth century, have regarded Macedonia with relative indifference. A number of reasons, not necessarily related to archaeological priorities, can be held responsible for this apparent lag in entering the area of collective archaeological imagination. The political adventures of the region, since the beginning of the century, were, without any doubt, a crucial factor. Successive wars in the region practically ended in the 1950s, and prior to that, in 1922, a huge wave of refugees from Asia Minor had settled in this land. Ethnic and social conflict had been dominant in Macedonia since the end of the nineteenth century when it became the theatre of fiercely competing nationalisms (Danforth 1995; Kofos 1997). Hence there were only brief periods of political stability to permit long-term projects. Nevertheless, similar – although perhaps less acute – vicissitudes did not prevent the intensive exploration of the rest of Greece, mostly by Europeans, but occasionally also by Greeks, and the development of the grand projects in the main centres of Hellenism, which gave to classical archaeology its distinctive quality (Petrakos 1982; Morris 1994). More than the political instability, it was the particular character of Macedonia which kept this region away from the main course of archaeological research.

Macedonia, however, was not totally outside the European vision of the Hellenic past. Even from 1784, Stuart and Revett in their famous work *Antiquities of Athens*, included drawings of the 'Incantadas', a Roman monument of Thessaloniki which was subsequently taken to the Louvre in 1864. M. Cousinéry, in his work *Voyages dans la Macédoine* (1831) and M. Leake, *Travels in Northern Greece* (1835) added Macedonia to the idealised geography of Hellenism. In 1839, Theophilus Tafel published in Berlin his collection and critical discussion of ancient sources on Thessaloniki and, in 1841, a study on the Roman 'Via Egnatia'. It was Léon Heuzey who initiated proper archaeological investigations in the region with his work in Western Macedonia, which culminated in the identification of what came to be known in later years as the city of Aegae, the ancient capital of the Macedonian Kings, now near the modern village of Vergina. His book *Mission archéologique de Macédoine* (1876) presents the results of this expedition, among which stands the excavation of both a Macedonian tomb, the first to be discovered in the region, and of the eastern part of a palace, according to Heuzey's dating from the time of Alexander.

All this initial research was more or less forgotten, and apart from minor issues of ancient topography of a historical, rather than archaeological, character, little further work was undertaken in Macedonia in subsequent decades. In the meantime, the great discoveries of Southern Greece, in Mycenae, Olympia, Delphi, Delos and the other centres of Classical Greece (Petrakos 1987) provided a wealth of finds and a direct link with ancient literary sources which eclipsed the modest finds of those first explorations and the sparse references of the classical writers to Macedonia. The philological model of archaeology and archaeology as history of art (Shanks 1996) were at that time very powerful to allow the meek archaeology of Macedonia a significant role in the formation of the Hellenic past. Thus

Macedonia gradually became the Other of Southern Greece, a view which persisted until very recently (Andreou, Fotiadis and Kotsakis 1996).

I would like to propose that the Otherness of Macedonia was a result of the tension between the geopolitical situation of the region, which at that period had a shifting and undetermined ethnological makeup (Mackridge and Yannakakis 1997: 4–5), and the concept of a well-defined Hellenic past that had been shaped in classicism and in classical archaeology in particular, and had a strong ethnic quality (Skopetea 1997). Their conflict formulated a stereotype of Macedonia that, for obvious reasons, could only marginally incorporate potentially meaningful similarities and differences to the rest of Greece other than those deriving from within the context of Hellenism. Briefly, the modern inhabitants of Macedonia, contrary to those of the South, could not safely, in Herzfeld's words 'accept the role of living ancestors of European civilization' (1987: 19). This ethnological obstacle of the present was intensified by the presumed silence of the past.

The prehistory of the region followed suit: it was conceived mainly as an absence of traits recognised long ago in the prehistory of Southern Greece. There was no Helladic culture here, no bronze age culture equal to the Mycenaean, nor even proper Geometric and Archaic phases, which as recently as 1932 were lumped together under the generic name 'pre-Persian' (Robinson 1932). Instead, this was an area of later colonisation from the south, the relations of which to the local population were, curiously enough, never considered. This notion of backwardness was a recurring theme in the archaeological literature of that period (Andreou, Fotiadis and Kotsakis 1996: 560–61). Even the coming of the Greeks, although at that time viewed as a migration from the north (Crossland and Birchall 1973; Haley and Blegen 1928; Sakellariou 1970) did not offer an identifiable progeny to this idiosyncratic culture, the main distinctive quality of which remained its geographic position in 'cross-roads', i.e. in a state of becoming, but not really of being a culture which could be directly related to Southern Greece.[1] This was the current opinion when Heurtley began his major project on the prehistory of Macedonia in the 1920s, following a line of research which had started a few years earlier during World War I, by the Allies stationed in Greece (Heurtley 1939).

Not all archaeologies practised in Macedonia had similar reservations. During the years that followed its incorporation into the Greek state, the Greek Archaeological Service of Macedonia was organised and numerous archaeological projects were initiated. Excavation and restoration was carried out on a number of monuments in Thessaloniki, the capital of Macedonia, and particularly on Byzantine churches which had been used as mosques during the Ottoman period. Most of these interventions had a 'purist' character, aiming at restoring the initial – 'Byzantine' – integrity of the monument (Theocharidou and Tsioumi 1985). Regional research and excavation was also carried out in the hinterland of

Macedonia. Notable among this is the regional research of A. Keramopoullos in western Macedonia, in the areas of Kozani and Kastoria. K. A. Romaios, Professor of the University of Thessaloniki, founded in 1926, resumed Heuzey's excavations at Palatitsa where, in the meantime, a refugee village called Vergina was established near the site. A. Sotiriadis, again Professor of the University of Thessaloniki, started excavations at the sacred city of the Macedonians, Dion, at the foothills of Mt Olympus. These excavations still form the main part of the University's archaeological project.

Considerable opportunity was given, therefore, to Greek archaeologists who were working in Macedonia at that time. The relative lack of interest from European archaeology was undoubtedly leaving the field open. But, above all, it was the pressing needs of the new political circumstances which provided the main impetus to Greek archaeology. These demanding circumstances evidently gave a sense of mission to those archaeologists working with limited resources in difficult times. Still, it was more than that, as Romaios revealingly observes, opposing subtly the cosmopolitanism of modernism to the ethics of nationality (Miller 1995):

> Generally speaking, Tsountas did not regard archaeological places, as every foreign scholar does, as merely an invaluable and sacred focal point of the universal civilisation, but also as our own places, which either from a distance or from a closer examination speak to us always about our national history. . . . It is customary in Greek excavations, or at least it should be, that the director does not remain, like the foreign archaeologist, enclosed in his mysterious wisdom, without any spiritual contact with workmen. . . . In this instance the workmen were refugees . . . who knew something of our national history . . . so that their exclusion from the spiritual labour of the excavation was never to be permitted.
>
> (my translation, Romaios 1941)

There was at least one area where Macedonia was construed as an archaeological subject, even from the nineteenth century, and which brought foreign and Greek archaeologists together. That was Byzantine archaeology, which was focused on the city of Thesalloniki, the second city of the Empire after Constantinople, and the former capital of Emperor Galerius. Excavations started here in 1917 on the palace of Galerius and were promptly carried out on most of the important Byzantine monuments of the town. An international consensus of scholars, such as Gabriel Millet, Charles Diehl and David Talbot-Rice, were soon canonising Byzantine art by defining schools and styles, as well as artists, which were active in Macedonia, Serbia and Mount Athos between the thirteenth and fifteenth centuries (Bryer 1997). The Greek side would follow, if only to defend the Greek heritage of the Schools and the ethnic origins of these artists (Prokopiou 1962).

The identification of Thessaloniki with the multicultural, multi-ethnic character of the Byzantine Empire was in deeper accordance with the political, cultural and economic character of the city which, throughout the Ottoman period, had developed into a cosmopolitan centre of administration and commerce. Nevertheless, multiethnicity, which nowadays forms the main slogan of Thessaloniki as the Cultural Capital of Europe for 1997, was not in the least the main concern in the decades that followed the annexation of Macedonia to the Greek state. On the contrary, the Byzantine character of the city was closely related to the Greek assumption that Byzantium was 'a purely Greek civilization' which secured the continuity with the Greek past, albeit indirectly (Mackridge and Yannakakis 1997: 12–15). An unmistakeable symbol of this historical construction was the University of Thessaloniki which, although named after the Greek philosopher Aristotle, adopted Saint Demetrius as its main emblem.

The quest for continuity with the past, which had grossly supported the ideological construction of the Greek state during the nineteenth century (Kalpaxis 1990; Kotsakis 1991; Skopetea 1984) was thus transferred to Macedonia. The Otherness of Macedonia, which we referred to earlier, was tacitly circumvented and the Byzantine cultural heritage was used as an indirect, but powerful, link which would bind together both areas of the Greek state, the old South and the new North, and would restore the primordial character of the nation. The project of the construction of a new Greek Macedonian identity thus became part of the general project of nation-building. Aiming at the ethnologically diverse population of the region, it took the form of an assimilationist policy through Hellenisation (Carabott 1997; Karakasidou 1997; Koliopoulos 1997). That was then the ideological – and political – space within which archaeology was invited to work in Macedonia soon after it became part of the Greek Kingdom.

A quest for continuity: the formation of modern Greek national identity

The complicated issue of the formation of modern Greek national identity has been the subject of recent discussions that place the Greek experience within the general argument of the construction of modernity (Herzfeld 1987; Friedman 1992). Following a somewhat different lead, modern Greek historiography in recent years has examined ethnic collectivities laying more emphasis on the circumstances and conditions for the construction of national identity. To this end modern Greek historiography is approaching the subject, not from the synchronic view of the deconstructionist, but from the diachronic position of the historian (e.g. Kitromilidis 1997; Koliopoulos 1997b; Veremis 1997). In this attempt the new Greek historians are furthering the work of the previous generation of historians such as Svoronos and Dimaras (Kitroef 1997).

According to Kitromilidis (1997) the origins of nationalism in the Balkans must be sought during the period of Enlightenment when, through a process of cultural change, national consciousness was imprinted on the identities of different groups in the Balkans. The main ideological drive behind this process, usually described by nationalist historiography as an 'awakening' of national identities, was a concept of primordialism, according to which the nation existed long before any state formation was achieved. This was the basis of the national history of the nineteenth century in Southeastern Europe, which pursued ethnic identities into the past, projecting them onto a national identity of the present. Rejecting the 'awakening' of an eternal continuity, Kitromilidis discusses critically the formation mechanisms of a homogenising national identity, most important among them, education, a well-known and very effective tool in the construction of the normative discourse of nationalism (Anderson 1991: 67–72; see Özdoğan, Chapter 5; Roth, Chapter 12; Hassan, Chapter 11). In the Greek experience, education was not addressed solely to populations within the limits of the Greek state, but also to Orthodox communities living in the Balkans and in the Asian provinces of the Ottoman Empire (Kitromilidis 1997: 92–103). One should emphasise, incidentally, the close relation of education to history, archaeology, and to notions of ethnic antiquity that are founded on archaeological arguments, an element with strong nationalist overtones which survives even in present day education in Greece (Fragkoudaki and Dragona 1997).

The mechanisms of national integration, through institutions such as consulates, educational institutions and the army, were applied to the region of Macedonia by the young Greek state (Kofos 1997: 202). The region at that time was inhabited by a population 'of an indefinite ethnological composition . . . with a historical heritage open to disputed and conflicting interpretations' (Kofos 1997: 200). The extent to which this population belonged to recognisable collectivities is a matter of conjecture. The application of fixed criteria for defining ethnicity is questionable, at least since Barth (1969) introduced the concept of boundaries of ethnic groups, shifting the critical focus from the 'cultural stuff that [the group] encloses' to the maintenance of social dividing lines (Barth 1981: 204). If this is so, any a priori existence or stability in the contents of the group is meaningless (Banks 1996: 12). Most efforts to categorise these collectivities by recognised normative criteria based on essential traits reflect more the obsessions of the respective nationalist historiographies than the identities of those populations. They, therefore, represent a record of the claims expressed in competing narratives (Danforth 1995; Karakasidou 1992; 1997). However, the convoluted historical issues related to the struggle of conflicting nationalisms in the region from the late nineteenth century onwards are too complicated to be discussed here without the risk of serious oversimplification. The situation became even more complex when the Republic of Macedonia was formed within Yugoslavia (see Brown, Chapter 3) in 1944, and eventually, in 1991, as an independent state. From that period on, the Macedonian identity became the official expression of yet another nationalism in the Balkans.

The archaeological reaction to the antiquity and the continuity of ethnic identities in the Balkans has taken the form of *ethnogenesis* (Dolukhanov 1994; Dragadze 1980). As a concept, the tracing of the antiquity of the ethnic constituent of a present nation restores a pseudo-historical sense of continuity and legitimises the present. In reality, it is a question of definitions, in an almost Aristotelian manner. Somehow, if one has defined the start (past) and the culmination (present) of a trajectory, all that goes in between is, in some miraculous manner, insignificant (Lekkas 1994: 40). To a large extent, this description could apply equally well to nineteenth-century Greece. Archaeology in Greece was not immune to ethnogenetic or, to put it more generally, culture historical discussions (Kotsakis 1991; n.d.). As mentioned above, it was the issue of the 'arrival of the Greeks' which provided the initial impetus. But the question of the origins of Greek culture was a recurrent theme which appeared in Greek archaeology even from the nineteenth century. The archetype was *The History of the Greek Nation* by Konstantinos Paparrigopoulos, a monumental nine-volume work describing the trajectory of Greek history from prehistoric times up to the War of Independence (1821), which was concluded in 1885. Greek scholarship justly considers this major work of synthesis a turning point, not only for modern Greek historical thought, but also for modern Greek identity in general. For the first time, the concept of a unified Hellenic civilization found here its official, clear and forceful expression. The first volume contains a chapter dedicated to prehistory. The object was the tracing of the early stages of the Greeks, and the sources were limited to classical and later mythology and classical historiography. No particular reference was made to archaeology, although at that time Schliemann's discoveries had changed dramatically the landscape of Aegean archaeology (Paparrigopoulos 1925).

In so much as it represents the domination of historical thinking, this work is very much a product of the nineteenth century (Trigger 1989). In keeping with the demands of that time, the ethnogenetic flavour is here unmistakable: the focus is on the taxonomy of ethnicity, on the boundaries and demarcations about which ancient literary sources are so articulate and seem to be so much preoccupied. Out of this fragmented universe came a history in which resided a society perceiving itself in its perfect totality in space and time (Anderson 1991: 22–36; Fabian 1983), a comforting self-assertion of an uninterrupted sequence, fulfilling ideally in the past what is expected in the present and the future. In other words, the narrative of nationality.

The grip, however, of ethnogenesis on Greek archaeology was never particularly strong, especially on classical archaeology which possessed categories of ethnic identity that were formulated and sanctified in Europe and were perceived as self-evident (Morris 1994). Besides, it was this European gaze on the continuity of Greece which made the question of definition of the Hellenic ethnicity redundant and permitted classical archaeology to develop as a 'neutral' history of an art which was simultaneously a Greek and European referent (Shanks 1996). The Balkan nations had to construct their own antiquity based upon their own theoretical constructions of continuity (Vryonis 1995) and, in this respect, ethnogenetic considerations were more or less a prerequisite. Moreover, ethnogenesis had a long ancestry in the archaeological theory of Eastern Europe and a prominent genealogy related to the culture historical approach and to influential names, such as those of Ratzel, Kossina and, above all, Childe (Bailey, Chapter 4; Davis 1983; Härke 1991; Klejn 1977; Slapöak and Novakovic 1996; Trigger 1989). In a sense, much as ethnography was a narrative for peoples without history in the eyes of western observers, so ethnogenesis was the answer to nations without history, or rather to nationalisms constructing their own historical continuities for a domestic and a foreign audience. In the decades after World War II, a proliferation of research touching upon issues of ethnic identification in the archaeological record was manifest in the Balkans.

In its ethnogenetic quality, the *History of the Greek Nation* inspired much subsequent work, establishing a persistent culture historical tradition. Notable among this is an ambitious multi-volumed edition which appeared a hundred years later and, not surprisingly, bearing the same title *History of the Greek Nation* (Christopoulos *et al.* 1970). The sixteen volumes cover the totality of the history of Greece, from the Palaeolithic to modern times. In the same tradition, and with the same historical breadth, the impressive volume on Macedonia (Sakellariou 1982) compiled by eminent members of the Greek and international academia had similar aims, but focused on a smaller entity, the region of Macedonia. The title of the book is revealingly straightforward: *Macedonia: 4,000 Years of Greek History and Culture*. In this large volume, there are only fifteen pages devoted to prehistory, 194 to ancient history and archaeology, 127 to the Byzantine period and seventy one to modern Greek history. Eventually, it was not prehistoric or Byzantine archaeology which assumed the responsibility for confronting the ethnogenetic claims advanced from the Macedonian state. The apparent reason was that the controversy was about the ethnic identity of ancient Macedonians, the Greek component of which was forcefully questioned.[2]

Archaeology as defence: the 'Vergina Syndrome'

In the heyday of the Vergina bewilderment, a university professor described the course that archaeological matters had taken in Macedonia as 'the Vergina syndrome'. As one would expect, the accusation prompted an immediate response from Professor Andronikos (1987), who pointed out that the Vergina finds were primarily 'archaeological facts which contribute to historical knowledge'. Andronikos was of course right: the deeper significance of the unique finds of Vergina lay not in their spectacular richness, not even in their undeniable artistic value, but in the historical evidence they were offering and in the spell they cast on the public. Ever since 1977, when the royal cemetery of Vergina was excavated, a rush of excavations overwhelmed Macedonia. The academic community was flooded with reports on excavations and new finds which were quickly filling the gap of decades of neglect and of the courageous but marginal efforts of the first pioneers. Suddenly, the centre of archaeological research shifted to the North and, for the first time, the finds of archaeologists acquired a prominent place in the popular press and the media. Vergina placed archaeology at the centre of public interest and attracted popular imagination by force.[3] State interest was soon to follow. Most of the research received state financial support on a scale largely unknown to archaeological matters, at least in this part of the country. In the opening address to the first meeting of the archaeologists working in Macedonia and Thrace (1987) the Minister of Macedonia and Thrace expressed the political argument very clearly:

> I need not repeat that we will continue to support your work steadily, both morally and materially. We believe that beyond their value as a means of aesthetic and spiritual culture of our people . . . [your finds are] the most prestigious interpreter of the essence and the uniqueness of Greek history. . . . We need this historical function of art now more than in any other time in order to answer to the attempted, on an international scale, falsification of our history.
>
> (my translation, Papathemelis 1987: xvi)

The results of this archaeological cosmogony are gathered in a series of bulky volumes published by the University of Thessaloniki and the Ministry of Culture.[4] The seven volumes that have appeared so far include 308 papers which represent the impressive outcome of approximately forty projects every year, covering the whole of Macedonia. They offer, therefore, an excellent panorama of the directions and goals of archaeological research which, for the first time since the annexation of Macedonia to the Greek state, operated within an environment of administrative attention that gave first priority to its needs. Although it is obvious that the administrative concern was not about archaeological research *per se*, but about arguments of historical nature, the positive outcome was a proliferation of research which gave the archaeologists a unique opportunity to advance their own objectives and purposes.

I will not reiterate here the well-known discussion concerning the political role of the discipline of archaeology (Fowler 1987; Gathercole and Lowenthal 1990; Miller *et al.* 1988; Trigger 1984; 1989; Ucko 1995). It is a general conclusion that archaeology, just like history and anthropology, is often endorsed, directly or indirectly, by political claims which in many instances have drawn arguments supporting their political narratives, although the degree of joint responsibility of archaeology and archaeologists can be contested. As Fowler (1987: 241) points out '[the] interpretations of the past . . . are seldom value neutral.' Note the word 'seldom', which implies the responsibility of the discipline.

In this light, it is interesting to examine the contents of these seven volumes in more detail. Of the papers published, 210 (68 per cent) discuss projects related to classical and roman antiquity, 51 (17 per cent) to prehistory and only a meagre 47 (15 per cent) to the Byzantine period. The marked variance between projects related to the classical period and those related to prehistory and the Byzantine period is striking. To some extent the preference is a predictable outcome of the attempt to counter the claims of nationalist historiography of the Macedonian republic. The challenge was historical in nature, and the answer had to rely on the appropriate 'facts'. The notion of an archaeology offering historical 'facts' rather than interpretations of the past is probably beyond the point, and will not be discussed here. Whatever the concepts defining archaeological practice, it is obvious that projects related to prehistoric periods would not be promoted in this context. Greek nationalism never had much use for prehistoric studies anyway, except for those cases where prehistory could somehow be related to the Greek world, either directly, as in the case of the Mycenaean civilization, or indirectly through Greek myths and legends, as in the case of Minoan civilization (Kotsakis 1991: 70–1).[5] However, the same argument is not directly relevant to the scarcity of projects dealing with the Byzantine period. Not only was the Byzantine past in an equal position to offer historical arguments, but it had also been a powerful model for the identity of Macedonia, inasmuch as classicism and the perception of a well-defined Hellenic past were, for a number of reasons, not easily applicable in the case of Macedonia, as we have seen.

To understand this ideological preference, one probably needs a deeper grasp of the perplexities of the social and historical conditions in which this narrative took place. The issue is vast, and I can only hope to raise few points here. It is well-documented that historians and archaeologists, among other intellectuals, create the symbolic capital which is used to construct a national culture, a fundamentally political process (Bourdieu 1977). In the particular case of Greece, this symbolic capital had two distinct parts already shaped in the nineteenth century: that which I will describe as 'extrovert', addressed primarily to an international audience, and that which by analogy could be termed 'introvert', mainly meant to reach a domestic or, more generally, a Greek-orthodox audience. I suggest that the 'extrovert' part of the symbolic capital was primarily concerned with the classical past, while the 'introvert' relied heavily upon the Byzantine heritage. This last was the basis of the Greek irredentism of the nineteenth century which became known as the 'Great Idea', introduced in 1844 by Koletis, and having as its main concern the reconstruction of the State in its original lands (Kofos 1997: 208–10; Koliopoulos 1997b: 165–7; Skopetea 1984). Moreover, the young Bavarian monarchy found in the Byzantine Empire a legitimisation of its own political authority (Skopetea 1984: 161–7).

In this sense, we can perhaps understand more clearly the emphasis on Byzantine monuments and culture which followed the annexation of Macedonia to the Greek state in the early twentieth century. It was primarily an instrument for national integration, and for the assimilation of the orthodox local populations living in the region, a basically domestic affair of extreme complexity. On the other hand, the recent dramatic shift to the classical past, the basic constituent of the 'extrovert' symbolic capital since the nineteenth century, was a reaction to a challenge which formed part of international politics, and consequently issued a response which was addressed to an international audience. If, following Gellner (1983: 89–95), nationalism is about identification with a high culture which covers the totality of a given population, than the imposition of classical Greek civilization as a central element of Macedonian identity should be understood accordingly.

Bounded entities: in search of identities

The above description is deliberately schematic and has more phenomenological than analytical value. It avoids touching on the real issues that are driving the revival of the quest for national identities in this part of Greece. A variety of explanatory factors should probably be invoked, such as the economic and social structure of post-war Greece, or the degree of homogenisation of the population, the result of the fate of the region before and after the War (Koliopoulos 1997). These questions, and others that are perhaps of equal importance, require specialised historical scrutiny which I prefer to leave to the better qualified. Nevertheless, it must be pointed out that the uses of the past and the concept of continuity in Greek culture have been questioned by modern Greek historiography – at least parts of it – either indirectly, by ascribing them to the general project of nation-building (e.g. contributions in Mackridge and Yannakakis 1997) or to aspects of the nationalist ideology (Lekkas 1992; 1994; 1994b) or directly, by questioning the validity of the very concept (Liakos 1994, 1995). Archaeology in Greece has not shown a similar reflexivity.[6]

In this context, the main project of archaeological research, as it has developed in the last twenty years or so, is to offer material evidence concerning the ethnic identity of the ancient Macedonians and the Hellenic character of their culture. This is a recurring theme in the recent archaeological literature, and is subtly amplified by museum exhibitions, some of them organised abroad, and by high quality publications offering a panorama of archaeological research (e.g. Vokotopoulou 1988; 1993; Pandermalis 1992). In these publications a plethora of artifacts are presented in evocative photographs accompanied by texts which comment on their significance as evidence for the cultural identity of ancient Macedonians. The implicit argument here is that these artifacts are directly comparable, or identical, to those which characterize the undisputed Greek areas of Southern Greece.[7] The history of the Macedonians is constructed on the basis of ancient narratives concerning the ethnic identity of 'tribes', and the Macedonians themselves are perceived as a 'population' with a defined geographic distribution (Vokotopoulou 1988: xvii–xviii; 1993: 12). Cultural change, in as much as it is considered deducible from the archaeological record, is primarily a factor of movement of people, migration or colonisation. The close relationship of artifacts and people in this context is considered, of course, plainly self-evident.[8]

This assumed relationship between artifacts and people is an often described and an easily recognisable typical feature of the culture historical approach (Trigger 1989: 167–74). Similarly, the ideas of migration and the association of ethnic groups with particular geographical areas are part of the same archaeological tradition, which is closely knit to historical reconstruction. Within this tradition, the perception of the past as consisting of bounded entities, whether these are called 'peoples' or 'tribes' or even 'cultures', with archaeologically definable and stable characteristics, is a logical deduction from the theoretical premises of culture history. Nonetheless, leaving aside the explanatory value of these theoretical constructs, around which revolved the whole argument of the New Archaeology of the 1970s, the content of these concepts is still a very central, and very ambiguous, issue (Balibar and Wallerstein 1991). For the moment it is sufficient, following Wolf, to point out the historicity of their content and of the concomitant people's sense of belonging to an identity, be it cultural or ethnic: 'history . . . feeds back in various ways upon the ways people understand who they are and where they might be at any given historical point in time.' (1994: 7).

The perception of any culture – Greek culture, in this instance – as a discrete, bounded and homogenous unit which retains its unalienable character so that it can be recognized in time and space, is not only a concept which has been criticized as part of the culture historical approach in archaeology, but also one which has received considerable critique in the field of anthropology. Wolf has described this very aptly:

> We can no longer think of societies as isolated and self-maintaining systems. Nor can we imagine cultures as integrated totalities in which each part contributes to the maintenance of an organised, autonomous, and enduring whole. There are only cultural sets of practices and ideas, put into play by determinate human actors under determinate circumstances. In the course of action these cultural sets are forever assembled, dismantled, and reassembled.
>
> (Wolf 1982: 390–1)

In a similar vein, Banks (1996: 12–13), following Barth's dereification of culture and ethnic group, stresses the futility of the list of features, or contents, approach, which often serves as the basis for the characterization of such groups. The point is that these lists are in no sense finite in length. It is quite the opposite in that the social actors have the freedom to choose features according to given situations. It is not, therefore, fixed and stable features, such as dress, material culture or language etc., which identify a group, but its boundaries against the other groups, as well as the maintenance of these flexible boundaries which form its distinctive characteristic (Barth 1969; 1981).

There is no need to stress further the relevance of these remarks to the archaeological approaches to ethnicity and to collective identity as a list of traits. Contrary to what was happening in anthropology in the period before World War II, when the culture historical approach was formed, the view of cultures as fixed and bounded entities of shared traits is no longer generally accepted (Stolcke 1995: 12). Obviously, an archaeological approach which aims at collecting features in order to compare them with an idealised culture conceived, in its turn, as a fixed and bounded entity is seriously erroneous. It also misses one of the most useful descriptions of ethnicity that has been described as 'instrumentalist', namely 'a position . . . that is adopted to achieve some specific end or . . . as the outcome of a set of particular historical and socio-economic circumstances' (Banks 1996: 185). Accordingly, in the particular case of Macedonia, we should be asking not simply which are the traits that point to a particular fixed ethnic identity but what were the ends and purposes of these groups choosing from the variable possibilities they obviously had and, in addition, what was the extent of the variability of this choice? There is no doubt that the quest for the ethnicity of ancient Macedonians – from both sides of the border – is not following this track.

It has been proposed that both anthropologists and nationalists tend to depict the world as made of bounded, homogeneous cultures (Spencer 1990). The philological revolution and the education of the nineteenth century marginalised and eventually killed off minority languages and dialects in favour of one vernacular language of the state (Anderson 1991: 77–8). By analogy, archaeology is aiming to produce one national 'idiom' out of antiquity, by establishing a uniform construction of the past coterminous with the political geography of the country.[9] The inherent impossibility of this endeavour might explain the relative demise of interest in the study of aspects that are less canonised than art and literary sources such as, for example, rural settlements and hamlets, the archaeology of the landscape, or even regional analysis, which, in most parts of the world, form an important component of archaeological research. It might explain also the official relative marginalisation of prehistoric research.[10] A long tradition of history of art in Greek classical archaeology has kept the discipline away from contact with anthropological discussion and has developed an atheoretical, empiricist approach (Kotsakis 1991; Shanks 1996).

Recent research has extensively discussed the close relationship between archaeology and nationalism in modern Europe (Díaz-Andreu and Champion 1996; Kohl and Fawcett 1995). A central theme of this discussion is state patronage in the form of financing research and providing the legal and insti-tutional framework for archaeological work. In countries like Greece, where very little archaeology is happening outside the state monopoly, the boundaries between the two areas can be at times blurred. On the other hand, we should not underestimate the positive effects of this relationship: irrespective of inter-pretations, which are temporary, state support leads to the creation of a more robust body of evidence and the growth of a powerful professional archaeology which can confront extravagant claims by archaeological arguments (Díaz-Andreu and Champion 1996: 19). No doubt this is also a process very much evident in Greek Macedonia.

Returning to the conflict, central for Macedonia, over the issue of ethnic identities, it must be stressed that they are, among other things, related to the everyday experience of people which is lost in historical narrative. This is a well iterated ground, which forms part of contemporary archaeological discourse (Shanks and Tilley 1987). According to Bourdieu (1977), the complex habitual actions, what he calls *habitus*, form the kernel of social identifications. In this respect, archaeology – and anthropology, see, for example, Karakasidou's analysis of the Macedonian family structure (1997) – maybe more than history, is in a position to study the everyday practice of people and, through their common experience of the everyday, reconstruct their cultural identity. Rather than relying on normative categories, as does the culture historical approach, contemporary archaeology seeks to approach the shared experiences of people and offer not just the material support for arguments of historiographic character. Although this last point is not totally without merit – see, for example, the points on the physical character of archaeological evidence in Díaz-Andreu and Chapman (1996: 19–20) – it somehow degrades archaeology as a supporting discipline, where material culture gives support to concepts that have been formed outside the discipline. Is this the way to circumvent nationalism in archaeology and face the responsibility for the objectivity of the discipline (Carrithers 1990; D'Andrade 1995; Scheper-Hughes 1995; Spencer 1990)? It is certainly a way to approach a complex issue. In the meantime, we remain sceptical about an archaeology publicised widely by the media and the press, creating a popular perception of archaeology as offering the ultimate 'proof' of a national argument (Kotsakis *et al.* n.d.).

Epilogue

Throughout the foregoing discussion, the latent feature characterising Greek archaeology was the domination of a classical archaeology which had purified herself from association with anything but classics, and so effectively neutralised herself from any relation with the emerging broader discipline of archaeology (Shanks 1996). The other side of the coin was an archaeology that was anthropological and, by definition, in a better position to face problems of ethnicity, such as those that were perceived as posing a threat to the perfection of the idealised Hellenism. But I disagree with Morris (1994: 11) that, because Greece was considered as 'continental', i.e. belonging to Europe, archaeology could not be used for nationalist purposes. Quite the contrary, this 'continentalism' promoted arguments of cultural superiority not only over the Europeans, but also over the rest of peoples of the wider region. In short, this perception allowed Greece to become indirectly one of the culturally dominating nations of Europe. Hence, the reaction on the uses of the Greek past by other nationalisms.

For the state of Macedonia, Greece is the dominant Other who sets the goal of imposing her objectivity and eventually defining the historical past of another people, just as European philhellenism had done for her (Herzfeld 1987). It is no surprise that the state of Macedonia is trying to escape from this imposed objectivity, by constructing its own 'objective' past in negation to anything Greek. With an established background of historical and archaeological research covering almost two centuries, Greece has entered the authoritative space of European modernity long before any of the Balkan states did. It is not therefore an issue of contesting historical evidence: imposing objectivity refers to hegemony, and here the political aspect becomes transparent. The 'communities' of the others may be 'imagined' (Kofos 1997), therefore distorted and by implication false. But does this mean that a community can reserve for itself the objective truth, the accurate description of a true world? Perhaps Friedman's (1992: 852) comment is an appropriate end and a reminder to this long discussion: 'In all these cases, modernism has come into direct confrontation with others' construction of their identities. . . . One cannot combine a strategy of empirical truth-value with a sensitive politics, simply because the former is also a political strategy.'

Kostas Kotsakis

Acknowledgement

The author wishes to thank Professor I. Koliopoulos for bibliographic help.

Notes

1 Consider for instance the opening remarks of G. Mylonas' report on the excavations of the Neolithic settlement of Olynthus:

> Macedonia is apt to prove one of the most interesting prehistoric regions of mainland Greece. Situated between southern Greece and the northern regions of the Balkan peninsula, countries where a great civilization flourished in prehistoric times, she holds the secret of the great wanderings of the prehistoric tribes in the Balkans and the key to racial formation of that peninsula in the Dawn of History
>
> (Mylonas 1929: xi)

This 'geographic' view persists today in a slightly modified form: 'The similarities observed in material evidence between Thessaly, Western Macedonia, Albania and Pelagonia reflect communications between geographically neighbouring regions. As regards this particular geographical unit, N. Hammond has pointed out that it 'represents the easiest natural passage that leads from Thessaly to the Adriatic' (my translation, Anagnostou *et al.* 1993: 14).

2 See Danforth (1995: 169–71) for a presentation of the controversy concerning the Greek ethnicity of ancient Macedonians which juxtaposes the allegations of crude versions of Greek nationalistic historiography with Borza's (1990) highly selective arguments.

3 The famous star of Vergina, the symbol which the Macedonian state decided in 1992 to place on its new flag, had already been used extensively from the Greek side in many different circumstances, ranging from institutions like the Macedonian Press Agency, banks, public buildings and 100-drachma coins to trademarks of insurance companies, buses, taxi companies, even take-away shops. This secularisation may seem to run completely contrary to the strong feelings which drove the large rallies and demonstrations against the 'usurpation' of this 'national symbol' by foreigners. On the other hand, *pace* Bourdieu (1977), it may also reveal a familiarity, signifying complete appropriation and eventually complete authority on the symbol. On 18 February 1993 it became the national symbol of Greece. For similar phenomena in Greece, see Hamilakis and Yalouri (1996, esp. figs 1 and 2) and (Boulotis 1988).

4 To Arhaeologiko Ergo sti Makedonia kai Thraki (The Archaeological Work in Macedonia and Thrace) appears annually as the proceedings of an annual meeting held in Thessaloniki. Up to now it has published seven volumes covering the years 1987–93.

5 In this context the attempt to link the prehistoric past of Macedonia to the Mycenaean world is very significant (Andreou and Kotsakis 1992: 269–70, esp. n. 26; Andreou and Kotsakis n.d.).

6 However, not everyone would agree with this description of Greek historiography in the particular case of Macedonia. See e.g. Konstantakopoulou 1994.

7 'This is because the objectivity of archaeological data enable us to reassess [the ancient Macedonian's] cultural past from a different perspective . . . and also because the material remains of a people . . . now truly reflect their cultural identity, above and beyond any arbitrary interpretations' (Saatsoglou-Paliadeli 1994: 29). 'This fact, together with the other finds which reflect the religion, art and burial customs of the inhabitants of ancient Macedonia, lead to the inescapable conclusion that the Macedonians . . . had long been exponents of the Greek culture, participating in and contributing to it in ways which are characteristic of the Greeks as a whole' (Saatsoglou-Paliadeli 1994: 39).

8 Consider, for example, the following: 'Furthermore, a group of matt-painted vases found at Aiani provides evidence for the movement of the Dorian Macedonians: Matt-painted pottery was used by the northwestern Greek nomadic tribes which according to the written evidence (Hdt. I, 56), moved southwards.' (Karamitrou-Mentesidi 1989: 71). Also, 'Of particular importance is the epigraphic testimonia from the Archaic and the Classical period . . . for these constitute tangible evidence of the Macedonians' *ethnic identity*' (my emphasis, ibid.: 34).

9 In this sense, the attempt to transfer the terminology of periods of Southern Greece (e.g., Protogeometric, Archaic etc.) to Macedonia is very significant.

10 The archaeological museum of Thessaloniki, where the finds of Vergina are exhibited has up to date no permanent prehistoric collection on display.

Bibliography

Anagnostou, I., Thomaidou, S., Stratouli, G., Sofronidou, M. and Touloumis, K. (1993) 'Anaskafi Dispiliou Kastorias: To Hronologiko Provlima', *Archaiologiko Ergo Sti Makedonia Kai Thraki* 7: 13–17.

Anderson, B. (1991) *Imagined Communities*, London: Verso.

Andreou, S. and Kotsakis, K. (n.d.) 'Mikinaiki Parousia?' 'Mikinaiki Perifereia?'

I Toumba Thessalonikis, Mia Thesi Tis Epohis Tou Halkou Sti Makdonia ('Mycenaean Presence?' 'Mycenaean Periphery?' Toumba Thessalonikis, a Bronze Age Settlement in Macedonia). International Multidisciplinary Symposium *The periphery of the Mycenaean World*, 25–29th September 1994.

—— (1992) 'Anaskafi Toumbas Thessalonikis', *To Arhaiologiko Ergo Sti Makedonia Kai Thraki* 6: 259–72.

Andreou, S., Fotiadis, M. and Kotsakis, K. (1996) 'Review of Aegean Prehistory V: The Neolithic and Bronze Age of Northern Greece', *American Journal of Archaeology* 100: 537–97.

Andronikos, M. (1987) 'Epeteios', *To Vima,* 8 November.

Balibar, E. and Wallerstein, I. (1991) *Race, Nation, Class. Ambiguous Identities*, London: Verso.

Banks, M. (1996) *Ethnicity: anthropological constructions*, London: Routledge.

Barth, F. (1969) *Ethnic Groups and Boundaries*, Boston: Little Brown and Co.

—— (1981) 'Ethnic Groups and Boundaries', in *Process and Form in Social Life,* London: Routledge and Kegan Paul, pp. 198–227.

Borza, E. N. (1982) The History and Archaeology of Macedonia: Retrospect and Prospect, in *Macedonia and Greece in Late Classical and Early Hellenistic Times*, Washington, DC: National Gallery of Art, pp. 17–30.

—— (1990) *In the Shadow of Olympus: The Emergence of Macedon*, Princeton, NJ: Princeton University Press.

Boulotis, C. (1998) 'I archaiologia sti diafimisi (Archaeology in commercials)', *Archaiologia* 27: 22–9.

Bourdieu, P. (1977) *Outline of a Theory of Practice*, Cambridge: Cambridge University Press.

Bryer, A. (1997) The Rise and Fall of the Macedonian School of Byzantine Art (1910–1962), in P. Mackridge and E. Yannakakis (eds) *Ourselves and Others: The Development of a Greek Macedonian Cultural Identity Since 1912,* Oxford: Berg, pp. 79–87.

Carabott, P. (1997) The Politics of Integration and Assimilation Vis-à-Vis the Slavo-Macedonian Minority of Inter-War Greece: From Parliamentary Inertia to Metaxist Repression, in P. Mackridge and E. Yannakakis (eds) *Ourselves and Others: The Development of a Greek Macedonian Cultural Identity Since 1912,* Oxford: Berg, pp. 59–78.

Carrithers, M. (1990) 'Is Anthropology Art or Science?', *Current Anthropology* 31, 3: 263–82.

Christopoulos, G., Bastias, I., Simopoulos, K. and Daskalopoulou, C. (eds) (1970) *Istoria Tou Ellinikou Ethnous* (History of the Greek Nation), Athens: Ekdotiki Athinon.

Crossland, R. A., and Birchall, A. (eds) (1973) 'Bronze Age Migrations in the

Aegean', *Proceedings of the First International Colloquium on Aegean Prehistory, Sheffield*, London: Duckworth.

Danforth, L. M. (1995) *The Macedonian Struggle. Ethnic Nationalism in a Transnational World*, Princeton, NJ: Princeton University Press.

Davis, R. S. (1983) 'Theoretical Trends in Contemporary Soviet Palaeolithic Archaeology', *Annual Review of Anthropology* 12: 403–28.

Díaz-Andreu, M. and Champion, T. (eds) (1996) *Nationalism and Archaeology in Europe,* London: University College London Press.

Dimaras, K. Th. (1985) *Neoellinikos Diafotismos (Modern Greek Enlightenment)*, Athens: Ermis.

Dolukhanov, P. (1994) *Environment and Ethnicity in the Ancient Middle East*, Aldershot: Avebury.

Dragadze, T. (1980) 'The Place of "Ethnos" Theory in Soviet Anthropology', in E. Gellner (ed.) *Soviet and Western Anthropology*, London: Duckworth, pp. 161–70.

D'Andrade, R. (1995) 'Moral Models in Anthropology', *Current Anthropology* 36, 3: 399–408.

Fabian, J. (1983) *Time and the Other*, New York: Columbia University Press.

Fowler, D. D. (1987) 'Uses of the Past: Archaeology in the Service of the State', *American Antiquity* 52, 2: 229–48.

Fragkoudaki, A., and Dragona, Th. (eds) (1997) *'Ti ein' i Patrida Mas'; Ethnokentrismos Stin Ekpaideusi*, Athens: Alexandria.

Friedman, J. (1992) 'The Past in the Future: History and the Politics of Identity', *American Anthropologist* 4: 837–59.

Gathercole, P. and Lowenthal, D. (eds) (1990) 'The Politics of the Past', *One World Archaeology*, Vol. 12. London: Unwin Hyman.

Gellner, E. (1983) *Nations and Nationalism*, Oxford: Blackwells.

—— (1987) *Culture, Identity and Politics*, Cambridge: Cambridge University Press.

Haley, J. B. and Blegen, C. W. (1928) 'The Coming of the Greeks', *American Journal of Archaeology* 32: 141–54.

Hamilakis, Y. and Yalouri, E. (1996) 'Antiquities as Symbolic Capital in Modern Greek Society', *Antiquity* 70: 117–29.

Härke, H. (1991) 'All Quiet on the Western Front? Paradigms, Methods and Approaches in West German Archaeology', in I. Hodder (ed.) *Archaeological Theory in Europe,* London: Routledge, pp. 187–222.

Herzfeld, M. (1987) *Anthropology Through the Looking Glass*, Cambridge: Cambridge University Press.

Heurtley, W. (1939) *Prehistoric Macedonia*, Cambridge: Cambridge University Press.

Kalpaxis, Th. (1990) *Archaeologia Kai Politiki I: Samiaka Archaeologika 1850–1914*, Rethymno: Panepistimiakes Ekdoseis Kritis.

Karakasidou, A. (1997a) 'Women in the Family, Women of the Nation: National Enculturation Among Slav-Speakers in Northwest Greece', in P. Mackridge and E. Yannakakis (eds) *Ourselves and Others: The Development of a Greek Macedonian Cultural Identity Since 1912,* Oxford: Berg, pp. 91–110.

—— (1997a) *Fields of Wheat, Hills of Blood: Passages to Nationhood in Greek Macedonia, 1870–1990.* Chicago: University of Chicago Press.

Karamitrou-Mentesidi, G. (1989) *Aiani of Kozani. Archaeological Guide,* Thessaloniki.

Kitroef, A. (1997) 'Sineheia Kai Allagi Sto Syghroni Elliniki Istoriographia (Continuity and Change in Greek Historiography)', in Th. Veremis (ed.) *Ethniki Taftotita Kai Ethnikismos Sti Neoteri Ellada (National Identity and Nationalism in Modern Greece)*, Athens: Morfotiko Idrima tis Ethnikis Trapezis, pp. 271–321.

Kitromilidis, P. (1997) ' "Noeres Koinotites" Kai Oi Aparhes Tou Ethnikou Zitimatos Sta Balkania ("Imagined Communities" and the Origins of the National Cause in the Balkans)', in Th. Veremis (ed.) *Ethniki Taftotita Kai Ethnikismos Sti Neoteri Ellada (National Identity and Nationalism in Modern Greece)*, Athens: Morfotiko Idrima tis Ethnikis Trapezis, pp. 53–131.

Klejn, L. (1977) 'A Panorama of Theoretical Archaeology', *Current Anthropology* 18 (1 March 1977): 1–42.

Kofos, E. (1994) *The Vision of Greater Macedonia*, Thessaloniki: Friends of the Museum of the Macedonian Struggle.

—— (1997) 'Ethniki klironomia kai ethniki taftotita sti Makedonia tou 19^{ou} kai tou 20^{ou} aiona' (National Heritage and National Identity in Macedonia of the 19th and 20th centuries), in Th. Veremis (ed.) *Ethniki Kai Ethnikismos Sti Neoteri Ellada (National Identity and Nationalism in Modern Greece)*, Athens: Morfotiko Idrima tis Ethnikis Trapezis, pp. 199–269.

Kohl, P. L. and Fawcett, C. (1995) *Nationalism, Politics and the Practice of Archaeology*, Cambridge: Cambridge University Press.

Kokkou, Angeliki (1977) *I Merimna Gia Tis Arhaiotites Kai Stin Ellada Kai Ta Prota Mouseia (The care for antiquities in Greece and the first Museums)*, Athens: Ermis.

Koliopoulos, J. S. (1997) 'The War Over the Identity and Numbers of Greece's Slav Macedonians', in P. Mackridge and E. Yannakakis (eds) *Ourselves and Others: The Development of a Greek Macedonian Cultural Identity Since 1912*, Oxford: Berg, 39–58.

—— (1997b) Listeia Kai Alitrotismos Stin Ellada Tou 19^{ou} Aiona (Brigandage and Irredentism in Greece of the 19th Century), in Th. Veremis (ed.) *Ethniki Taftotita Kai Ethnikismos Sti Neoteri Ellada (National Identity and Nationalism in Modern Greece)*, Athens: Morfotiko Idrima tis Ethnikis Trapezis, pp. 133–97.

Konstantakopoulou, A. (1994) 'Themata Balkanikis Istoriographias Kai Ethnikistikis Ideologias', *Syhrona Themata* 50–1: 11–23.

Kotsakis, K. (1991) 'The Powerful Past: Theoretical Trends in Greek

Archaeology', in I. Hodder (ed.) *Archaeological Theory in Europe*, London: Routledge.

—— (n.d.) 'Heterotopia', paper presented at the 1993 *TAG*, Durham.

Kotsakis, K., Vokotopoulos, L., Lekka, A. and Fourlinga, E. (n.d.) 'Politistiki Klironomia Kai Topiki Koinonia: I Anaskafi Tis Toumpas Thessalonikis', paper presented at the conference *Monument and society*, Athens.

Lekkas, P. (1992) *I Ethnikistiki Ideologia*, Athens: EMNE-Mnimon.

—— 1994 'Ethnikistiki Ideologia: Paradosi Kai Eksighronismos', *Sihrona Themata* 50–1: 39–46.

—— 1994b 'O Ipertaxikos Haraktiras Tou Ethnikistikou Logou', *Mnimon* 16: 95–106.

Liakos, A. (1994) 'I Proskollisi Sto Megalexandro (The Attachment to Alexander the Great)', *To Vima*, 23 January.

—— 1995 'To Parelthon Os Epiheirima (The Past as an Argument)', *To Vima*, 12 February.

Mackridge, P. and Yannakakis, E. (eds) (1997) *Ourselves and Others. The Development of a Greek Macedonian Cultural Identity Since 1912*, Oxford: Berg.

Miller, D. (1995) *On Nationality*, Oxford: Clarendon Press.

Miller, D., Rowlands, M. and Tilley, C. (1988) *Domination and Resistance*, London: Unwin Hyman.

Morris, I. (1994) 'Archaeologies of Greece', in I. Morris (ed.) *Classical Greece: Ancient Histories and Modern Archaeologies*, Cambridge: Cambridge University Press, pp. 8–47.

Mylonas, George (1929) *Excavations at Olynthus*, Baltimore, MD: The Johns Hopkins University Press.

Pandermalis, D. (ed.) (1992) *Macedonia: The Historical Profile of Northern Greece*, Thessaloniki: University of Thessaloniki.

Paparrigopoulos, K. (1925) *Istoria Tou Ellinikou Ethnous*, Athens: Eleftheroudakis.

Papathemelis, St. (1987) 'Omilia Tou Ypourgou Makedonias – Thrakis', *To Arhaiologiko Ergo Sti Makedonia Kai Thraki* 1: xv–xvi.

Petrakos, V. (1982) *Dokimio Gia Tin Arhaiologiki Nonmothesia (An Essay on Archaeological Legislation)*, Athens: Ministry of Culture.

—— (1987) *I en Athinais Arhaiologiki Etaireia. I Istoria Ton 150 Hronon Tis (The Archaeological Society of Athens. A History of Her 150 Years)*. Athens: Arhaiologiki Etaireia.

Prokopiou, A. (1962) *The Macedonian Question in Byzantine Painting*. Athens.

Robinson, D. M. (1932) *Excavations at Olynthus*, Baltimore, MD: The Johns Hopkins University Press.

Romaios, K. (1941) 'Anaskafi Sto Karampournaki Thessalonikis', in *Epitimvion Hristou Tsounta*, Athens: Arhaiologiki Etaireia, pp. 358–87.

Saatsoglou-Paliadeli, Ch. (1994) 'The Excavation of the Great Tumulus', in *Vergina. The Great Tumulus. Archaeological Guide*, Thessaloniki: Aristotle University of Thessaloniki, pp. 13–39.

Sakellariou, M. (1970) 'Oi Glossikes Kai Ethnikes Omades Tis Ellinikis Proistorias (The Language and Ethnic Groups of Greek Prehistory)', in G. Christopoulos *et al.* (eds) *Istoria Tou Ellinkou Ethnous,* Athens: Ekdotiki Athinon, pp. 356–79.

—— (ed.) (1982) *Makedonia: 4000 Hronia Ellinikis Istorias Kai Politismou (Macedonia: 4000 Years of Greek History and Civilisation)*, Athens: Ekdotiki Athinon.

Scheper-Hughes, N. (1995) 'The Primacy of the Ethical: Propositions for a Militant Anthropology', *Current Anthropology* 36, 3: 409–40.

Shanks, M. (1996) *Classical Archaeology of Greece*, London: Routledge.

Shanks, M. and Tilley, C. (1987) *Re-Constructing Archaeology: Theory and Practice*, Cambridge: Cambridge University Press.

Skopetea, E. (1984) *To Protypo Vasileio Kai i Megali Idea (The Model Kingdom and the 'Great Idea')*, Thessaloniki: University of Thessaloniki.

—— (1997) *Falmerayer, Tehnasmata Tou Antipalou Deous*, Thessaloniki: Themelio.

Slapöak, B. and Novakovic, P. (1996) 'Is There National Archaeology Without Nationalism? Archaeological Tradition in Slovenia', in M. Díaz-Andreu and T. Champion (eds) *Nationalism and Archaeology in Europe*, London: University College London Press, pp. 256–93.

Spencer, J. (1990) 'Writing Within: Anthropology, Nationalism, and Culture in Sri Lanka', *Current Anthropology* 31, 3: 283–300.

Stolcke, V. (1995) 'Talking Culture. New Boundaries, New Rhetorics of Exclusion in Europe', *Current Anthropology* 36, 1: 1–24.

Theocharidou, K. and Tsioumi, X. (1985) *I Anastilosi Ton Bizantinon Kai Metabizantinon Mnimeion Sti Thessaloniki (The Restoration of Byzantine and Postbyzantine Monuments of Thessaloniki)*, Athens: Tameio Archaeologikon poron kai apallotrioseon.

Trigger, B. G. (1984) 'Alternative Archaeologies: Nationalist, Colonialist, Imperialist', *Man* 19: 355–70.

—— (1989) *A History of Archaeological Thought*, Cambridge: Cambridge University Press.

Ucko, P. J. (1995) 'Introduction: Archaeological Interpretation in a World Context', in P. J. Ucko (ed.) *Theory in Archaeology. A World Perspective*, London: Routledge, pp. 1–27.

Veloudis, G. (1982) *O Jakob Philipp Fallmerayer Kai I genesi tou ellinikou istorismou (Jakob Philipp Fallmerayer and the Birth of Greek Historicism)*, Athens.

Veremis, T. (1997) 'Apo to Ethniko Kratos Sto Ethnos Dihos Kratos. To Peirama Tis Organosis Tis Konstantinoupoleos', in Th. Veremis (ed.) *Ethniki Taftotita Kai*

Ethnikismos Sti Neoteri Ellada, Athens: Morfotiko Idrima Ethnikis Trapezis, pp. 27–52.

Vokotopoulou, I. (ed.) (1988) *Macedonia from Mycenaean Times to Alexander the Great*, Athens: Ministry of Culture.

—— (1993) *Greek Civilization. Macedonia Kingdom of Alexander the Great*, Athens: Ministry of Culture.

Vryonis, S. (1995) '*Prior Tempore, Fortior Jure:* Ethnogenetikes Diergasies Stin NA Evropi Kata Ton 200 Aiona (Ethnogenetic Processes in SE Europe During the 20th Century)', *Egnatia* 4: 189–220.

Wolf, E. (1982) *Europe and the People Without History*, Berkeley: University of California Press.

—— (1994) 'Perilous Ideas: Race, Culture, People', *Current Anthropology* 35, 1: 1–12.

Contests of heritage and the politics of preservation in the Former Yugoslav Republic of Macedonia

K. S. Brown

Introduction

This chapter explores theories of the symbolic maintenance of collectivities, and seeks to demonstrate their applicability to questions concerning the material environment. It considers the ways in which architecture, construction and reconstruction can serve as a temporal map, not just of relations between individual citizens and governments, but also as indicators of other oppositions that are subsumed by, or partially overlap with, that dichotomy. The focus of the chapter is on what might be called a speculative archaeology of sites in the neighbourhood of Krushevo, a town in the Former Yugoslav Republic of Macedonia. The history of Krushevo demonstrates how landscapes are always bound up with politics, not just for the states that seek to control them, but for the people who inhabit them. While most of the contributions to this book are offered by professional archaeologists, and describe the activities of professionals, this chapter deals with the involvement of local communities with the landscape and its meaning. It thus seeks to take an ethnographic approach to the social relations within a state which are built around the landscape.

Political background

The Former Yugoslav Republic of Macedonia is home to approximately two million people who are classified both within the state and by outside agencies as constituting a number of different ethnic groups. As well as Macedonians, who are in the majority, there are Albanians, Turks, Serbs, Roma and Vlachs. The census of 1994 relied on self-identification and primary language to draw lines between these communities. While some political parties, supported by various NGOs, strive to establish a multi-cultural model of 'civil society' within the Republic (Schwartz n.d.), other local actors promote the virtues of the nation-state, and argue that the only viable political units are those characterised by cultural homogeneity. Their agenda is served by the various external observers who stress the existence of 'ancient hatreds' in the region.

Within the Republic, the division that attracts most focus is that between the Macedonian Orthodox majority and the large Albanian minority, who are mostly Muslim. Albanian demands are various, and range from greater use of the Albanian language in higher education, through constitutional changes to make Macedonia a bilingual and bicultural state, to secession of regions with a local Albanian majority. Some claim discrimination of the kind suffered by Albanians in Kosova, although on a lesser scale. In all of this activism, the world community and those segments of it which particularly promote minority rights are part of the audience (Danforth 1995). Macedonian political parties respond in different ways, some by seeking compromise settlements, others by refusing to brook any departure from the ideal nation-state of ethnocracy.

The disputes are played out in a territory which bears the marks of a turbulent history. It remained part of the Ottoman Empire until 1912, when an unholy alliance of new Balkan states first defeated Turkish forces, and then collapsed in quarrels over the spoils. Serbia emerged from World War I with control over what is now the Republic of Macedonia, and treated it as an undeveloped area for colonisation. In World War II the territory was split between Albanian and Bulgarian control before being united again, within the pre-war borders, as one of the constituent republics of the new federal Yugoslavia.[1]

History, politics and Balkan landscapes

Visiting Skopje, the capital of the Republic in the 1950s, the geographer H. R. Wilkinson considered that Skopje's urban landscape provided a striking commentary on the various phases of its growth, and the varied backgrounds of its peoples (1952: 399). He stressed the juxtaposition of the markers of previous regimes – the mosques and baths of the Ottoman period, the finery of the interwar Serbian aristocracy – with those of the new socialist regime. He also noted the contrasts in private dwelling space in the Republic, as Albanian *kulas* jostled for space with Greek mansions. The juxtapositions became more striking after the catastrophic earthquake of 1963, when Skopje underwent modernisation and massive expansion.

The impression that Wilkinson received has persisted. Macedonia as a whole has come to be considered a place of heterogeneity, contradictions and historical ruptures. Commentators delight in the linguistic quirk that means that the French term for fruit salad is *macédoine*, and metaphors of medley, chessboard or mosaic are commonplace in descriptions of the territory. This aspect of the region is taken by political analysts to be a sure sign that Macedonia is another Bosnia-in-waiting; in a parallel set of descriptions, Macedonia is a powder keg, a fault-line, or a seething cauldron of historical conflicts, all bound to explode into outright conflict (see also Kotsakis, Chapter 2).

In these descriptions, little analytical distinction is made between the levels at which heterogeneity is observable. This blurring of the properties of states, cities, ethnic groups and, at the last resort, individuals, has recently been described as the product of a discourse of 'Balkanism' (Todorova 1994, 1997). Drawing on Said's model of Orientalism, itself suggestively applied to descriptions of the Yugoslav War (Bakic-Hayden and Hayden 1992), Todorova argues that the term 'Balkan' has been progressively shorn of the conditions of its invention, and taken as a category of explanatory force. Originally, the term Balkanisation was coined to describe the intrusive state-making of the Western Great Powers; now that the long-term consequences of foreign intervention are working themselves out, the observable violence is considered to be the home-made product of inherent and permanent confusion.

In a recent article on the destruction of cultural sites in the former Yugoslavia, John Chapman (1994: 120) draws attention to what this impression of a natural or irredeemable diversity of cultural elements misses. In stressing the importance of human agency, he emphasises the active processes that have sedimented into the region's material appearance in the following terms:

> The physical and social landscape of a region is more than a palimpsest of long-term settlement features; it is an imprint of community action, structure

and power on places. The significance of place in the landscape is related to place-value created by individuals and groups through associations with deeds of the past, whether heroic and transient or commonplace and repeated.

Chapman goes on to note that in the war zones of Croatia and Bosnia-Hercegovina in 1992–3, sites that had acquired significance were then targets for those who sought in turn to create a homogeneous landscape of the nation-state. Indeed, any commitment to the protection of a site because it had cultural significance often appeared simultaneously to mark it out for destruction. Chapman thus focuses on the wilful and deliberate targeting of sites with particular historical resonances in the course of recent fighting, in what he calls, following Joel Halpern (1993: 6), an 'ethno-archaeology of architectural destruction.' He alludes also to the paradoxical effect of such targeting, which at times appeared to enhance the symbolic value of what was destroyed, by introducing a dimension of victimhood. Ruins can, at times, carry more meaning than their intact predecessors (Chapman 1994: 122; following Povrzanović 1993).

What Chapman's formulation additionally offers, though, is a reminder that one can also conduct an ethno-archaeology of construction. In the citation given above, he also points toward a suggestive line of inquiry for such an enterprise. He marks events that are commemorated as at least potentially separable into two categories – 'heroic and transient or commonplace and repeated.' The two categories identified here resonate clearly with those of Fernand Braudel; the *événementielle*, the motivated and wilful historical interventions of powerful actors, and the *longue durée*, the working out, with no implication of self-consciousness, of collective mentality.

In a perceptive review of Braudel's argument in *The Identity of France* (1989 [1986]), Perry Anderson (1992 [1983]) suggests that the notion of the *longue durée* lends ideological valency to the nation, while another concordance can be drawn between the *événementielle* and state initiatives. In this respect, the work of the *Annales* school, from which much of the impetus to a new 'social' history came, has at times come to serve the purposes of those in search of an enduring *volk*, which has survived the predations and prestations of any particular individuals or states from above.

The political use of such a notion of the processes of history is apparent when one reads works about the break-up of Yugoslavia. Below is an example of appropriation of Braudel's division from an article by Peter Vodopivec (1992: 223):

Yugoslavia passed its seventy years in accordance with Braudel's schema: on the political surface, seemingly turbulent in terms of events, with numerous splits and sudden changes; on the level of economic and social history there is the rhythm of gradual but persistent modernisation; and as regards the collective mentality, behavioral patterns and norms of value are caught in a cycle of lengthy duration.

The effect of the division here is that 'Yugoslavia' is reduced to an epiphenomenon of history – an irrelevance to those with the 'long perspective'. Implicit in the argument here is that the sites of 'collective mentality' are such groups as Slovenes, Serbs and Croats.

Examples such as this demonstrate the political utility of long-term history which is predicated on the existence of distinct groups. The claiming of such broad, deep roots has come to be a key part of the ideological project of many nation-states. Benedict Anderson suggests that the biographies of nations are fashioned 'up-time . . . wherever the lamp of archaeology casts its fitful gleam' (1991: 205). The notion that drives such narratives is that nation-ness has no origin point, but is immanent in a population which has existed for as long as one can imagine. In such formulations, there is still room for identifiable political figures. Their importance is celebrated through rhetorics of awakening and the teaching of national self-awareness: their biographies fit within a larger frame, subordinate to that of the entity into which they were born.

As with time, argues Benedict Anderson, so with space. In this regard, though, the subordination of particular politics into a general unfolding of destiny could be argued to operate less smoothly. Arjun Appadurai (1995: 213–14) identifies the paradox that a state faces in seeking to create this vision of space as follows:

> The nation-state conducts on its territories the bizarrely contradictory project of creating a flat, contiguous and homogeneous space of nationness and simultaneously a set of places and spaces (prisons, barracks, airports, radio stations, secretariats, parks, marching grounds, processional routes) calculated to create the internal distinctions and divisions necessary for state ceremony, surveillance, discipline and mobilization.

Benedict Anderson suggests that the nation-state's power lies in its ability to blur the distinction that Appadurai marks here. Within the territory of the state, national churches are sacred, as are the homes of national citizens. Legitimacy thus resides in two potentially distinct locations. In one sense, it lies in the mundane; in the other, in the punctate occasions marked out by authority, of one kind or another. What Appadurai offers here, then, is a clarification of the very different modes in which space and place within a nation-state acquire historical resonances and meaning.

Modern Macedonia: the levels of opposition

By focusing on the different modes that are involved in the shaping of a national landscape, it becomes possible to chart more specifically the politicisation of landscape that has taken place in post-Yugoslav Macedonia. In an earlier article (Brown 1994) I sought to highlight some of the influences at work in debates over state symbols. I focused there on the external and internal tensions surrounding the replacement of the Yugoslav *petokratka* – the five-pointed star of the socialist period – on the state flag. I argued that the initial selection of a symbol associated with ancient Macedonia was a response to internal pressures, especially those arising between Macedonian and Albanian political parties, rather than a deliberate provocation of Greece. I went on to trace the extent to which tensions between domestic groups are apparent in the built environment of Skopje, the Republic's capital city.

Yugoslav socialist monuments and symbols did not recall any ancient past so much as celebrate more recent history and political unity. Indeed, it could be argued that novelty and nonconformity were constituted as defining characteristics of Yugoslavia as a whole. There was no rhetoric of an ancient Yugoslav past: to be sure, it was acknowledged that South Slavs were groups that had been in the Balkans since the sixth century, but there was no suggestion that there had ever been such a 'Yugoslavia' before. The state of the same name which had existed on the same territory between 1929 and 1941 played no part in the new state's self-image. Instead, the post-World War II leadership constituted Yugoslavia along very different lines, as a federation of people's republics. The slogan of brotherhood and unity evolved from a partisan movement which began its struggle only after the invasion of Russia by Germany. It had never aimed at the restoration of a pre-war nation but, rather, had striven to establish a post-war federation of the Yugoslav peoples.[2]

The agency that had led to the state's establishment, then, was part of a recent past. The will of the citizens of Yugoslavia was at the forefront of the state's charter, which emphasised ties forged by struggle and common purpose, rather than assumed to derive from any prior history. In so far as 'Yugoslav nationalism' existed, then, it did so in a form which drew attention to its own novelty and its own volition – in short, to its own constructedness, rather than its naturalness.[3]

Philip Kaiser, in a study of Southeastern European archaeology, states the extent to which the profession in socialist countries was influenced by three interwoven ideologies; ethnicity, nationalism and Marxism. He argues that with the collapse of socialist regimes since 1989 the importance of the latter has all but disappeared. Regarding Yugoslavia in particular, he suggests that ethnicity was always a dominant concern which wrapped itself in the guise of regional specificity until the 1980s. He takes as an example of the increasing involvement of archaeology with national politics recent Serbian initiatives to disprove any historical relationship between ancient Illyrians and modern Albanians as well as to preserve and protect Orthodox churches and monasteries in Kosova (1995: 114–15). All this has accompanied an increasing Serbian police presence in Kosova, as well as steps to settle Serb refugees in the region.

Kosova offers an extreme case of opposing claims to legitimate ownership of territory. The Serbian government controls the apparatus of power and celebrates various sites, such as the battlefield of Kosova and frescoed churches and monasteries, as markers of the region's deep, historical connection with the Serbian nation. The demographics of the region tell a different story, as the inhabited landscape is predominantly Albanian. Two distinct varieties of *force majeure* meet, and the ideologues of each side challenge the basis of the other's claim.[4] The Albanian majority, according to some Serbian sources, is a recent phenomenon, brought about only by the terrorisation of Serbian inhabitants and a higher birth-rate among Albanians. The present Serbian regime is accused by Albanians of operating a police state in the present, and justifying it by the falsification of history.

Such a view is perhaps schematic, but it demonstrates the extent to which the battle-lines of legitimacy in Kosova are more or less fixed. In the Former Yugoslav Republic of Macedonia, however, a broader set of players make claims to sovereignty in various realms. The two analytically distinct ways in which links are constructed between territory and people – as aggregate of individuals or households, or as collective entity – resonate with claims and counter-claims about the built environment. As noted above, there are calls for some form of self-government to be granted to areas in the north west of the Republic where Albanians constitute a local majority in cities such as Tetovo, Debar and Gostivar. One basis for such calls is an allegedly simple arithmetic of population statistics and the practices of everyday life.

However, Albanian activists have also worked to contend for legitimacy at another level, by seeking to invest particular sites with symbolic status. In the 1980s, for example, Albanian writers claimed that Macedonian authorities carried out a concerted offensive to prevent Albanian households from maintaining high-walled courtyards in front of village houses (Biberaj 1993: 5, 16). Whatever the official justification, this was presented as oppression by denying a particular cultural expression of Albanian identity. This reaction can be grouped with accusations of routine discrimination and state interference in Albanian private lives. Recent events in Tetovo, where an officially unapproved Albanian university was founded and defended against police intervention to close it down, demonstrate an extension of the grounds of dispute to include particular places of value (Schwartz 1996). The attention paid to mosques by all parties in Macedonia is a further reminder of the impact and significance of such punctate markers of collective presence.

At the institutional level, the Macedonian Republic faces other challenges. Although a compromise was finally reached on the state flag in late 1995, the protracted debate with Greece over the final name that the Republic should bear remains unresolved at the time of writing. Greek determination to make clear the absolute non-connection of a modern, Slavic state with that of Philip II and Alexander seems set to rule out a straightforward name like that of any of the other successor states to Yugoslavia. The use of 'Macedonian' to designate ethnic identity also remains problematic in the face of objections from Greece and Bulgaria, voiced by individuals from both states who claim the term for themselves (Danforth 1995).

A different level of dispute again arises with respect to one of the new bulwarks of national identity, the Macedonian Orthodox Church. Recognised within Yugoslavia after 1967, the church benefited from a state policy which acknowledged the cultural heritage of Orthodoxy. The property of the church in Macedonia was largely expropriated, but it was also preserved. In the twenty five year period 1945–70, 841 Orthodox churches and forty eight monasteries throughout Yugoslavia were repaired or restored, including the frescoed churches of Macedonia (Alexander 1979: 274). This could be argued to have been an inscription of an ethnic or religious identity in the Republic, which took place alongside the project of creating other sites, both ceremonial and everyday, where ideals of atheistic socialism were promoted. Now that the state's relationship with religion has changed and the Orthodox church is regaining control of these sites they appear set to play an influential role in the politics of the present. However, the Serbian Church never recognised the Macedonian, and nor did the rest of the world's Orthodox churches. The complication that this brings in its wake is that the Serbian church lays claim to all church property in the Republic that is dated prior to 1967. In so doing, it reprises the role it played when Serbia controlled the area between 1919 and 1941; a claim to proprietorship of cultural capital thus carries with it, implicitly, a claim to the control of the territory in which it stands.[5]

None of these disputes are new. Clashes with Greece over the name of the Republic and its Slavic inhabitants began in the 1940s (Kofos 1964); the Serbian church mounted opposition to the Macedonian church's bids for autocephaly throughout the 1960s (Alexander 1979); and Albanian citizens of Yugoslavia made the claims to the status of *narod* that Albanian citizens of Macedonia do today (Biberaj 1993; Poulton 1995: 126–36).

What gives these old confrontations new and critical salience is the passing of a Yugoslav regime that sponsored the construction of solidarity in the present, rather than its location in the past. Under its sway, the emphasis was thus not on excavation so much as construction. The result was a set of memorials and buildings that were self-consciously modern, marking a continuity with universal humanistic ideals. These ideals then informed an emphasis on reading the recent past. In the Republic of Macedonia academic energies were devoted mainly to history and, in particular, to that of the late nineteenth and early twentieth centuries when the region was the base of revolutionaries with clear connections to those of the rest of Europe. Their activism was held to anticipate the founding not only of Macedonia, but of the federal socialist Yugoslavia of which it was a part. More distant history, obviously, raised greater problems in the location of such connections. Nonetheless Philip Silberman, visiting the archaeological site of Stobi, south of Skopje, in the late 1970s, found a largely abandoned excavation, and a young archaeologist who located not a proto-Macedonia, but a proto-Yugoslavia in the ruins (Silberman 1989: 20). More so perhaps than any of the other republics, Macedonia's history and solidarity were tied up with Yugoslavia.[6]

Local consequences

Perhaps the single most important historical site within the Republic in Yugoslav days was Krushevo, a town of around 3,000 people, mostly Macedonians and Vlachs. It has retained its significance today. Krushevo became a significant populated settlement in the eighteenth century when Vlach refugees from the city of Moschopolis fled to the area. Although they remained Ottoman subjects until 1912, the inhabitants were able to purchase the land on which their town was built as a result of the *tanzimat* reforms in the mid-nineteenth century. By 1900 it was one of the richest towns in the Balkan peninsula. The church of St Nikolas was the seat of an Orthodox bishopric and boasted an iconostasis that was ranked with the best in the region (Ballas 1962 [1905]).

In 1903, Western Macedonia was the site of an armed uprising against Ottoman rule and Krushevo was the seat of a provisional rebel government. The town was quickly recaptured by Ottoman forces and sacked: over 150 houses were burned, as well as the church. Although many people left to make homes elsewhere, the church and many houses were rebuilt. Because of the symbolic significance attached to the Ilinden Uprising by the new regime of Yugoslavia and Macedonia after World War II, the town in its entirety was designated a *spomen grad* – a memorial town. Partly as a consequence of this designation, although some building programs were undertaken in the town centre, much of the town remained as it had been. Tito visited the town in 1969 and within a few years the road up from the valley had been improved, a ski-lift added at one end of the town and, in 1974, a monument at the other. On the basis of research conducted in the town during 1992–3, I offer a speculative archaeology of three particular sites in the neighbourhood of Krushevo. These are based largely on the narratives given by people of the town when asked about history. The parameters according to which they constructed their narratives reveal very clearly the kind of connection that space and architecture has with the recollection of the past, as well as the continual processes of construction and destruction at work on the material of a town.

The unmaking of community: the destruction of Trstenik

Trstenik, a village lower in the hills than Krushevo, was also established by Vlach refugees from Moschopolis in the eighteenth and nineteenth centuries. According to local accounts it had ninety three houses at its largest. The livelihood of its inhabitants came from their work abroad, either as tinsmiths or masons or in other trades. In keeping with practices that were common among the Christian population of the area throughout the nineteenth and twentieth centuries, men travelled abroad to work while their families stayed at home.[7] Over an extended period, though, Trstenik was abandoned, as family after family left for Krushevo. This gradual erosion of the village, again according to local versions, was caused by the proximity of the village to two others, Vrboec and Aldanci, whose inhabitants terrorised the residents of Trstenik, and made their lives intolerable. This took place during the Ottoman period, when various sources report that Christians had little recourse to the law if their complaint was against a Moslem. Krushevo, as a Christian town which enjoyed a privileged position, including the protection of an Ottoman garrison, offered greater security to the householders of the village.[8]

Following Ottoman rule, Trstenik was still inhabited. It remained so until World War II when there were still three houses there. By the end of the war, only one house was inhabited. The story of its destruction is that its owner was a supporter of the partisans and that someone indicated this by writing a partisan slogan on the wall. When Bulgarian forces, who occupied the area between 1941 and 1944, passed by the village they set fire to the last house. Similar marks of resistance are recorded in an account of World War II by Ristevski (1983), who records his workers' group painting slogans at the various springs of the town. Within the town of Krushevo the Bulgarian response was to wash them off because they aimed to convert rather than oppress the population. In Trstenik, elsewhere reported as a partisan stronghold, conditions were different and historical destruction was a result.

As a social unit, the village of Trstenik was depopulated by a system which made it impossible for the Christian villagers to hold their ground. The final house was destroyed because it was used to make an explicit statement of resistance to the Bulgarians. In this narrative of the physical destruction of Trstenik, two different processes are clearly marked: the last house was burned in response to a wilful provocation, but it was the last house only because longer term processes had already been at work, in which a regime created conditions under which one group was forced to relocate to escape oppression. Who or what, then, destroyed Trstenik? Two processes, set in motion by different kinds of human interaction, combined with the effects of time and natural decay to efface the village as a practised space.

Now in the 1990s, the old man who provided this narrative is seeking to reclaim something of his family's local heritage. There is no question of his returning to live in the village – his initiative, and that of the collective to which he belongs, is to reclaim the *symbolic* space. He is heading a local initiative to rebuild the village church. One of the threads of his narrative is the difficulties that they face in acquiring money for their project; it is not state-funded, but relies on local labour and contributions. Their goal is to reclaim a ruined site, and turn it back into a site of collective activity. Although a national church is involved, this activity lies outside the purview of the state – it is local activism, which responds to a loss in the past.

The presence of the past: a private destruction

A few days after hearing this story, I watched the destruction of a house in Krushevo. It was built in traditional style near the bottom of the ski-lift, which has helped make the town into a ski-resort. As one of the few houses that had survived the onslaught of 1903, it had been inhabited for some years following that year before being abandoned and falling into disrepair. In 1992 the old grey slate roof was still more or less intact and it topped walls made of a latticework of massive stones, dirt and mud, and over eighteen inches thick in order to support the weight of it. Like most of the other houses in the upper part of the town which survived the town's destruction in 1903, it had small barred windows and a central downstairs hallway.

A great-granddaughter of the inhabitants of the house in 1903 told me the story of the day that Krushevo was destroyed. When the others fled the town, her great-grandparents barricaded themselves in; but the 'Turks', apparently villagers from the local area, broke in. After locating and taking the family's hidden wealth, they took the couple into the downstairs hallway and shot them. Somehow, the wife survived, and stayed in the same house. One of her sons offended one of the local leaders of the Revolutionary Organisation, which had led the Uprising of 1903. She hid him on the top floor of the house, and, in order for him to hide, she rigged up a bell that she would ring if the Organisation came looking for him. On one occasion he hid under a coverlet but his boot showed and the Organisation killed him and took his body away to bury in the mountains. His brother had to return from the USA, where he had been working, to find the body and give it a proper burial in one of the town's graveyards.[9]

These stories illuminate not only the 'official' history of the town, which honours those who were victims of Ottoman reprisals in 1903, but also the less nationally palatable history of internecine strife within the town's community in the Uprising's aftermath. Part of the stories' currency derives from the immediacy with which they could be connected with their location. One could, for as long as the house stood, imagine their taking place.[10]

With the destruction of the house which was the site of these episodes, though, it could be said that the stories' place is taken. The circumstances of the destruction that I witnessed are straightforward; enemy shelling was not responsible, nor a bureaucratic government. A young couple, the husband of whom had inherited a share in the house and the land on which it stood, preferred to live in a new bungalow with modern conveniences. In a detail which could be argued to give force to the notion of the *longue durée*, the new house was to be financed from the young husband's work in the building trade in Switzerland. As Krushevo's young male inhabitants have done for at least a hundred years, he spent a substantial period of time abroad as a *pechalbar* before returning to invest his earnings in his hometown. In thus financing the destruction of a part of his own family's past, the young man inscribes a new message of individual industry and of prosperity regained after long struggle in the town's landscape.[11]

Monumental memories: the intervention of the state

Between 1968 and 1974 a monument to the Ilinden Uprising of 1903 was commissioned and built on the outskirts of the town of Krushevo. In keeping with the usual practices in Yugoslavia, noted above, the monument is self-consciously modern, designed to serve as a national monument to an uprising that was widespread. Its construction itself was a process which was illuminative of various tensions in the Yugoslav-Macedonian vision of history and the connections between socialist and nationalist ideals (Brown 1995).

This construction did not occur in a vacuum. The monument stands at the north-western corner of the town on the hill known alternatively as *gumenja* in Slavic, and as *alonia* in Greek. The words themselves have histories, but the space has even more. When the town was burned in 1903, the lower part of the town where the wealthier families lived suffered most. The area at the top of the town, around the hill, was left largely untouched. Yet it was also the site on which in 1903 the Ottoman commander set up his headquarters, to which townspeople had to go to plead that their town be spared (Ditsias 1904). Despite these entreaties, the commander conducted inquiries into the Uprising that led, in some cases, to public hangings.

In more peaceful days the area was the threshing-floor of the town. Two middle-aged men recalled playing at this site as children, and recounted how the wheat was threshed by a horse tied to the central pole which ran around in circles, breaking the wheat with its hooves.[12] From the 1930s, at least, it was a site where people of the town would take their *korzo*, or promenade, the very public exercise that is central to urban sociability. *Gumenja* was thus a practised site which carried in its periodic use for agricultural purposes a link between the town of Krushevo and surrounding villages. In its more regular guise it was the forum for maintaining social relations between townspeople. By these mundane means, the people of Krushevo reclaimed the space from its temporary service as a place of terror, and domesticated it.

The Ilinden monument in turn effaced this history, replacing it with a national narrative. It aspired to represent the struggle of the Macedonian people – the *makedonski narod* – for their freedom and self-rule. In so doing, it represents the investment of space with an imposed significance. Instead of a sense of unmanaged continuity, driven by unreflective practices of the local economy and society, it refers self-consciously to larger issues. In style it represents the kind of socialist triumphalism that Krushevo otherwise largely escaped, but which characterises the public spaces of Skopje. The monument's very existence could thus be said to represent concretely the writing-in of a state's perspective into a town's landscape.

The people of Krushevo were far from unanimous in welcoming this state recognition of their town's significance. This was in part a reaction to the dominance of outsiders in overseeing the construction.[13] However, perhaps more significant in people's objections was the style of the monument, which was abstract in design and massive in scale. It has been called 'lifeless' by some critics in the town, while others suggest that it is not a source of national pride but rather of international shame, as it does not bear comparison with monuments elsewhere in the world.

All these shortcomings contributed toward making this monument, supposedly a great unifying symbol, a place where critical townspeople read all that was wrong with the whole regime that constructed it. In time, the unhappy reception led to further material changes in the commemorative landscape of Krushevo. In 1983, a statue was unveiled on Mechkin Kamen, a battleground from the 1903 Uprising outside Krushevo. The statue was a product of a town initiative, and was figurative in style, on the site where one of the more famous of Krushevo's participants in the Uprising met his death. In April 1990, the remains of another of the Uprising's leaders were interred within the monument on Gumenja. A space created to promote certain Yugoslav ideals, with an explicit agenda of socialist modernity, thus received a symbolic makeover. A Macedonian leader, most famous for his socialism, was laid to rest in a religious service conducted by Orthodox priests. A space which had previously included only abstract reliefs with titles such as 'freedom' now has a grave marker bearing the name of an individual.[14]

These two interventions in a state project of remembrance were attempts to respond to popular sentiments in the Republic as a whole. The interment described above was a response to a campaign orchestrated by the national news-paper, *Nova Makedonija*. In 1992 the same newspaper called for greater attention to be paid to the material condition of monuments throughout the Republic, and renovation was carried out on the monument on *Gumenja* in the summer of 1993, before the ninety-year anniversary celebrations of Ilinden in August. But ultimately, these initiatives have not kept pace with changes in people's commemorative practices. The main celebrations of Ilinden, at least in 1992 and 1993, were conducted at the base of the new figurative statue on Mechkin Kamen. The state monument on *Gumenja* now plays only a supporting role in the yearly rituals of remembrance.

Conclusion: the ethnography of built landscapes

These three sites were selected for analysis because each represents a different kind of contemporary engagement with the material landscape. In Trstenik, a local community organisation is seeking to renovate a ruined church; within the town of Krushevo, a young married couple seek a more comfortable life; on the town's outskirts, a state tries to keep a monument meaningful. Each, additionally, represents a different interaction with narratives of the past. In the first, an old man speaks for a village community, driven out of their homes: his present activism symbolically marks their return. In the second, the narrative is that of a single family and its tragedies, in some sense redeemed by the material success of the present generation that the new house shows. At the third site, the narrative of a nation was put in place, and then buttressed by the inclusion of its charismatic leaders. Even then, though, the constructedness of the site and its narratives remained a salient aspect for townspeople who made their own responses to establish more locally meaningful means of recall.

The village of Trstenik, and the old house at the foot of the ski-lift in Krushevo, play roles in narratives of the past that are local in currency. They occupy a place in histories that appear to lie beyond any state rhetorics of national or socialist activism, highlighting instead stories of human suffering. In each case, though, the present seems to provide some form of closure to the narratives. The state monument in Krushevo, by contrast, seems by its design to have emphasised its distance from the events it commemorates. Its narrative is that of official event-history rather than the lived history of a community – although it strives to lay the past to rest, it cannot.

These three sites around Krushevo represent different modes in which it could be argued that communities in the present engage in dialogues with a set of pasts. Local activism to produce and reproduce locality lies outside the control of states, and where government agency seeks to create meaning in landscapes, its initiatives may, if anything, be less successful than those that originate within a town's community.

The particular processes described here are perhaps specific to Krushevo. Its destruction in 1903 was sufficiently shocking and extensive to be reported in the Western press, and various regimes of the past twenty years have made particular investments in its status as a symbol of the nation's ordeals and ultimate success. But I would argue that almost any small town in the Balkans has, in the course of the last century, been through its share of transformations on the local scale. In Bosnia in recent years these have been violent and destructive. But such destruction, historically, has been preceded and succeeded by the less obvious but equally powerful processes of continuous construction and reconstruction. Almost one hundred years after the town was sacked and largely abandoned, the inhabitants of Krushevo continue to make and remake their environment. It is they, and not the interventions of any states, who preserve and produce locality in the material and narrated landscape.

Acknowledgements

The research on which this paper is based was assisted by a grant from the Joint Committee on Western Europe of the American Council of Learned Societies and the Social Science Research Council, with funds provided from the Ford and Mellon Foundations. I am grateful to Lynn Meskell and Yannis Hamilakis for their comments.

Notes

1 The borders of the Republic have never followed specific geographical features, and so their exact locations have always been disputed. These disputes have often centred on the ownership of specific and highly-charged symbolic sites in the contested region. The monastery of St Naum, for example, at the base of Lake Ohrid, was included briefly in Albania after World War I (West

1941: 739) while the monastery of Prohor Pchinski, close to the border between the former republics of Serbia and Macedonia, is also a contested cultural monument.

2 For many of its citizens, especially those in what would later become the Republic of Macedonia, the 'first Yugoslavia' which existed between 1929 and 1941 was a Serbian-dominated police state. This perception, and the state initiatives which prompted it, was certainly tied to the existence of pro-Bulgarian sentiment in the area, clearly evident in the encounters that Rebecca West (1941) describes.

3 In this respect, Yugoslav nationalism differed decisively from that of its southern neighbour Greece within which the ancient past remains a primary source of symbolic capital in the present (Green 1989; Hamilakis and Yalouri 1996; Herzfeld 1982; Silberman 1989).

4 The clear distinction between the two rhetorics of legitimacy is neatly highlighted in a response offered by Elez Biberaj to potential Serbian fears over the survival of cultural monuments in the region. He suggested that international organisations take over the stewardship of the various monasteries and churches, thus in one stroke acknowledging claims that they represent a 'world class' heritage, and simultaneously denying their use to justify continuing Serbian military presence (1993: 22).

5 The particular dispute over church property in Macedonia has not yet been documented, but is currently being researched by Professor Stephen Batalden.

6 Silberman juxtaposed his description of Stobi's excavation with that at Vergina, site of the Macedonian Royal Tombs in Northern Greece. The historical fact that the peoples known as Slavs came to the Balkans only in the sixth and seventh centuries after Christ plays a significant role in discourses of legitimacy and heritage in the region. Significant, too, is the cross-cutting importance of the Christian heritage, which complicates the celebration of links to pagan predecessors. The result is that both Greece and the Republic of Macedonia at times strain to construct simple narratives of deep continuity.

7 The term used to decribe such migratory labour in modern Macedonian is *pechalba*.

8 It should be noted that this narrative of local emigration to higher ground from a village with Moslem neighbours is repeated elsewhere in the region of Macedonia. In the summer of 1997, I encountered a cognate version in the village of Akritas, formerly known as Buf, in Northern Greece.

9 Labour migration of *Pechalba* has been identified as a cultural practice distinctive to the region (Cvijić 1966: 459, cited in Schierup and Ålund 1987: 65–6; Schwartz 1996). North America became a prominent destination in the years following the Ilinden Uprising, as young men sought to elude the pressures of

what have been called the 'converging nationalisms' (Karakasidou 1992) and involvement in escalating levels of violence between local factions.

10 The sense of connectedness with the events of 1903 is commonplace in Krushevo and is often expressed with reference to its very tangible legacies. In another house I was told how the inhabitants had doused the walls with water to stop them catching alight in the flames, and shown the hiding places for valuables artfully constructed by past generations.

11 Prosperity, it should be noted, is expressed in the building of a new house, rather than the restoration or preservation of an older dwelling. One might argue that there are parallels with the processes described by Schierup (1973) in a Yugoslav village of migrants, whereby ducats are replaced by tractors and modern houses as markers of prestige in local contests.

12 This practice has been recorded throughout the region but was not always recalled so fondly. A visitor to Bardovci describes the open space, or '*gumno*', as a place to which peasants brought their crops to be taken by others – 'So much for the Sultan's taxes, so much for the beg, and so much for the peasants themselves.' (Edwards 1938: 94–5).

13 The commission responsible for the monument's construction included more people from Skopje than from Krushevo.

14 The hero of Mechkin Kamen was Pitu Guli, whose death there has been commemorated within Yugoslav Macedonia as an embodiment of the slogan of the Uprising, 'Freedom or Death'. The leader whose remains were interred in the monument was Nikola Karev, contentiously identified as the principal author of a manifesto in 1903 which represented the Uprising as an attempt to win social justice for all. I deal with the status of both figures more fully elsewhere (Brown 1995).

Bibliography

Alexander, S. (1979) *Church and State in Yugoslavia since 1945*, Cambridge: Cambridge University Press.

Anderson, B. (1991 [1983]) *Imagined Communities: Reflections on the Origin and Spread of Nationalism*, London: Verso.

Anderson, P. (1992) *A Zone of Engagement*, London: Verso.

Appadurai, A. (1995) 'The production of locality', in Fardon, R. (ed.) *Counterworks: Managing the Diversity of Knowledge*, London: Routledge, pp. 204–26.

Bakić-Hayden, M. and Hayden, R. (1992) 'Orientalist variations on the theme "Balkans": Symbolic geography in recent Yugoslav cultural politics', *Slavic Review* 51, 1: 1–15.

Ballas, N. (1962 [1905]) *Istoria tou Krousovou*, Thessaloniki: Institute of Balkan Studies.

Biberaj, E. (1993) *Kosova: The Balkan Powder Keg*, London: Research Institute for the Study of Conflict and Terrorism.

Braudel, F. (1989 [1986]) *The Identity of France*, New York: Harper and Row.

Brown, K. S. (1994) 'Seeing stars: character and identity in the landscapes of modern Macedonia', *Antiquity* 68: 784–96.

—— (1995) 'Of Meanings and Memories: The National Imagination in Macedonia', unpublished PhD dissertation, University of Chicago.

Chapman, J. (1994) 'Destruction of a common heritage: the archaeology of war in Croatia, Bosnia and Hercegovina', *Antiquity* 68: 120–26.

Cvijić, J. (1966) *Balkansko Poluostrvo i Juznoslovenske Zemlje: Osnovi Antropogeografije*, Beograd: Zavod za izdavanje udzbenika.

Danforth, L. (1995) *The Macedonian Conflict: Ethnic Nationalism in a Transnational World*, Princeton, NJ: Princeton University Press.

Ditsias, G. N. (1904) *I Katastrofi tou Krousovou*, Athens: S. Vlastos.

Edwards, L. F. (1938) *Profane Pilgrimage*, London: Duckworth.

Green, P. (1989) *Classical Bearings: Interpreting Ancient History and Culture*, New York: Thames and Hudson.

Halpern, J. M. (1993) 'Introduction', in D. Kideckel and J. M. Halpern (eds) *The Anthropology of East Europe Review, Special Issue: War Among the Yugoslavs*, 11, 1–2: 6–15.

Hamilakis, Y. and Yalouri, E. (1996) 'Antiquities as symbolic capital in modern Greek society', *Antiquity* 70: 117–29.

Herzfeld, M. (1982) *Ours Once More: Folklore, Ideology and the Making of Modern Greece*, New York: Pella.

Kaiser, P. (1995) 'Archaeology and Politics in South-East Europe', in P. Kohl and C. Fawcett (eds) *Nationalism, Politics and the Practice of Archaeology,* Cambridge: Cambridge University Press, pp. 99–119.

Karakasidou, A. (1992) 'Ethnic Imagery in the Shadows of Nationalist History in Greek Macedonia', paper presented at the Eighth Annual Conference for the Council of European Studies, Chicago.

Kofos, E. (1964) *Nationalism and Communism in Macedonia*, Thessaloniki: Institute for Balkan Studies.

Poulton, H. (1995) *Who Are the Macedonians?* Indianapolis and Bloomington: Indiana University Press.

Povrzanović, M. (1993) 'Ethnography of a war: Croatia 1991–2', in D. Kideckel and J. M. Halpern (eds) *Anthropology of East Europe Review Special Issue: War Among the Yugoslavs*, 11, 1–2: 54–62.

Ristevski, K. P. (1983) *Mojata Revolucionerna i partiska rabota pred i za vreme na NOB*, Krushevo: unpublished manuscript.

Schierup, C.-U. (1973) 'Houses, Tractors, Golden Ducats. Prestige Games and Migration: A Study of Migrants to Denmark from a Yugoslav Village', Arhus Universitet.

Schierup, C.-U. and A. Ålund (1987) *Will they still be Dancing? Integration and Ethnic Transformation among Yugoslav Immigrants in Scandinavia*, Umea: Department of Sociology.

Schwartz, J. (1996) *Pieces of Mosaic: The Making of Makedonija*, Højbjerg: Intervention Press.

—— (n.d.) 'Civil Society and Ethnic Conflict in the Republic of Macedonia', unpublished manuscript.

Silberman, N. A. (1989) *Between Past and Present: Archaeology, Ideology, and Nationalism in the Modern Middle East*, New York: Henry Holt and Company.

Todorova, M. (1994) 'The Balkans: from discovery to invention', *Slavic Review* 53, 2: 453–82.

—— (1997) *Imagining the Balkans*, New York and Oxford: Oxford University Press.

Vodopivec, P. (1992) 'Slovenes and Yugoslavia, 1918–1991', *East European Politics and Societies* 6, 3: 220–41.

West, R. (1941) *Black Lamb and Grey Falcon*, New York: Viking.

Wilkinson, H. R. (1952) 'Jugoslav Macedonia in transition', *Geographical Journal* CXVIII, 4: 390–405.

Chapter 4

Bulgarian archaeology

Ideology, sociopolitics and the exotic

Douglass W. Bailey

Introduction

The common Western perception of Bulgarian archaeology is of a blinkered, nationalist discipline, either dominated by Party Congress reports or slowed by theoretically challenged practitioners. Soviet and Marxist–Leninist inspired reasoning is often blamed for both conditions. In the background of the Western perception we glimpse an archaeological record of colossal depth and variety. There are few important developments of European (and Eurasian) human existence which have not left traces in the modern territory of Bulgaria: from the earliest appearances of Anatomically Modern Humans in Europe to the developments of plant and animal management, the earliest explosion of metallurgy and the dynamism of nomadic Iron Age warriors to Medieval Kingdoms.

Despite the depth and breadth of its past, the modern nation-state has remained enveloped in an atmosphere of isolation. Isolation is evident in political and economic progress, in the presence of linguistic and political barriers and in many traditions of scientific research. The sense of archaeological isolation is heightened by limited Western publication coverage of Bulgarian prehistoric and historic developments and by the absence of Western (or Eastern) historiographies of

Bulgarian archaeology. In the rash of recent English language publications on developments in archaeological thought and method across Eurasia, there have appeared few accounts of the Bulgarian scene.[1] One of the aims of this chapter is to seek the reasons for the West's apparent ignorance of Bulgarian archaeology as a discipline and as part of a European past. This is not a chapter about nationalist uses of archaeology in totalitarian or fascist states. Nor is it a review of local political battles over ethnogenesis (e.g. the question of the origins of the Slavs). It is not to excuse, nor to apologise, nor to condemn. Quite simply, it considers Bulgarian archaeology as it is currently practised. Where relevant, it refers to the discipline's development over the past one hundred years and, where necessary, it outlines the potential for the discipline's future.

The thesis I propose has three components. The first is that Bulgarian archaeology is best characterised as an exotic other. It is exotic in the eyes of the (mostly Western) outsiders and, perhaps more surprisingly, it is exotic in the Bulgarian perception of its own internal organisation, methodology and development. Second, I contend that as a discipline, Bulgarian archaeology perceives (and actively conceives) its object of study (i.e. the past) as an exotic: a rich, at times technically and aesthetically brilliant, element of a national past. The third component of my thesis is more active. Through it I suggest that the elements of exoticism be exorcised from Western perceptions of the tradition as well as from internal Bulgarian perceptions of their objects of study. The agenda proposed is that by dissolving the double exoticism (which in fact defines the praxis of Bulgarian archaeology), Bulgarian archaeology, archaeologists and their object of study (the Bulgarian past) should no longer be given ideological priority. This means that archaeology be viewed, and employed, as a tool for studying diversities of human behaviour and not as a weapon in battles of ethnic or political genesis. This requires that archaeologists (and politicians) use the past, not as powerful building blocks for modern political or territorial claims, but as a tool to understand ourselves in the here and now.

To make these points requires an understanding of the reality of the praxis of Bulgarian archaeology. To do this I consider the exotic condition of Bulgarian archaeology in the following manner. I argue that Bulgarian archaeology is part of a geographic and political region which is perceived by the Western community (and which actively promotes itself) in images of exoticism. I investigate the identity of the discipline of Bulgarian archaeology as an ideology, a socio-politics and an arbiter. I suggest that the participation in the discipline (both in terms of practitioners and audiences) follows rigid ideological criteria. I examine how the discipline has formulated particular capacities to contain the danger inherent in archaeological data and its interpretation. And finally, I argue that, because of its exotic condition, Bulgarian archaeology contains the potential to revolutionise not only the study of Bulgaria's past but, more importantly, the modern and future perception of Bulgarians of themselves and their relations to others.

Exoticism: The Balkans, Bulgaria and the past

The American-based Bulgarian historian and historiographer Maria Todorova has illustrated how Western perceptions of southeastern Europe have developed in a marginalising, and mainly negative, manner (M. Todorova 1994). Todorova examines the invention and use of the term 'Balkan' from its origins in the Turkish phrase for 'wooded mountain' and notes the word's early use, in the late eighteenth century, to describe the Stara Planina mountains which run across the middle of modern Bulgaria (M. Todorova 1994: 462). From the 1820s, the term was commonly used for the geography of the region as a whole. By the beginning of the twentieth century, however, the term had come to connote a political atmosphere as well as a geographic region, and featured in discussions and debate on the Russo-Turkish War of 1877–8 and the First and Second Balkan Wars at the start of the twentieth century. Todorova also suggests that in these discussions a stereotype arose in which the inhabitants of the Balkans were identified as superstitious, irrational and backward peasant societies (M. Todorova 1994: 460–70).

Foreign marginalisation

In the romanticism and evolutionism of the late nineteenth and early twentieth centuries, the people of the Balkans appeared as objects for study, as scientific specimens and as targets for ridicule in the popular arts. Maria Todorova reminds us that George Bernard Shaw's *Arms and the Man* (1894) was set in Bulgaria and portrayed Bulgarians as romantic, ignorant and only just emerging from a state of barbarism (M. Todorova 1994: 471–2).[2] In 1887, the German Julius Stettenheim published a multi-textual (opera-mock correspondence-narrative) work, *Bulgarische Krone gefällig? Allen denen, welche Ja sagen wollen, als Warnung gewidmet* (*Would you care for a Bulgarian crown? To all those who would like to say yes, dedicated as a warning*) as a political statement ridiculing Bulgaria and southeastern Europe as disorderly and backward. The events leading up to World War I and the efforts of German racists in the 1920s added to the identification of the Balkan people as trouble making inferiors (M. Todorova 1994: 474).

The divisions of Europe after the Cold War and the stereotypes which the West attached to the Soviet-bloc extended the negative image of the Balkans into the late 1980s. The pervasiveness of this negative perception is found even in the post-1989 press coverage of some countries' re-election of former communists. The

Douglass W. Bailey

American scholar, Gerald Creed, has noted how Western press reports of the
1994 parliamentary elections portrayed Bulgaria either as an early exception or
as a laggard and 'trend surfer' riding the regional tide which swept former
communists back to power. Creed demonstrates that a more accurate picture
should portray Bulgaria as a member of the political avant-garde (Creed 1995:
853–4).

Thus, the West has long considered, and continues to consider, the Balkans in
general, and Bulgaria in particular, as an exotic other, a primitive poor relation, an
object worthy of study, much like an anthropological tribe. This Western stance
has developed over the past century to include the discipline of archaeology in its
gaze. Indeed Tim Kaiser concludes his recent essay on archaeology and ideology in
southeastern Europe with the observation that Balkan archaeology 'provides an
interesting case study' (Kaiser 1995: 119).

Internal auto-exoticisation

The characterisation of the Balkans (and Bulgaria) as exotic is not, however, a
phenomenon inspired purely from Western bias: it is as much the product of
internal events and political strategies as it is the imposition of foreign prejudices.
Much effort has been expended from within to position modern Bulgaria as a
separate and exotic element within Europe. This auto-exoticism or self-
marginalisation runs through the long trajectory of the country's political
and economic development. Indeed the history of modern Bulgaria is one of
auto-exoticism.

Bulgarian auto-exoticism has entailed efforts to create a modern nation-state by
illuminating its distance (ethnic, historical, linguistic) from other states as well as
to eliminate any internal alternative pockets of cultural or ethnic exoticism
(thus the internal campaigns of forced resettlement and name-changing of 'non-
Bulgarian' Bulgarians). While roots of the auto-exoticism may be most obvious in
the much romanticised struggle against a Turkish presence in the Balkans (in the
area that was modern Bulgaria from 1396 to 1878), one can see a continuous line
of foreign powers exerting influence almost until the present day.[3] Through each
of these periods of external influence, efforts have been concentrated to establish
and maintain a Bulgarian national identity. Not surprisingly, such efforts are
evident in the demarcation of modern political boundaries (via common mechanisms of most nation states – for example, visa restrictions). They are also evident
in the use of alternative archaeological terms for individual groups of material
culture which, in terms of modern political geography, happen to straddle
national borders.[4] Thus, both from a Western perspective and through an internal
drive towards isolation, the political state of Bulgaria has developed as an exotic
modern state within modern Eurasia.

In light of the external and internal exoticising of Bulgaria as a nation, it is not surprising that Western scholars commonly view the discipline of Bulgarian archaeology as exotic. From the West, the discipline appears to exist solely to glorify the ethos of a magnificent past through a fascination with the art and culture of extinct peoples. From this perspective it is confirmed as a discipline born in the spirit (and the period) of modernism: it seeks to study the primitive in its past and it relegates matters of causal explanation to the epiphenomena of descriptive ideas of cultural progress.

Thus, Bulgarian archaeology itself considers its object of study (i.e. the past) as exotic. In this sense, the more mundane elements of the material record hold little interest: common practice on excavations is to discard coarse-ware pottery without concern or quantification. The emphasis of research remains firmly centred on the most sensational and emotive sectors of the archaeological record (i.e. burials, figurines, metal-work, fortresses and fine-ware pottery). Most surprisingly, perhaps, the tradition of Bulgarian archaeology-as-romanticism has remained in place through the post-1989 period of the region-wide opening of intellectual borders, research resources and collaborative strategies.

I suggest that to fully understand the current condition of Bulgarian archaeology and to appreciate the continuing desire for, and complacency with, the exotic requires an investigation of the practice of archaeology in Bulgaria. It is to this task that the remainder of this chapter is dedicated.

The praxis of Bulgarian archaeology

Bulgarian archaeology is an historical discipline. In her incisive study of Bulgarian historiography Maria Todorova details the central territory which history has occupied in the national consciousness (M. Todorova 1992a: 1105). Todorova illustrates how, through its development, even before the birth of the Bulgarian nation (i.e. from 1878 *de facto*, from 1908 *de jure*), the practice of history has remained inseparable from political practice.

In the period of early nationhood (between 1878 and the end of World War I) most historical effort was directed to the discovery, recovery and study of a common heritage (ibid.: 1106). Indeed, in his review of Balkan archaeology, Kaiser has noted that at the end of the Ottoman Empire Balkan states needed to 'sift' the remains of the pre-Ottoman eras in order to recover previous territorial boundaries. As with most of southeastern Europe, the Bulgarian historical machine operates to produce indigenous histories. Balkan history is largely ethnic history, a history of ethnic movements and ethnic conflicts. Modern existence is inseparably constituted in terms of ethnic history and ethnic boundaries. The same is the case for archaeology (Kaiser 1995: 104–109). As Shnirelman has argued, in employing ethnonational ideas and facts or fictions of ethnic history, effort is concentrated to establish an ideological background and basis for modern politics (Shnirelman 1996: 220).

Maria Todorova has argued that the modern study of history in Bulgaria is more of an ideology than it is an academic discipline (M. Todorova 1992a: 1106). History and the other historical sciences have developed as active ideological and political factors in Bulgarian social life. Furthermore, historical scholarship was highly politicised from a very early period, well before the communist period. Walsh has documented the close ties which existed between scholarship and politics during the inter-war years (Walsh 1967). Following M. Todorova, I suggest that Bulgarian archaeology itself is an active socio-politics and ideology: it is not a passive tool of socio-political, nationalist, totalitarian, or other state-level political structures. Bulgarian archaeology's long-established position as a socio-political ideology is one of the conditions which makes it appear exotic to Western eyes.[5]

As an historical subject and thus as active socio-political ideology, Bulgarian archaeology occupies an unrivalled position as justifier and legitimator. In this sense, the past is an arbiter of the present and those who can read the past are arbiters of justice and, as such, possess considerable power. The ideology of the past as arbitration is not limited to the recreation of national histories and prehistories: it drives a social logic through the reality of all elements of daily life. A particularly strong recent manifestation of this logic was the enthusiastic (and in most cases successful) drive by Bulgarian families, in the early 1990s, to reclaim property confiscated by the communists during their forty-five years in power. Property reclamation rested on the simple principle that proof of ownership in the past justified the right to regain ownership in the present. The past arbitrates the present.

Archaeological participants: audience and practitioners

In simplest terms there are two categories of participants in Bulgarian archaeology. On the one hand, there is a massive public audience. On the other hand, there is a much smaller group of professional practitioners. The former group includes members of the public who attend museums (either as children, via education, or as adults with a genuine interest about the past) and members of the public who visit sites (either in response to an inherent curiosity about their own past, or in the case of foreign visitors, out of the curiosity of the tourist).[6]

One of the most successful contributions to the development of the archaeological machine in Bulgaria since 1944 was the co-ordinated investment in museum construction and dissemination of knowledge about the past to the Bulgarian public.[7] Major regional cities without museums received funding for their construction or for the acquisition of appropriate premises.[8] Public dissemination of archaeological discoveries was achieved via museum display, televisual news items and film shorts. The organisation of travelling exhibitions of Bulgarian finds to foreign countries (e.g. of the Thracian silver hoards or the Varna gold grave inventories) increased the audience, literally, along global dimensions.[9] Driving these investments was a national cultural policy in which the cultural disciplines like archaeology played a central role (Bailey forthcoming; Popov 1981). Cultural workers co-operated to awaken national consciousness. Themes in the fine arts were explicitly detailed to have immediate relevance to working life, offering edifying lessons from Bulgaria's heroic past of the struggle against foreign rulers and invaders. Indeed, a central tenet of Bulgarian cultural policy in the communist period was the use of past monuments and material culture in the construction of socialism.

Major national celebrations put archaeological output in the public spotlight. The celebrations of 1,300- and 800-year anniversaries of the founding of the First and Second Bulgarian Kingdoms, respectively, drew heavily upon archaeological knowledge. Indeed, the late Velizar Velkov, formerly director of the Archaeological Institute and Museum (AIM) noted that the political enthusiasm (indeed as detailed in Party directives; Ovcharov 1976: 2) and funding invested in the preparations for these festivals directed the AIM to carry out excavations on medieval capitals (Pliska, Preslav and Turnovgrad) when other sites with greater scientific claims for funding were neglected (Velkov 1993: 127).

Practitioners as ideologues

The line between audience and practitioner is not as simply drawn as I have implied above. There are large numbers of the audience who might count as part-time practitioners. A large minority of the populace have practised archaeology. These accidental practitioners include teenagers who spent their summer expeditions in the youth brigades working on archaeological excavations. Also included are young men, who during their national service, were conscripted to provide labour for rescue excavations. An additional group consists of local villagers (most often pensioners, but also young students) who are frequently employed on large, mainly foreign-financed, projects.

While these part-time practitioners may give pause for thought in assessing the expertise of the archaeological workforce, they are peripheral to the main focus here (i.e. the professional, full-time practitioners). Furthermore, while education, public exhibition, broadcasts and hands-on involvement bring the experiences of archaeology to a majority of the population, the direction of its study is restricted to the few. If, as I have argued above, Bulgarian archaeology is an ideology, then these full-time practitioners of Bulgarian archaeology are best characterised as ideologues.

The case that Bulgarian archaeologists are ideologues rests on several important facts. The first is a long-standing link between politicians and members of the scientific and cultural intelligentsia. The second link connects two separate roles which Bulgarian archaeologists play: on the one hand they are scientific field-workers; on the other they are custodians and, as mentioned above, arbiters of the nation's past. These links raise (and suggest answers to) important questions about the power of archaeological data and its interpretation. In turn they raise a debate surrounding the personnel of Bulgarian archaeology, most particularly the question of who is allowed (as opposed to who is qualified) to study the past. Furthermore, it is through an examination of the practitioners of archaeology that one comes to understand the unchanging condition of archaeological interpretation in Bulgaria. Such an understanding is especially enlightening in the absence of either processual or post-modern developments in Bulgarian archaeologies.

Archaeologists and political institutions

It is often assumed that the linkage between science and politics in eastern Europe is a factor of the soviet-communist influence in the region and thus that the strength of such links only came to significance after 1945. As Walsh has shown, this is clearly not the case: science and politics were firmly allied in the pre-1945 period (Walsh 1967). The early Balkan historians of the eighteenth and nineteenth centuries produced their work within wider movements towards political (re)awakening of national sentiments. In the early twentieth century, the Bulgarian Academy of Sciences (BAN) held a position of eminence in the country's scientific organisation.[10] Indeed, one of the main goals in the formation of BAN was to provide an institution which would co-ordinate all intellectual activities in the country. BAN was formally approved by the Bulgarian parliament in July 1912. Thus, well before the traditional start of communist centralisation in the 1940s, Bulgarian science was establishing its own centralised organisation.

The connections between the activities and membership in BAN and the government were formalised in the law which set up the academy. It required BAN to provide the Ministry of Public Education with lists of members and reports on activities (ibid.: 140). In the first decade of BAN's existence the government provided it with substantial financial support. The main teaching institution of archaeology (the Historical-Philological Faculty in Sofia University) also played a significant role during the inter-war period of acute social and political conflict.

The university was autonomous but felt political pressure accompanying its dependence on state funding (M. Todorova 1992a: 1107).[11]

Walsh has also noted how the academies of East European countries provided institutional links between intellectuals and a country's political élite (ibid.: 139). From the 1940s, the goals of scientific work carried out by BAN were increasingly proscribed: to reconstruct science on dialectical materialistic foundations and to link work with the economic plans of the state (ibid.: 143). From the 1950s, Communist Party organisations were active within BAN to ensure that the scientific tasks of the academy were carried out properly and that members of the academy were well versed in fundamentals of dialectical and historical material-ism, the history of the Communist Party in the USSR and in Bulgaria (ibid.: 146).[12]

Archaeologists as political intelligentsia

The study of the particularities of one's own ethnic group is a common target of political intellectuals. The attentions of members of the intelligentsia (priests, teachers and writers) have often focused on producing textbooks and histories of their people (e.g. the Bishop of Sofia, Petur Bogdan Bakshev's *A Description of the Bulgarian Empire* (1640) and *History of Bulgaria* (1668) and the monk, Paissi Hilendarski's, *History of the Bulgarian Slavs* (1762) (see Shnirelman 1996: 226). Ethnic intellectuals frequently consider that they are obliged to build an admirable historical-mythological image of their ethnic ancestors (Shnirelman 1996: 238).

Both the early intellectuals' efforts to study and write their past and the early links between the Bulgarian government and academy are not surprising in the pre-1945 period of state formation. The active roles which many academicians played in national and party politics, however, are more unexpected. More than half of the 1938/9 membership of BAN held or had held positions (many at high levels) in state offices and ministries (e.g. Ministry of Foreign Affairs, Justice, Education, Public Health) and some members had sat in the national parliament (Walsh 1967: 141). Ivan Geshov, who served as the first president of BAN was a Prime Minister. Bogdan Filov, a founding father of modern Bulgarian archaeology served as the last pre-World War II president of BAN, held the office of Minister of Education as well as that of Prime Minister and was one of the advisors to Prince Simion, the Prince Regent, following the death in 1943 of King Boris III.

In more recent times, academics and intellectuals have occupied high political offices. A dissident philosopher, Zheliu Zhelev, led the first post-1989 opposition party: he became President of the new Grand National Assembly in 1990. A month later, an economist, Andrei Lukanov, was elected Prime Minister. The 1996 presidential elections pitted a divorce lawyer (the Union of Democratic

Forces candidate and eventual winner, Petar Stoyanov) against an archaeologist–art historian (Professor-Dr Ivan Marazov, the candidate of the Socialist Party – the former Communists). A less well publicised, but perhaps more sensational, indicator of the natural acceptance of a link between politicians and archaeologists occurred in 1995 when a Western polling organisation carried out a survey of potential mayoral candidates in a major city in north-eastern Bulgaria. The winner was the director of the local historical museum. The victory was spectacular in that she had not been a listed candidate: she had won as a write-in.[13] To understand why these long-standing links between archaeologists and national politics have survived, it is necessary to consider the archaeologist as a custodian of the national past, as an arbiter and, most importantly, as a manager and interpreter of powerful, and perhaps dangerous, data.

Archaeologists as custodians, arbiters and interpreters

The control of archaeological activities in Bulgaria is centred in the AIM, a member institution of BAN. Additional responsibilities for the preservation of cultural monuments rest with the Ministry of Culture. Since 1969, the sole power to grant permission for excavation, and the responsibility for organising excavations, has rested with the AIM (Velkov 1993: 126). The centralised, and closely controlled, legal power to grant permission to carry out fieldwork reflects the AIM's (and in turn BAN's) role as chief custodian of the national past. The need for a centralised custodian of the past and its investigation is rooted, I suggest, in the power inherent in archaeological data and its interpretation.

Díaz-Andreu and Champion have argued that the power of archaeological information rests in its physicality. It is powerful because it offers both the opportunity and the materials for people to produce an alternative knowledge and version of the past: it generates and values knowledge (Díaz-Andreu and Champion 1996: 20).

In a tightly controlled socio-political reality, sources of alternative knowledges (of any kind) were unacceptable and thus required control. After 1944, in a reorganisation of BAN, the AIM was created by uniting the Archaeological Institute (originally founded in 1923) with the National Archaeological Museum. The latter lost its previous financial independence and its funding reserves were confiscated. Previously, the AIM had relied successfully upon donations in order to build up substantial reserves, the interest from which covered funding for research and overheads. Indeed, the Institute was originally formed on the directions of King Boris III and enjoyed enormous funding from the government. Money for wages and excavation now came from BAN, although this pattern changed slightly when the Ministry of Culture gained responsibility for allocating funds through local administrative authorities.

As a consequence of the position of history and archaeology as ideologies, the selection of personnel deemed 'qualified' to be practitioners of either discipline required investigation into sensitive aspects of individuals' family history and political affiliation (M. Todorova 1992a: 1115). This was one of the reasons that few students were drawn to study history in the 1960s and 1970s. The best students went into the hard sciences while the top students graduating from language schools went into the diplomatic services, foreign trade and the governmental elite (ibid.: 1116). M. Todorova suggests that there was not the 'critical mass' of high calibre intellectuals which would have been necessary to influence the discipline. Todorova sees a continuity of personnel between the pre- and post-1989 periods with scholars from newly eliminated programmes (e.g. the study of the history of the Bulgarian Communist Party) being absorbed by other institutions (ibid.: 1114). The same trends may be seen in the staffing histories of the archaeological institutions and museums.

Trends in interpretation

If Bulgarian archaeology proceeds according to ideological precept and is firmly rooted in early state formations of the late nineteenth and early twentieth centuries, then what can be inferred about contemporary trends in archaeological interpretation in Bulgaria? Bulgarian archaeological interpretation is deeply rooted in a descriptive and a culture historical approach. It seeks answers in terms of the formal typologies of artefacts to questions of ethnic movement, migration and invasion. Interpretations of eco-determinism have recently gained favour (see recent explanations of the 'Neolithisation' of the Balkans and of the demise of the Copper Age – H. Todorova 1986).

What is most striking is the absence of the scientism which bore processualist traditions in the West during the late 1950s, 1960s and 1970s. This absence feeds Western perceptions of Bulgarian archaeology and archaeologists as exotic. The absence of a processualist move in the development of Bulgarian archaeology is significant for two reasons. First, it helps to explain why interpretation (and, hence, research designs) have remained cosseted in the descriptive warmth of culture history. Second, without a processualist trend, postprocessualism has nothing against which to struggle and to measure itself and thus remains still-born.

Why has Bulgarian archaeology developed in this way? One answer is that it is stuck in a retarded stage of development in the evolution of archaeological theory: it hasn't yet caught up. Surely this answer is both naïve and condescending. Not only does it rely on unacceptable applications of linear evolution onto socio-political trends but it also assumes a pretentious Western righteousness of method. A more accurate answer is to recognise current and contemporary Bulgarian archaeology as a synthesis of the discipline's culture historicism (descended from the discipline's modernist origins) with its position as a socio-political ideology.

A processualist approach can never develop within a synthesis of culture history and political ideology such as that present within the development of Bulgarian archaeology. This is because processualism threatens both the culture historical approach and, perhaps more importantly, the control of knowledge and interpretation which lies at the heart of ideological archaeology. One of the fundamental advances of processual archaeology was its demand for, and provision of, explicit, objective standards for evaluating archaeological interpretation.

While it is clear that a processual approach to archaeology is incompatible with ideological archaeology because the former threatens the existence of the latter, the absence of processualist archaeology in Bulgaria makes sense for another reason. In its quest for objectivity, a processual approach to archaeology claims that archaeology (like all sciences) is separate from politics. Clearly, the very long links between Bulgarian archaeology (like all Bulgarian sciences) and Bulgarian politics make Bulgarian archaeology, by definition, ineligible for any approach to science which claims apolitical status.

The absence of objective criteria for the assessment of alternative archaeo-logical explanations raises a related issue: the larger goals of the scientific process within Bulgarian archaeology. In Bulgarian archaeology, explanation is pre-determined: often archaeological research entails little more than recovering more and more data which can be assigned to pre-determined chronological and social stages. The definition of these stages and their relative positioning are pre-set within the mono-paradigmatic reconstruction of social organisation derived from the Leninist–Marxist–Morgan–Engels model of human social development. An editorial applying the decree of the Central Committee of the Bulgarian Communist Party and the Council of Ministers for the development of Bulgarian science and the tasks of Bulgarian archaeology calls for archaeologists to use their data to 'prove the progressive evolution of societal development' (Arkheologiya 1960: 1).

Related to the pre-set interpretation of social stages is the absence of any serious, critical, self-reflective studies by Bulgarian archaeologists on the developments of archaeology in Bulgaria. The absence of self-reflection within archaeology is part of a larger trend which reaches across the historical disciplines in Bulgaria. In her study of Bulgarian historiography, Maria Todorova despairs over the almost complete absence of interest by young historians, even in post-1989 research, in the methods and suppositions of their profession (M. Todorova 1992a: 1112). The same can be argued for archaeology. Despite a number of articles on the history of Bulgarian archaeology (Chichikova 1960; Dimitrov 1964; Ovcharov 1962; Vaklinov 1969), I could find no critical assessment of current (or past) methods or interpretations. The articles which purport to provide historiographies of archaeology offer little, other than selective description of the study of individual periods (e.g. Rumen Katincharov on the Bronze Age – Katincharov 1975; H. Todorova on the Chalcolithic – H. Todorova 1986), or programmatic statements applying Party Congress results to the discipline (Arkheologiya 1960, 1963, 1967; Dimitrov 1955; Ovcharov 1976; Vaklinov 1971), or necrologies of deceased archaeologists of high status (see Georgieva and Velkov 1974: 400–6). The Bronze Age specialist, Ivan Panayotov, suggests that accurate comment on current practices is not possible due to the 'impossibility of gaining an objective perspective on a period in which one is working [and] to the imprecise formulation of the trends in current research goals' (Panayotov 1995: 246). Bibliographies abound (see Georgieva and Velkov 1974: 407–8 for a listing of those published between 1878 and 1966) but critical interrogation of existing methods and assumptions are significant in their absence.

The absence of disciplinary self-criticism, and the straight-jacketing of explanation inherent in pre-set interpretation, exemplify Bulgarian archaeology as distinct from the post-processual trends in recent Western archaeologies. In light of the inherently political nature of Bulgarian archaeology, this distinction from post-processualism appears at first to be a paradox: if a major goal of post-processualism is the injection of politics into archaeology, then surely Bulgarian archaeology has long contained a basic tenet of post-processualism. The politics inherent in Bulgarian archaeology, however, are not the politics of post-processualism, which are the politics of empowerment and revolution. Rather, the politics of Bulgarian archaeology are the politics of centralised ideology.[14]

The absence of a desire to inject an interpretation of politics (i.e. of exploitation and confrontation) into archaeological discourse may also be a reaction against the constant official demands made by Party Officials for archaeologists to be more politically focused in their work. Indeed, the demand for archaeologists to develop and apply theory to archaeology (and to practice self-critique) are common themes in the editorials published in the main Bulgarian archaeological journals (*Arkheologiya*: *Izvestia na Arkheologiya Institut*) which converted the directives of the five-yearly National Communist Party Congresses to the work of archaeologists (Arkheologiya 1963: 3, 4; Dimitrov 1955: 5; Ovcharov 1976: 4). A silent reaction by the majority of archaeologists against any demand made in such disciplinary distillations of party dictates may well be a major reason for the atheoretical nature of Bulgarian archaeology.

De-exoticising Bulgarian archaeology

Bulgarian archaeology has remained an exotic species, isolated, in the main, from contemporary developments in archaeological practice. Exoticism rests on

Bulgarian archaeology's position as an ideology, on its auto-marginalisation and on its vision of the past as a romantic object. The future of the discipline both as a legitimate academic discipline and as a potential nexus for the development of a civil society will only be assured if the atmosphere and restrictions inherent in these exoticisms are lifted. Success in de-exoticising Bulgarian archaeology relies equally upon internal action of the discipline as with external collaboration and commitment.

Internal action

Internally, de-exoticisation requires a move away from the romantic approach to the past, a recognition by the majority of archaeological practitioners of the power they possess to help construct a civil society, and a commitment by archaeologists to build their own archaeology without recourse to the implementation of pre-packaged schools of thought or bodies of practices.

In rejecting the romantic vision of the past, Bulgarian archaeology needs to turn to investigate and understand human behaviour and belief in a credibly scientific fashion. Perceptions of brilliant periods of past technological achievements (e.g. the earliest appearance of Anatomically Modern Humans or the first use of gold) need to be replaced with more complex and valuable considerations of human behaviour (e.g. what were the cognitive abilities which enabled Anatomically Modern Humans to outlast Neanderthals?; what, if any, inherent physical characteristics of materials such as gold and copper made them obvious media for expressing personal identity?). Indeed, the falsely inflated valuation of 'earliest' and 'first' will collapse once they are no longer employed as artefacts in glorification of a past. Internally, culture history must be recognised as bankrupt and the pursuit of patterns in human behaviour and cognition must be engaged without delay.

Unlike much in Bulgaria since 1989, archaeology has not been affected by import. It stands outside the sphere of disciplines (economics, sociology, law) and activities (banking, insurance, investment) which have been injected via the syringe of Western funders and foundations. Neither history nor archaeology are the subjects which new programmes of foreign funding bodies have targeted most actively. Internally, the new, independent universities and institutes which have recently arisen do offer archaeology (indeed the New Bulgarian University has an Archaeology department with its own publication series). However, the courses most popular among students (and thus among parents, I presume) are not in the historical sciences. The popular courses are in business studies, political science, law.

Thus, one could argue that the marginalisation of archaeology both by the explosion of post-1989 foreign funders and by newly created internal institutions is a negative consequence of the 1989 changes. On the other hand, and perhaps less obviously, the marginalisation of archaeology has kept the discipline clear of association with potential sources of negative images (e.g. the scandals over profit-making in the privatised utilities). Marginalisation has thus kept archaeology clean of the flood of changes, aspects of which many Bulgarians find unacceptable, catastrophic and of foreign influence (the staggering increase in the crime rate is a good example).

The final internal ingredient in the de-exoticisation of Bulgarian archaeology concerns the nature of the archaeological school(s) into which it invests effort or looks for advice. It is clear that the most disastrous approach which could be followed is a relativist one. In the first place, relativism fosters and reinforces the exotic (via its inherent condescension). It does this by accepting alternative traditions, and their goals and methods, on their own terms without reference to external standards. Perhaps much more importantly in the light of Bulgaria's history of ethnic struggle and authoritarian disregard for basic human rights, a relativist approach to the past would be an ethnic catastrophe. Chernykh has emphasised this point better than I have any ability or right to. In discussing the emergence of archaeological and historical consciousnesses of previously colonised people and the frequent contemporary emergence of long traditions of ethnic prejudices, he alerts us to the dangers of

> being fuzzy-headed, of uncritically romanticising formerly colonised peoples, or of uncritically facilitating their empowerment by supporting their often questionable "readings" of their own pasts. . . . Little fascists eager to distort their pasts to further their own, often violent, political ends are capable of sprouting up like weeds everywhere, and one must recognise them for what they are and not excuse them away on the basis of some slippery relativist standard.
>
> (Chernykh 1995: 148)[15]

External action

In parallel to the internal development of Bulgarian archaeology, the task of de-exoticisation must engage people and policies outside Bulgaria. At the heart of the external development is the recognition that archaeology defined in terms of modern nation-states is futile. While the recent relationship between Bulgarian and foreign archaeologists and institutions has been tightly controlled and at times strained, earlier periods in the discipline's history reflect an easier, more open relationship.[16]

The earliest developments in Bulgarian archaeology benefited from foreign influence. The Škorpil brothers (Karel, Hermengild and Vladimir) were

Czechoslovaks working in Bulgaria during the creation of the new nation-state at the end of the nineteenth century. They collected information about a range of archaeological topics from all regions of the country and published a substantial number of papers and books.[17] This early period also included the excavations by the French archaeologists Jerôme, Seure and Degrand. Indeed, many of the early archaeologists working in Bulgaria had received their training in Austria or France. Raphail Popov and Gavril Katsarov were both trained abroad. Bogdan Filov was German educated. Indeed, one could argue that the very origins of Bulgarian archaeology, including the founding of the Archaeological Institute by Boris III (who had been born in Bulgaria as the son of the Prince Ferdinand of Saxe-Coburg-Gotha when the latter was King of Bulgaria), was heavily influenced by western and central European traditions and individuals. More striking, perhaps, is the work of the American, James Gaul, who travelled widely in the country before World War II. His book *The Neolithic in Bulgaria* (Gaul 1948) was published posthumously and stood, until very recently (Todorova and Vajsov 1994), as the only synthetic monograph on the Neolithic in Bulgaria. The British archaeologist, Dorothy Garrod, carried out work on the Palaeolithic site Bacho Kiro in 1938 (Garrod 1939), work continued by a Polish–Bulgarian team from 1971–5 (Kozlowski 1982).

While a substantial proportion of post-1944 projects involved partners from the former Warsaw Pact countries, collaboration in more recent times has included major projects involving west European, American and Japanese archae-ologists. After 1976 international excavations were encouraged on the initiative of BAN and the Ministry of Culture, with teams from western Europe and Japan invited to take part (Velkov 1993).[18]

In light of the internal opposition to foreign influence, the extent of the inter-national collaboration which has occurred over the past fifty years (and beyond) must be recognised for the achievement which it represents. This becomes especially clear when viewed against the official line delivered to archaeologists from the Party ideologues in the 1950s and 1960s. This held that the major goals of Bulgarian archaeology were to assist in the struggle towards the final victory against the capitalist world (Arkheologiya 1963: 2; Dimitrov 1955: 8), to criticise the Western bourgeois archaeologists (ibid.: 5) and to fight against alien influences (ibid.: 5). Indeed, according to Party dictate, archaeologists were at the front line of the 'gigantic struggle of peace-loving people against the Anglo-American monopolists, the war-mongers of the World War' (ibid.: 8). Despite the move away from the xenophobic nationalism displayed in the Party-directed statements and the recent expansion of international collaboration, it remains illegal for a foreign national to have his or her name on a permit for excavation in Bulgaria.

More telling perhaps is the almost complete absence of Bulgarian archaeolo-gists working on projects in other countries. The recent work of a team of

Palaeolithic archaeologists in Vietnam, led by Nikolai Sirakov, is a notable exception. A major component of the de-exoticisation of Bulgarian archaeology is the practical integration of Bulgarian archaeologists into field projects in other archaeological traditions. Integration into the fieldwork of non-Bulgarian traditions requires an expansion of the discipline from its current blinkered perspective as a national archaeology (only concerned with traces of the past as they relate to the territory within the modern borders of the nation-state) to a broader perspective which is not concerned with traces of ethnic originality of primacy, but which searches for patterns of human behaviour, regardless of border, political boundary or territory. Such an expansion could begin in the classroom and in the editor's office with courses and publications on the archaeology of pan-European regions and beyond. All this requires investment and contribution (in the hard reality of publications) from outside Bulgaria.

Each of these proposals circle around the character of the role best played by foreign archaeologists in the praxis and future of Bulgarian archaeology. One alternative would be to take up a passive, hands-off position. This is the role of the relativist. It accepts Bulgarian archaeology as a self-contained and self-regulating entity. This position is unacceptable, dangerous and reckless. The preferred alternative is that foreign archaeologists roll up their sleeves and get their hands dirty.

The task to be taken in hand is the removal of the false distinction which has been erected over the past century-and-a-half and which nominates Bulgarian archaeology as the exotic other, best left to its own devices.[19] The alternative, preferred in this essay as an example, is to treat colleagues as peers and offer them the respect of critical comment on their work, their methods and the social consequences of their doctrines. To do otherwise is to abrogate any responsibility for the impact which archaeology has on the reality of modern existence in Bulgaria or in any place that archaeology is practised. The time to accept that responsibility is now when, as a discipline, Bulgarian archaeology drifts without proper financial ballast, having been orphaned from a long-exploitative family.

Acknowledgements

I am grateful to many Bulgarian archaeologists at the Archaeological Institute in Sofia and in the regional museums who had the patience to speak with me about the condition and history of Bulgarian archaeology. Critical comments by the editor and Alasdair Whittle helped me to refine my thinking about this topic. The opinions expressed in this essay remain my own.

Notes

1 The only two of which I know are the late Velizar Velkov's short piece in a section of *Antiquity* devoted to central and east European archaeology (Velkov 1993) and an introductory chapter in an edited volume on Bulgarian prehistory (Bailey and Panayotov 1995). Critical comment on other countries in the region and across Europe are accumulating quickly with considerations of the development of archaeology in the countries of the former Soviet Union especially well represented. (For central, eastern and southeastern Europe, see Bogucki 1993; Bökönyi 1993; Kaiser 1995; Kobyliński 1991; Kotsakis 1991; Laszlovszky and Siklódi 1991; Milisauskas 1990; Miraj and Zeqo 1993; Neustupný 1991, 1993; Rączkowski 1996; Schild 1993; Sklenář 1983. For the former Soviet Union, see Chernykh 1995; Dolukhanov 1993, 1996; Kohl and Tsetskhladze 1995; Puodžiuas and Girininkas 1996; Shnirel-man 1995, 1996; Trigger 1989. For Western Europe and Eurasia in general, see d'Agostino 1991; Bogucki 1985; Champion 1991; Cleere 1993; Cleuziou *et al.* 1991; Díaz-Andreu and Champion 1996; Gringmuth-Dallmer 1993; Härke 1991; Hodder 1991; Kohl and Fawcett 1995; Myhre 1991; Sklenář 1983; Trigger 1989; Vázquez Varela and Risch 1991; Veit 1989; Whitley 1987.

2 The Austrian Oskar Strauss (1870–1954) based the libretto of his comic opera *Der Tapfere Soldat [The Chocolate Soldier]* (1908) on Shaw's play.

3 Turkish influence was replaced by Russian, German, Soviet, US–Western European.

4 A good example is the way in which the Danube manages to bisect internally consistent archaeological phenomena such as the fifth millennium Gumelnitsa and Karanovo culture complexes.

5 The language of the editorial précis and the application of Party Congress theses as they appeared in the main archaeological journals are heavy with archaeologists' active role in the struggles of the 'ideological front' (Arkheologiya 1963: 4; Dimitrov 1955: 8).

6 One may include in the audience-group a transitional category: foreign archaeologists (either practicing professionals or students).

7 For a detailed proclamation of Bulgaria's national cultural policy prior to 1989 see Costadine Popov's volume, *Bulgarian Cultural Policy* (1981), published in the UNESCO series Studies and Documents on Cultural Policies.

8 'Appropriate' premises include Revival Period houses, the architecturally imposing, former law courts in Sofia for the National Historical Museum, the Buyuk Mosque in Sofia for the home of the collections of the Archaeological Institute and Museum.

9 In many cases the best publication of the Varna or Thracian material comes from foreign produced (and financed) exhibition catalogues (British Museum 1976; Cook 1989; Fol and Lichardus 1988; Musée des Antiquités 1989). For possible negative consequences of international display of exotics as a stimulus for looting sites and trading in antiquities, see Bailey (1993).

10 BAN was founded in 1911 on the basis of an earlier institution (the Bulgarian Literary Society which had been founded in 1869), nine years before Russian armies liberated Bulgaria from the Ottomans and thirty-nine years before Bulgaria was formally recognised as a nation).

11 In the post-1945 period, the relationship between the academy and the universities changed. Where research had aligned teaching in previous periods, Soviet practices of separating research from teaching were followed in Bulgaria. Research became the priority of BAN and not the university (M. Todorova 1992a: 1112).

12 The report applying the theses of the eleventh congress of the Bulgarian Communist Party stresses the importance of the role of the party within the Archaeological Institute (Ovcharov 1976: 4).

13 The link between political office and archaeological occupation is noticeable in many regions of eastern Europe and the former Soviet Union. See Chernykh (1995: 143) for examples from the Caucuses, Belarus, Armenia, Abkazia, and see the recent news from the political struggles in Albania.

14 There is yet another side to the paradox of the absence of interpretive politics in Bulgarian archaeology. This is that the majority of Bulgarian archaeologists strive not to engage political issues in their archaeologies. They do this, they believe, to preserve their archaeology as one of the only apolitical zones in their lives. For them, the world of archaeology, and especially that of archaeological interpretation, remains a world of escapism, free of the worries, political and otherwise, of life in very difficult personal and eco-nomic conditions. See M. Todorova (1992b: 162) for a well-argued discussion of potential causes for this.

15 Kohl and Tsetskhladze make the same point in their consideration of nationalism in the archaeology of the Caucasus (Kohl and Tsetskhladze 1995: 168).

16 As an example, see the recent scandal over the Bulgarian expulsion of a US archaeologist under trumped up charges of spying (Bailey 1995; Steele 1995; THES 1995).

17 Between the 1880s and the early 1940s the Škorpils produced over a hundred works in Bulgarian, Russian, German and Czech.

18 Collaborative projects included Italian work at Ratiaria, British work at Nicopolis ad Istrum, Austrian work at Karanovo, German work at Drama, French work at Kovachevo and Dutch and Japanese work at Dyadovo.

19 It is this attitude of relativist abandonment that has much to answer for in the abuses of archaeology and archaeological data in the ethnic tragedies of the former Yugoslavia. Colin Renfrew has made this point in his keynote address to the inaugural meeting of the European Archaeological Association in 1994 in Ljubljana (Renfrew 1994).

Bibliography

d'Agostino, B. (1991) 'The Italian perspective on theoretical archaeology', in Hodder, I. (ed.) *Archaeological Theory in Europe: The Last Three Decades*, London: Routledge, pp. 54–62.

Arkheologiya (1960) 'Postanovlenieto na TsK i BKP i MS za razvitieto na bulgarskata nauka i zadachite na bulgarskata arkheologiya', *Arkheologiya* 2, 1: 1–2.

—— (1963) 'Osmiyat kongres na BKP i zadachite na bulgarskata arkheologiya', *Arkheologiya* 5, 1: 1–4.

—— (1967) 'Devetiyat kongres na Bulgarskata komunisticheska partiya i nashite zadachi', *Arkheologiya* 9, 1: 1–4.

Bailey, D. W. (1993) 'Looting Bulgaria: a special report', *Archaeology* 46, 2: 26–27.

—— (1995) 'Checkmate', *The Times Higher Education Supplement*, September 22.

—— (forthcoming) 'Bulgarian culture', in Frucht, R. (ed.) *Encyclopedia of Eastern Europe (1815–1989)*, Denver, CO: Westview.

Bailey, D. W. and Panayotov, I. (1995) 'Introduction: the structure of Bulgarian archaeology', in Bailey, D. W. and Panayotov, I. (eds), *Prehistoric Bulgaria*, Madison, WI: Prehistory Press, pp. 1–9.

Bogucki, P. (1985) 'Theoretical directions in European archaeology', *American Antiquity* 50: 780–8.

—— (1993) 'Between East and West: archaeology in the new Eastern Europe', *Annual Review of Anthropology* 1, 2: 145–66.

Bökönyi, S. (1993) 'Recent developments in Hungarian archaeology', *Antiquity* 67: 142–5.

British Museum (1976) *Thracian Treasures from Bulgaria*, London: British Museum Publications.

Champion, T. (1991) 'Theoretical archaeology in Britain', in Hodder, I. (ed.) *Archaeological Theory in Europe: The Last Three Decades*, London: Routledge, pp. 129–60.

Chernykh, E. N. (1995) 'Postscript: Russian archaeology after the collapse of the USSR – infrastructural crisis and the resurgence of old and new nationalisms', in Kohl, P. L. and Fawcett, C. (eds), *Nationalism, Politics and the Practice of Archaeology*, Cambridge: Cambridge University Press, pp. 139–48.

Chichikova, M. (1960) '15 godini arkheologicheska nauka', *Arkheologiya* 2, 2: 67–8.

Cleere, H. (1993) 'Central European archaeology in transition', *Antiquity* 67: 121–2.

Cleuziou, S., Coudart, A., Demoule, J.-P. and Schnapp, A. (1991) 'The use of theory in French archaeology', in Hodder, I. (ed.) *Archaeological Theory in Europe: the Last Three Decades*, London: Routledge, pp. 91–128.

Cook, B. F. (1989) *The Rogozen Treasure. Papers of the Anglo-Bulgarian Conference, 12 March 1987*, London: British Museum Press.

Creed, G. (1995) 'The politics of agriculture: identity and socialist sentiment in Bulgaria', *Slavic Review* 54, 4: 843–68.

Díaz-Andreu, M. and Champion, T. (1996) 'Nationalism and archaeology in Europe: an introduction', in Díaz-Andreu, M. and Champion, T. (eds) *Nationalism and Archaeology in Europe*, London: UCL Press, pp. 1–23.

Dimitrov, D. P. (1955) 'Resheniyata na shestiya kongres na BKP i po-natatushnoto razvitie na bulgarskata arkheologicheska nauka', *Izvestiya na Arkheologicheskiya Institut* 20: 1–9.

—— (1964) 'Bulgarskata arkheologiya prez perioda 1944–1964 g.', *Arkheologiya* 6, 3: 1–6.

Dolukhanov, P. M. (1993) 'Archaeology in the ex-USSR: post-perestroyka problems', *Antiquity* 67: 150–6.

—— (1996) 'Archaeology and nationalism in totalitarian and post-totalitarian Russia', in Atkinson, J. A., Banks, I. and O'Sullivan, J. (eds) *Nationalism and Archaeology*, Glasgow: Cruithne Press, pp. 200–13.

Fol, A. and Lichardus, J. (eds) (1988) *Macht, Herrschaft und Gold*, Saarbrücken: Moderne Galerie des Saarland-Museums.

Garrod, D. (1939) 'Excavations in the cave of Bacho Kiro, northeast Bulgaria. Description, excavations and archaeology', *Bulletin of the American School of Prehistoric Research* 15: 46–75.

Gaul, J. (1948) *The Neolithic in Bulgaria*, Cambridge, MA: American School for Prehistoric Research.

Georgieva, S. and Velkov, V. (1974) *Bibliographiya na Bulgarskata Arkheologiya (1879–1966)*, Sofia: BAN.

Gringmuth-Dallmer, E. (1993) 'Archaeology in the former German Democratic Republic since 1989', *Antiquity* 67: 135–42.

Härke, H. (1991) 'All quiet on the Western Front? Paradigms, methods and approaches in West German archaeology', in Hodder, I. (ed.) *Archaeological Theory in Europe: The Last Three Decades*, London: Routledge, pp. 187–222.

Hodder, I. (1991) 'Archaeological theory in contemporary European societies: the emergence of competing traditions', in Hodder, I. (ed.) *Archaeological Theory in Europe: The Last Three Decades*, London: Routledge, pp. 1–24.

Kaiser, T. (1995) 'Archaeology and ideology in southeast Europe', in Kohl, P. L. and Fawcett, C. (eds) *Nationalism, Politics and the Practice of Archaeology*, Cambridge: Cambridge University Press, pp. 99–119.

Katincharov, R. (1975) 'Prouchvaniya na bronzovata epokha v Bulgariya' (1944–1974), *Arkheologiya* 17, 2: 1–17.

Kobyliński, Z. (1991) 'Theory in Polish archaeology 1960–90: searching for paradigms', in Hodder, I. (ed.) *Archaeological Theory in Europe: The Last Three Decades*, London: Routledge, pp. 223–47.

Kohl, P. L. and Fawcett, C. (1995) 'Archaeology in the service of the state: theoretical considerations', in Kohl, P. L. and Fawcett, C. (eds) *Nationalism, Politics and the Practice of Archaeology*, Cambridge: Cambridge University Press, pp. 3–20.

Kohl, P. L. and Tsetskhladze, G. R. (1995) 'Nationalism, politics and the practice of archaeology in the Caucasus', in Kohl, P. L. and Fawcett, C. (eds) *Nationalism, Politics and the Practice of Archaeology*, Cambridge: Cambridge University Press, pp. 149–76.

Kotsakis, K. (1991) 'The powerful past: theoretical trends in Greek archaeology', in Hodder, I. (ed.) *Archaeological Theory in Europe: The Last Three Decades*, London: Routledge, pp. 65–90.

Kozlowski, J. K. (ed.) (1982) *Excavation in the Bacho Kiro Cave (Bulgaria). Final Report*, Warsaw: Państwowe Wydawnictwo Naukowe.

Laszlovszky, J. and Siklódi, Cs. (1991) 'Archaeological theory in Hungary since 1960: theories without theoretical archaeology', in Hodder, I. (ed.) *Archaeological Theory in Europe: The Last Three Decades*, London: Routledge, pp. 272–98.

Milisauskas, M. (1990) 'People's revolutions of 1989 and archaeology in Eastern Europe', *Antiquity* 64: 283–5.

Miraj, L. and Zeqo, M. (1993) 'Conceptual changes in Albanian archaeology', *Antiquity* 67: 123–5.

Musée des Antiquités (1989) *Le Premier or de l'humanité en Bulgarie 5e millénaire*. Paris: Editions de la Réunion des Musées Nationaux.

Myhre, B. (1991) 'Theory in Scandinavian archaeology since 1960: a view from Norway', in Hodder, I. (ed.) *Archaeological Theory in Europe: The Last Three Decades*, London: Routledge, pp. 161–86.

Neustupný, E. (1991) 'Recent theoretical achievements in prehistoric archaeology in Czechoslovakia', in Hodder, I. (ed.) *Archaeological Theory in Europe: The Last Three Decades*, London: Routledge, pp. 248–71.

—— (1993) 'Czechoslovakia: the last three years', *Antiquity* 67: 129–34.

Ovcharov, D. (1962) 'Kum istoriya na purvoto arkheologichesko druzhestvo v Bulgariya', *Arkheologiya* 4, 3: 69–71.

—— (1976) 'XI congres na BKP i zadachite na arkheologicheskata nauka', *Arkheologiya* 18, 3: 1–5.

Panayotov, I. (1995) 'The Bronze Age in Bulgaria: studies and problems', in Bailey, D. W. and Panayotov, I. (eds), *Prehistoric Bulgaria*, Madison, WI: Prehistory Press, pp. 243–52.

Popov, C. (1981) *Bulgarian Cultural Policy*, Paris: UNESCO.

Puodžiuas, G. and Girininkas, A. (1996) 'Nationalism doubly oppressed: archaeology and nationalism in Lithuania', in Díaz-Andreu, M. and Champion, T. (eds) *Nationalism and Archaeology in Europe*, London: UCL Press, pp. 243–55.

Raçzkowski, W. (1996) '"Drang nach Westen?": Polish archaeology and national identity', in Díaz-Andreu, M. and Champion, T. (eds) *Nationalism and Archaeology in Europe*, London: UCL Press, pp. 189–217.

Renfrew, C. (1994) 'The identity of Europe in prehistoric archaeology', *Journal of European Archaeology* 2, 2: 153–74.

Schild, R. (1993) 'Polish archaeology in transition', *Antiquity* 67: 146–50.

Shnirelman, V. A. (1995) 'From internationalism to nationalism: forgotten pages of Soviet archaeology in the 1930s and 1940s', in Kohl, P. L. and Fawcett, C. (eds) *Nationalism, Politics and the Practice of Archaeology*, Cambridge University Press, pp. 120–38.

—— (1996) 'The faces of nationalist archaeology in Russia', in Díaz-Andreu, M. and Champion, T. (eds) *Nationalism and Archaeology in Europe*, London: UCL Press, pp. 218–42.

Sklenář, K. (1983) *Archaeology in Central Europe: The First 500 Years*, Leicester: Leicester University Press.

Steele, J. (1995) 'Bulgaria expels archaeologist', *The Guardian*, 5 September.

THES (1995) 'Spy row prompts dig halt', *The Times Higher Education Supplement*, September 8.

Todorova, H. (1986) *Kamenno-mednata Epokha na Bulgariya*, Sofia: Nauka i Izkustvo.

Todorova, H. and Vajsov, I. (1994) *Novokamennata Epokha v Bulgariya*, Sofia: Nauka i Izkustvo.

Todorova, M. (1992a) 'Historiography of the countries of Eastern Europe: Bulgaria', *American Historical Review* 97, 4: 1105–117.

—— (1992b) 'Improbable maverick or typical conformist? Seven thoughts on the new Bulgaria', in Benac, I. (ed.) *Eastern Europe in Revolution*, Ithaca, NY: Cornell University Press, pp. 148–67.

—— (1994) 'The Balkans: from discovery to invention', *Slavic Review* 53, 2: 453–82.

Trigger, B. (1989) *A History of Archaeological Thought*, Cambridge: Cambridge University Press.

Vaklinov, S. (1969) '25 godini bulgarskata arkheologiya', *Arkheologiya* 11, 1: 1–3.

—— (1971) 'Desetiyat kongres na BKP i bulgarskata arkheologiya', *Arkheologiya* 13, 3: 1–2.

Vázquez Varela, J.M. and Risch, R. (1991) 'Theory in Spanish archaeology since 1960', in Hodder, I. (ed.) *Archaeological Theory in Europe: The Last Three Decades*, London: Routledge, pp. 25–51.

Veit, U. (1989) 'Ethnic concepts in German prehistory: a case study on the relationship between cultural identity and archaeological objectivity', in Shennan, S. (ed.) *Archaeological Approaches to Cultural Identity*, London: Unwin Hyman, pp. 35–56.

Velkov, V. (1993) 'Archaeology in Bulgaria', *Antiquity* 67: 125–9.

Walsh, W. A. (1967) 'Politics and scholarship in Bulgaria', *Balkan Studies* 8: 138–49.

Whitley, J. (1987) 'Art history, archaeology and idealism: the German tradition', in Hodder, I. (ed.) *Archaeology as Long-term History*, Cambridge: Cambridge University Press, pp. 9–16.

Chapter 5

Ideology and archaeology in Turkey

Mehmet Özdoğan

Setting the stage

Archaeology, and the active interest in constructions of the the past, is an innovation that was initiated, and subsequently evolved, in Europe. One could define archaeology as a perspicacious perception of the past that developed as one of the key elements of modern "Western"[1] culture. As a concept, archaeology is closely linked with Western ideology and it is no coincidence that – in spite of the extensive field work taking place all over the world – ideas on how archaeological data should be evaluated are still being undertaken primarily in the West. At present, almost every state in the world, regardless of its economic status, cultural or historical background, is involved at some level in documenting, or at least in considering, the past. However, the type of archaeology that is being implemented differs considerably according to the ideological and/or political setting of each country (Arnold 1996; Banks 1996; Fleury-Ilett 1993; Mouliou 1996). One could say that while some nations are theorising archaeology, most nations are rather unconsciously practicing archaeology.

Archaeology began in Turkey as an imported concept. As such, it remained as an élite pursuit until it was integrated with the ideological framework of the Republic. At present, Turkey is one of the few countries where a local tradition in archaeology has developed. It also occupies a unique position being located between the West and the East. Turkey's position is not just a matter of geographical location – in the last two centuries it has vacillated between Western and marginal Western models. Throughout history, and at present, its position has had a decisive impact on the formation of Anatolian cultures. The impact of this intermediary position between the East and the West can also be traced in the ideological formation of archaeology in Turkey.

The events that led to the emergence of modern Turkey are poorly known in the West, and without this knowledge, neither the motives that stimulated the development of archaeology in Turkey, nor the status of its current problems, can be comprehended. Throughout this chapter occasional remarks are made to illustrate the historical background of these events.

The beginnings of Turkish archaeology go back to the early years of the nineteenth century, to the time when the traditional Ottoman state was experiencing what can be termed as a 'process of Westernisation'. Accordingly, archaeology in Turkey developed simultaneously through the events that led to the emergence of the modern Republic of Turkey.

Turkey is an Islamic country that for over half a millennia, as the only leading power of the Islamic world, had to confront European powers. Yet there are considerable discrepancies between Turkey and the other Middle Eastern and Islamic countries: these differences are not only restricted to distinct linguistic and ethnic origins, but Turks in general have never been orthodox in their religious beliefs.[2] In spite of sharing the same religion, Turks (having their origins in remote Asia) and Arabs (having totally different origins and social habits), never developed a genuine liking for each other. Both in the Seljuk and in the Ottoman Empires, while people of Turkic origin were a minority, members of the Eastern Christian churches were at least as populous as their Islamic counterparts. Thus, when compared with the contemporary states in Europe, all Turkish states were highly pluralistic, being composed of diverse ethnic, racial, linguistic and religious groups. This seems to have characterised Anatolia from prehistoric times to the present. With some justification it can be stated that the Turkish population of the Ottoman Empire accorded better with their local Orthodox subjects than with other Islamic populations. Consequently, the Ottomans had inherited both the traditional hatred and mistrust of its Orthodox subjects to the Catholic World and also the physical boundary between the East and the West.[3] This border endured, both physically and conceptually, for centuries.

The process of Westernisation in Turkey was not a linear development. As can be expected it was, and still is, full of controversies. First, it was a 'state oriented' process, mainly imposed by the newly emerging élite and even, in some cases, by the personal initiatives of the Sultans, implemented at the expense of confronting most of its subjects. Turkey's struggles to change its system to a European one coincided in Europe with the peak of "anti-Turkish" trends, motivated under the impact of highly romanticized Hellenism. While Turkey was trying to integrate within the European cultural system, Europe was, and still is, reluctant to accept it, occasionally resulting in double-standards.

The emergence and the development of archaeology in Turkey took place under constraints that are deeply rooted in history. Confrontation between the traditional Islamic framework and the Western model, the endeavor to survive as a non-Arabic nation in the Middle East while the Empire was disintegrating, the hostile and occasionally humiliating attitude of Europeans, and growing nationalism have all been consequential in this development. The extremely rich archaeological potential of the country served to stimulate a developing interest in archaeology. However, compared to other Middle Eastern states where similar potential exists, Turkey can claim to have developed a long tradition in archaeology. Turkey not only became the first Islamic country to develop a critical view on cultural heritage, but it is the only one where a continuum has been established between local politics and science. This is clearly demonstrated by the fact that Turkey offers a rare case where scientific research – both by foreigners and Turks – could endure, without any obstructions, for over a century.[4] I consider that the pace that archaeology took in Turkey is much more related to the ideology of the modern Republic than to the existing archaeological potential of the country.

The modern Republic of Turkey, founded in 1923, is the direct descendant of the Ottoman empire which, up to 1829 (the year when Peloponnese seceded from the Empire), extended over the Near East, Northern Africa, Caucasus, Cyprus and to most of the Balkan peninsula, including Greece and the Aegean islands. Almost all the regions that were considered the cradle of civilisation, thus appealing to the archaeologists, were dominated by the Ottoman Empire. During the incipient years of archaeology, at the time when the first European archaeologists took to the field, Turkey – or the Ottoman Empire – was the only non-Western European country to face the first wave of explorers and archaeologists. This inevitably had an impact on the Ottomans. The intelligentsia became engaged in archaeology, directly or indirectly, and came to consider it at a relatively early date. Like other modern institutions, archaeology began in Turkey as an imitation of that in the West. No efforts were spent either thinking about archaeological practices or adapting archaeology to local needs. It was oriented simply to the Near Eastern, Hellenistic, Roman and Byzantine cultures. The remains of the Seljuk or of the Ottoman periods were not considered as *antiquities* for a long period of time.

The traditional Ottoman perception of the past

The traditional Ottoman perception of the past, as in most other non-Western cultures, was less dependent on 'factual' evidence or, rather, the 'facts' did not necessarily have to be as concrete as they are in the Western way of thinking. The philosophical base of the Ottoman Empire, the forerunner of modern Turkey, can be considered as an amalgamation of Oriental and Islamic cultures, having its roots both in Central Asia and in the Near East. The conception of the 'past' was thus more putative than empirical. It was, in a way, an abstraction without a temporal dimension. Thus, "Antiquarianism . . . failed to develop in the Near East, where Islamic peoples lived in the midst of impressive monuments of antiquity" (Trigger 1989: 44). There is an interesting contradiction in the Ottoman system. More than any other nation, the Ottomans collected and meticulously kept documents and books – even those left over from the Byzantine Period were saved. Extremely accurate records were kept from all over the Empire, yielding minute details about historical events and daily activities. Written documents, regardless of their subject matter, were saved and archived. However, these documents were never used to write a "factual" history. History was more a tradition beyond the use of written texts or documents. It is not a coincidence, then, that the history of the Ottomans was inevitably written by Europeans.

A past based on "facts", or the perception that ancient remains constituted evidence from which to write a history, was a concept imported into the Ottoman Empire. Most of the "ancient buildings" were saved and esteemed, not because they were considered as indicators of the past, but because they were associated with an atavistic patrimony. For this reason, the traditional Ottomans considered inconceivable the interest shown to ancient ruins by the first generation of European archaeologists.

The first generation of European archaeologists and the Ottoman Empire

As mentioned above, the Ottoman Empire was the first and, for a considerable time, the only non-European state to meet the initial wave of European explorers and archaeologists. The latter were at first ignored, but in general their actions were taken to be the bizarre deeds of the Westerners. However, in time, the looting of sites and removal of antiquities by the Western explorers infuriated the newly emerging intelligentsia of the Empire.

As a part of the process of modernization in the beginning of the nineteenth century, a number of Western style institutions had already been established in the Ottoman Empire. Within that context, in 1846 a collection of antiquities was established in İstanbul (see Arık 1953). In 1868, this collection was to be inaugurated as the Ottoman Imperial Museum. As the Empire was still controlling the Near East and most of the Balkans, its collections grew rapidly and, in 1891, it moved to a new building, now the İstanbul Archaeology Museum. By the first decade of the twentieth century there were already a number of museums in the provinces, including Bursa, Selanik (present Thessaloniki), Konya and Sıvas.

As archaeology came to the Ottoman Empire as an imported concept through the impact of Classical archaeologists, most of the collections in the Ottoman Museums initially consisted of Hellenistic, Roman or Byzantine antiquities. In time, Near Eastern and Egyptian collections were added and since then all antiquities, regardless of their cultural origins, have been collected. The same trend can also be envisaged in selecting sites to be excavated. During the last decades of the nineteenth century, almost all the Turkish excavations were at sites of Greco-Roman period, such as Sidon, Nemrut Dağ, Alabanda, Sipar, Tralles etc. (Arık 1950: 4).

The most significant contribution made by the Ottomans to archaeology was prohibiting the export of antiquities which at that time might be considered as revolutionary. In 1884, Osman Hamdi Bey, the curator of the Imperial Museum and most eminent figure in the history of Turkish archaeology, formulated a new law for the protection of antiquities (see also Potts, Chapter 10). This law was so well formulated that it was maintained until 1972. Two important concepts were introduced by it: one considering all antiquities as the property of the state, and the other forbidding the export of all antiquities. The latter was strongly opposed and, to a degree, disregarded by Westerners until the establishment of the Turkish Republic. The major difficulty in the implementation of this law was the attitude of the Western archeologists and diplomatic services, not only because they wanted to enrich the museums of their own countries, but because they considered the Turks ineligible to possess such collections. There are numerous cases demonstrating this attitude, but H. Schliemann's smuggling of the finds from Troy is the most explicit case (see Esin 1993). Schliemann countered the claims of the Ottoman government by stating that "instead of yielding the finds to the government . . . by keeping all to myself, I saved them for the science. All the civilized world will appreciate what I have done" (ibid.: 185). This view is also expressed by Runnels (1997: 127): "He [Schliemann] shared the widely held dislike of the Ottomans that characterized Europeans in his day . . . his high-handed behavior . . . was excusable, even laudable." In Europe, no one seriously considered justifying their practices either in scientific or in intellectual circles.

At the turn of the twentieth century, the Ottoman Empire experienced considerable political and economical difficulties which led to a total collapse. Considering the situation, the ability to maintain museums without losing their collections was a significant achievement of the first generation of Turkish archaeologists. During the last episode of the Ottoman Empire, attempts were made by certain foreign diplomatic missions to receive, as a present, some of the outstanding pieces on display. Such attempts were, with certain tact and persistence, prevented. More significant were the events during the years of occupation following the collapse of the Empire. After World War I, when most of Turkey – and in particular İstanbul – was occupied by the British and French troops, the director of the Imperial Museum, Ethem Bey, was able to save the museums. After Turkey's War of Independence, the persistent claims of the government enabled archaeological material, excavated and removed during the occupation, to be partially repatriated. The most significant example of this is material from the Protesilaos-Karaağaçtepe excavations.

It should be emphasised here that the illicit export of antiquities from the Empire, as well as accusations of spying by some archaeologists such as T. E. Lawrence, inevitably resulted in foreign archaeologists being cast as disreputable characters. With the growing impact of nationalism, this image, at least among the general public, has been sustained up to the present.

Nationalism and archaeology in Turkey

Nationalism, both as a concept and as an ideology, developed in Western Europe and began impacting upon the Ottoman Empire by the first half of the nineteenth century. However, the Turkish population of the Empire were the last to contemplate this idea. For a considerable time, as late as the 1890s, even intellectuals educated in the West considered nationalism a very strange idea. The concept that Turkish speakers constituted a single nation is another idea that was imported from the West. Despite being customary for Europeans and other Middle Eastern peoples to identify Ottomans with Turks, throughout most of its existence the Ottomans not only rejected Turkish identity, but even considered it humiliating (see Güvenç 1996: 21–33).[5] Following the collapse of the Ottoman Empire and during the formation of the new Turkish state, one of the main concerns of Atatürk, the founder of the new republic, was to propagate Turkish identity. Given Turkey's situation in 1923 this seemed like an impossible achievement since for centuries being a Turk (and not an Ottoman) was considered degrading. Moreover, during the War of Independence there was no one, except a handful of intelligentsia educated in the West, who called themselves Turkish.

In creating a nation out of the ruins of the Ottoman Empire, it was essential to formulate an ideology that would assure national pride, give moral direction and identity. Most of the élite of the time were utterly desperate and had lost confidence as a result of the events that led to the collapse of the Ottoman system. They took a more retrospective view by looking back to the glorious days of history and to their Turkic origins in Central Asia. Thus, they promoted the Pan-Turkist ideology.

Atatürk was one of the few, if not the only person, who rejected Pan-Turkism and still had confidence in Anatolia. He developed an antithesis to the prevailing Pan-Turkist ideology and insisted upon Anatolia being the homeland. To substantiate this totally new concept, an ethnohistorical theory was formulated, relating

Sumerians and Hittites to the Turks, and integrated into the ideological framework of the new state. This approach considered Anatolia and the present population as an ethnic amalgamation of thousands of years. Pan-Turkists, who later became the ideologists of the racist movements of the present times, were rather pleased with the idea of affiliating Sumerians and Hittites to Turkish origins, but they never accepted a pre-Turkish history of Anatolia as a part of their heritage. In some respects, conflict between "Anatolianism" and Pan-Turkism continues to the present day – although there was some consensus, at least in history books, by stressing both the Anatolian heritage and over-stressing Central Asian origins. The latter, particularly in books written in the 1930s under the impact of prevailing nationalistic trends of its time, posited a Turkish exodus from Asian steps. Atatürk's view, summoning all the pasts of Anatolia – regardless of ethnic origin – as national, was incorporated into the ideology of the modern state.

The motive behind this ideology has survived, with some modifications up to the present. Remnants of all cultures that lived in Anatolia have been regarded impartially, either in issuing research permits or in the funding of archaeological expeditions; sites of Hellenistic, Byzantine or Turkish period were treated equally. For example, of the major excavations conducted in Turkey in 1995, twenty-four were on prehistoric and proto-historic period sites, thirty on Hellenistic, Roman and Byzantine, and only nine on Islamic period sites. Even during the last decade, the newly founded nationalist and fundamentalist political parties have not yet hampered, but have begun criticising the state for treating pre-Turkish or pre-Islamic remains no differently from those of the later periods. One of their arguments is based on the fact that in the Balkan countries Ottoman cultural heritage had been systematically destroyed and that asking for a permit to excavate sites of Ottoman period in most of these countries (Greece, for example) would be unthinkable.

Turkish views on foreign archaeological expeditions

Another political aspect of archaeology in Turkey has been the relationship between the "foreign" and local archaeologists. Turkish archaeologists, since the last quarter of the nineteenth century, have been active, not only in the field, but also in setting a legislative basis regulating archaeological activities. Particularly since the 1930s the number of archaeologists, museums and institutions has consistently increased. In spite of the presence of a local archaeological tradition Turkey is one of the few Middle Eastern or Balkan countries to maintain good relations between the local and foreign teams. With the exception of the 1920s, during the formation years of the Republic, there have always been foreign teams working in Turkey. Occasionally there have been short episodes of turmoil, but these stem primarily from problems such as spying and smuggling and not from ideological reasons.

The first generation of Turkish archaeologists

From the beginning, archaeology in Turkey had developed as an élite involvement. Almost all first generation Turkish archaeologists were educated in the "Western style" and belonged to aristocratic families (see Esin, forthcoming). Notable among them are Osman Hamdi Bey, Makridi Bey, Halil Ethem Bey, followed by Aziz Ogan and Arif Müfit Mansel, all eminent scholars with strong personalities. The principles set by them have continued to be the traditional standpoint of Turkish archaeology, regarding all past cultures as equally important. At the same time they have defended the legal rights of the country by the protection of antiquities, rejecting all sorts of trade and exportation of antiquities. They have also established as a tradition the maintenance of good relations with foreign archaeo-logical schools working in Turkey. Yet, two other serious implications of this tradition need to be mentioned. Due to their élitist background, these early scholars neither considered propagating archaeology to a more general public media, nor stimulating a consciousness for past heritage. Perhaps one positive consequence of this 'élitism' was to save archaeology from the political turmoils that the country experienced in the course of Westernisation.

Being extremely selective in issuing excavation permits by asking high scholarly standards is a tradition that was instigated by the first generation of Turkish archaeologists and later became the unwritten official policy. Unlike most Middle Eastern countries, where young and unexperienced archaeologists can easily get archaeological permits, the Turkish authorities have been selective, not only to foreigners, but even more to the Turkish archaeologists. While bringing higher excavation standards to Anatolia, it inevitably limited the number of excavated sites and, subsequently, our knowledge. Throughout the 1960s, when the number of excavated sites per year were counted in hundreds thoughout the Middle East and in the Balkans, the number remained below twenty in Turkey.

In the 1930s, Atatürk took a personal initiative to engage with archaeology. A group of students were sent to Europe, mainly to France, Germany and Hungary, to study archaeology, the Turkish Historical Society was founded, and Turkish excavations resumed in full. In the years preceding World War II, Atatürk invited German professors, fleeing from the Nazi regime, to Turkey. Most chairs in archaeology in the newly founded or reformed universities of the young Turkish Republic were allocated to migrant German professors. In 1939, this new influx of academics, coupled with the return of students educated abroad, led to a significantly high standard of teaching in archaeology. These students became the second generation of archeologists in Turkey. Even though archaeological excavations, such as Alaca Höyük, were promptly reflected in history books, the actual popularization of archaeology did not take place until the late 1960s.

The second generation and women in archaeology

The first of this second generation of Turkish archaeologists were educated in Europe. However, soon after World War II the new group of students in Turkish Universities took to the field. It was no longer a profession for the élite or aristocrats but their impact still persisted. An interesting aspect of this generation was the sudden increase in the number of active female archaeologists, a trend that still continues today. At present, Turkish archaeology is dominated by female archaeologists, and most archaeology departments are chaired by women. They also constitute a clear majority in museum-based archaeology. In this respect, at least in the Middle East, Turkey is a unique case.

Double standards in protection and cultural cleansing of Turkish heritage

On several occasions Turkey has been accused of the "selective destruction" of antiquities. As in all countries currently undergoing the process of industrialization, considerable destruction is unfortunately being inflicted upon sites and monuments. Turkey's cultural inventory has not been completed yet and, in spite of existing legislations, massive destruction of sites is taking place due simply to inefficient implementation of the law. Nonetheless, I would argue that the destruction is neither culturally nor religiously selective. It is either due to the growing pressure caused by expanding urban, industrial and tourist centers, industrialized agriculture etc., or is the result of illicit digging by treasure hunters. Intensive construction activities currently taking place in Turkey have clearly resulted in the destruction of sub-surface Byzantine deposits, but the same activities have devastated even more of the Ottoman remains. With justification we can claim that during the last decades more Ottoman archaeology has been destroyed than any of the earlier periods since public opinion still posits that Byzantine and Greco-Roman remains are antique whilst Ottoman ones are not. Even during conservative governments the only case that has been made public is that of St Sophia. This reputed Byzantine monument, after being used as a mosque for over 400 years, was converted to a museum by Atatürk. During the last twenty years conservative parties have occasionally demanded that it should again be used as a mosque as it symbolizes the conquest of the town. However, these demands have been met with such public rejection that the issue has now faded from current discussions.

It should be taken into consideration that the Ottoman Empire ruled in the Balkans and the Near East for over 600 years and, to the Ottomans, the heartland of the empire was in fact the Balkans, not Anatolia. As such, most of the monuments were erected there. As late as 1908, all Macedonia, Western Thrace and parts of Bulgaria were still part of the Ottoman Empire. Now, almost nothing of Ottoman heritage survives in most of the Balkan countries. What survived through this "cultural cleansing" are sample areas of civilian architecture preserved, not as markers of cultural heritage, but for the purposes of tourism. Some mosques have been saved, either by being converted into museums or churches, but other monuments, particularly the Turkish cemeteries, have been wiped out.

On the other hand, even a brief survey of the old territories of the Ottoman Empire shows that the area is still full of pre-Turkish remains. After 500 years of Ottoman rule, Greece is still full of ancient Greek and Byzantine monuments. There are numerous old churches and monasteries throughout the Balkans that were maintained and repaired during Ottoman rule. Turkey, particularly İstanbul, still has numerous Byzantine, Roman and Hellenistic monuments, and most museums have special departments covering these periods. Most of the universities with programs in archaeology or art history have Classical archaeology and Byzantine art departments. As previously stated, most of the current excavations and restoration programs are devoted to pre-Turkish periods. Research and excavation permits are not rejected for taking Byzantine sites or monuments as their subjects. In the Balkans, however, the situation is different. Besides the systematic destruction of Ottoman archaeological remains, the Ottoman period has been omitted as a field of research. Considering the claims of southern Cypriots (see Vermeule 1975), one is prompted to ask what remains of the 300 years of Ottoman heritage in Southern Cyprus?

There are often claims in Europe that Kurdish and Armenian cultural heritages in Turkey are being overlooked.[6] Excavation and research permits there are issued by the Antiquity Service and I suggest that it is misguided to consider that applications are processed according to potential ethnic import of a site. All over Eastern and Southeastern Turkey there are, and have been for a long period of time, numerous excavations covering the entire time span from the Neolithic to Medieval periods. Numerous Armenian sites, including Ani and Ahtamar, have been excavated and a number of Armenian churches have been restored. For the most part, archaeology has not been linked to contemporary polemics surrounding ethnicity. Yet what is intended by Kurdish heritage, or Kurdish archaeology, is not clear. Kurds have lived in that region for some millennia under different tribal names,[7] without establishing any state. The area now populated by Kurdish peoples has been part of numerous kingdoms and empires, including the Assyrian, Mittani, Urartian, Persian, Achaemenid, Roman, Byzantine, Armenian, Arab, Seljuk, Artuquid, Eyyubid, Mongolian, Ottoman and even the Crusader kingdoms. Which one of these should be considered Kurdish, Turkish or Arabic? Would such an approach not lead to a biased imposition of present conflicts onto the past? Is it our concern as archaeologists to use the past as a tool either to prove or disprove racial origins and claims which agitate present conflicts? Or should we engender the notion that the past is past and, whatever its character, it belongs to all of us?

Treasure hunting and the antiquities market

A final area where archaeology matters concerns the illicit looting of ancient sites to supply the demands of the art market. Cultural heritage in Turkey, like all "archaeologically rich" countries, suffers considerably from the exploits of treasure hunters. This phenomenon is provoked by the antiquity markets of the Western World and is not the result of any ideological reasoning. Turkey's government, like that of Northern Cyprus, has been desperately struggling to stop illicit digging but it seems that, as long as there is a market in the West, the destruction will continue. Given these attempts, the West should not accuse these authorities of being unconcerned with illicit digging.

To stop the illicit export of antiquities, buying them in Turkey (for Turkey) by paying sums comparable to the Western collectors has been suggested as a solution. For some years Turkish Museums bought from illicit diggers and, at the same time, private museums and collections were encouraged. This, of course, only encouraged further destruction of the sites. Museums attained important objects at the expense of losing scientific knowledge of their contexts. The most significant destruction took place in the East and, in a few years, thousands of Urartian cemeteries were looted.

Conclusions

In spite of its significant place in the development of local archaeological traditions Turkish archaeology, as a case study, has been largely omitted or ignored by Western scholars working on the history of archaeology. Considering the large number of my colleagues that are fluent in our language it seems evident that this negligence is more the result of political biases than of the inability to access documents written in Turkish. Here we can conclude with the quote that 'Third

World nations resent those in the West who would deny them their past while claiming history as their own' (McIntosh *et al.* 1989: 74).

Notes

1 Throughout this paper, "Western Countries" or "Western" is used, not in a geographical sense, but as a concept to indicate countries that are conceptually integrated with West European culture.

2 Inevitably, this does not imply that there were never cases of religious orthodoxy, but that they have all been short lived. It is no coincidence that at present Turkey is the only secular state of the Islamic World.

3 Here it is interesting to note that in the Ottoman Empire most of the bureaucrats were from the local Orthodox population. The traditional concerns of the local Orthodox subjects against the West did have certain consequences which hampered the process of Westernization (see Berkes 1975).

4 In some other Middle Eastern states, such as Jordan, Syria, Israel and during the previous regime of Iran, it was much easier for foreign teams to get research permits than in Turkey. However, in none of these countries has this situation been uninterrupted and, often, political concerns have been more influential in yielding permits to foreign teams. In yielding research permits, Turkey has been more selective and thus more difficult – but I would argue that the selection has been based on scientific concerns.

5 To the Ottomans, "Turk" signified nomadic Turkomans or simple villagers. The terms "Turk" and "Turkey" were introduced to Europe by the Crusaders. In the Ottoman Empire, Turk as the name of the nation was first suggested in 1874, and with great concern. After the introduction of nationalism and when, for the first time, it was suggested that the Turkish speakers constituted a nation, the Ottoman intelligentsia, to humiliate, named them "Turkists" (Berkes 1975: 64).

6 Three years ago in preparing an Anatolian archaeological exhibition for Belgium, the Belgian delegation asked specifically for Kurdish archaeology to be represented in the collection.

7 It should be noted that the term "Kurdish" was a general name given by other communities and not used by them. What is generalized as Kurdish actually consists of a number of different languages and dialects. In Turkey there are two main Kurdish languages, Zaza and Gırmançi. Kurds, until a few decades ago, identified themselves either with their tribal names or with language groups.

Bibliography

Arık, R. O. (1950) *Les fouilles archéologiques en Turquie*, Ankara: Milli Egitim Basim Evi.

——— (1953) *Türk Müzeciliğine Bir Bakiş*, Istanbul: Milli Egitim Basim Evi.

Arnold, B. (1996) "The Past as Propaganda: Totalitarian Archaeology in Nazi Germany," in R. Preucel and I. Hodder (eds) *Contemporary Archaeology in Theory: A Reader*, Oxford: Blackwell Publishers: 549–69.

Banks, I. (1996) "Archaeology, Nationalism and Ethnicity," in J. A. Atkinson, I. Banks and J. O'Sullivan (eds) *Nationalism and Archaeology* (Scottish Archaeological Forum), Glasgow: Cruithne Press: 1–11.

Berkes, N. (1975) *Türk Düşüncesinde Bati Sorunu*, Istanbul: Bilgi Yayinevi.

Esin, U. (1993) "19. Yüzyıl Sonlarında Heinrich Schliemann'in Troya Kazılari ve Osmanlılar'la İlişkileri," in Z. Rona (ed.) *Osman Hamdi Bey Ve Dönemi*, İstanbul: Tarih Vakfi Yurt Yayınları: 179–91.

——— (in press) "Cumhuriyet'imizin 73. Yılında Türk Arkeolojisi," *Cumhuriyet'in 73 Yılında Bilim*, Ankara: TÜBA yayinlari.

Fleury-Ilett, B. (1993) "The Identity of France: The Archaeological Interaction," *Journal of European Archaeology* 1, 2: 169–80.

Güvenç, B. (1996) *Türk Kimliği*, İstanbul: Remzi Kitabevi.

McIntosh, R. J., McIntosh, S. K. and Togola, T. (1989) "People Without History," *Archaeology* 41: 74–82.

Mouliou, M. (1996) "Ancient Greece, its Classical Heritage and the Modern Greeks: Aspects of Nationalism in Museum Exhibitions," in J. A. Atkinson, I. Banks and J. O'Sullivan (eds) *Nationalism and Archaeology* (Scottish Archaeological Forum), Glasgow: Cruithne Press: 174–99.

Runnels, C. (1997) "D. Traill, Schliemann of Troy: Treasure and Deceit," *Journal of Field Archaeology* 24: 125–30.

Shnirelman, V. A. (1995) "Alternative Prehistory," *Journal of European Archaeology* 3, 2: 1–20.

Trigger, B. (1989) *A History of Archaeological Thought*, Cambridge: Cambridge University Press.

Vermeule, E. (1975) "A Note on Cypriote Antiquities in Turkish Cyprus," *Archaeology* 28: 58.

Chapter 6

The past as passion and play

Çatalhöyük as a site of conflict in the construction of multiple pasts

Ian Hodder

Introduction

This article will include 'thick descriptions' of the site at Çatalhöyük as viewed from different perspectives. Recent work at the site has quickly become embroiled in a maelstrom of conflicting interpretations. 'The past matters', but to different people in different ways. The past can be erased or it can be forgotten, later to be picked up and reused with new meanings. The variety of currents in the Near East make this a complex and highly charged process. But it is all too easy to take a distanced stance which is itself part of the appropriation of the past for intellectual gain. Any analysis of the socio-politics of the past in the Eastern Mediterranean is itself a construction, an intellectualisation, an appropriation. This chapter attempts to counter this process by attempting to describe thickly the processes through which a particular site has become engaged in a practical struggle.

An underlying theme is that the kaleidoscope of interests that have converged on Çatalhöyük can be grouped into two broad categories, themselves a product of an underlying tension between, on the one hand, a global and multinational commercialism and homogenisation which views cultural difference as play and pastiche and, on the other hand, an increasingly fragmented world of competing identities, ethnicities and nationalisms within which the past *matters* very directly. 'Hotel Çatalhöyük' may be a long way from 'Hotel Auschwitz', but it raises some of the same concerns about the clash between, on the one hand, the past as play, postmodern façade, commodity, resource, and on the other hand, the past as passion, depth, history, ownership. It is argued that these two dimensions of experience of the past in the Near East interact in complex ways and that the past as commodity and as Oriental theme park does not undermine the use of the past in political engagement when local communities, as at Çatalhöyük, become re-engaged in their history.

The archaeological discourse

It is too easy, and at least to some extent incorrect, to say that archaeologists have excavated in the Near East in order to elucidate the prehistory and history of that region. Archaeological interpretation of the Near East has also been embedded within a Western construction which opposes the East or Orient as 'other'. The prehistory of the Near East has been constructed in a 'play of difference' within academic discourse.

As Said (1978) has shown more generally, the Orient has been constructed as the Other of Europe. Especially in the nineteenth and twentieth centuries the Orient came to be seen as stagnant and despotic in order to define the democratic dynamism of Europe (see Bahrani, Chapter 8). In the writing of the prehistory of Europe and the Near East these are not abstract ideas. In a very concrete way they came to define the dominant discourse of European prehistory as exemplified in its most important practitioner, V. G. Childe. In the Preface to the first edition of the *Dawn of European Civilisation* (1925), Childe said that his theme was the 'foundation of European civilisation as a peculiar and individual manifestation of the human spirit.' In Europe 'we can recognise already these very qualities of energy, independence and inventiveness which distinguish the western world from Egypt, India and China.' To Childe, the opposition between Europe and the Orient was especially clear in the Bronze Age because, unlike the Orient, 'European metalworkers were free. They were not tied to any one patron or even to a single tribal society. They were producing for an intertribal if not an international market.'

To exemplify the opposition in the Bronze Age, Childe compared Crete with Egypt and despotic Mesopotamia. He described the modern naturalism, the truly occidental feeling for life and nature that distinguish Minoan vase paintings and frescoes. Beholding these charming scenes of games and processions, animals and fishes, flowers and trees, we breathe already a European atmosphere. Likewise in industry the absence of the unlimited labour-power at the disposal of a despot necessitated a concentration on the invention and elaboration of tools and weapons that foreshadows the most distinctive feature of European civilisation.

Thus, the Near East was seen as the cradle from which agriculture and civilisation initially spread. But the main developments which laid the foundations for a dynamic, and ultimately capitalist, society took place in Europe during the Bronze Age. The Near East may have been the 'cradle' from which the 'birth' took place, but the Orient never 'grew up' (see Bahrani, Chapter 8). In Childe's view it became stagnant and despotic – it became the 'Other' of Europe, its inverse.

Anatolia has been placed in a difficult position in the traditions of research influenced by Childean Orientalism. Anatolia is not within the cradle but neither is it in the European centre of regrowth. As Özdoğan (1995: 27) points out, 'areas to the north of the Taurus range, the high plateau of Anatolia, are regarded as still being outside of the "nuclear zone".' One clear consequence of this has been the lack of theoretical discussion about the development of Neolithic societies in Anatolia. Equally, there has been a lack of serious attempt to look for sites in Anatolia and known site densities remain low for many areas and periods. Further, 'it is of interest to note that even after the recovery of Hacilar, Çatal Höyük and Asıklı in central Anatolia, these sites were considered for some time as trading posts for obsidian and salt trade, and not as indicators of a developing Neolithic culture on the Anatolian plateau' (ibid.: 28). There were similar implications of this Anatolian 'blindness' for the chronologies of Anatolia and Southeastern Europe. 3,000 BC had been set as the start of sedentary life in both areas. But with the large-scale application of C14 dates in Europe, the dates of Southeastern early Neolithic sites were pushed back 2–3,000 years. 'However no one considered the impact of the change in datings on the chronology of central Anatolian cultures' (ibid.). Renfrew's (1973) discussion of calibrated C14 dates created a 'fault-line' between Europe and Asia. The effect was to focus attention on developments in Europe at the expense of those in Anatolia. The latter remained caught uncomfortably between the emergent developments in Southeastern Europe and the long sequence of cultural developments in the Near East.

More recently Özdoğan (1995) has argued for a different Neolithic sequence in central Anatolia and for strong links between central Anatolia and Europe in the Chalcolithic. In the work by Turkish archaeologists such as Ufuk Esin (1991) at Asıklı Höyük and Refik Duru (1992) in the Burdur areas we begin to obtain a clear picture of a central Anatolian sequence which belies a simple Orient/Occident opposition. 'Central Anatolia should neither be considered as a nuclear nor as a marginal zone to the low lands of the Near East, but as a distinct cultural formation zone, developing on different lines from the Near East' (Özdoğan 1995: 54).

The global and the local

Research at Çatalhöyük and other work in central Turkey can help to counteract the Europe/Orient set of differences. But these archaeological examples are part of a wider movement which now challenges that opposition. The new discourse is globalism. 'Globalization has rendered much of the discussion of East and West in orientalism redundant' (Turner 1994: 183). The Orient was constructed as 'other'. With globalisation 'others' have become less strange and have been imported into all societies as a result of human mobility, migration and tourism. 'Otherness has been domesticated' (ibid.). With the collapse of communism and the traditional oppositions of cold-war politics of the post-war era, Islam may function as a substitute for the dangers of communism. But Islam is increasingly part of the 'inside' of the Western world. For example, the Rushdie affair in Britain forced a debate about the recognition that Britain was now a multicultural society. In Germany, Turkish migrants now pose a significant social issue. Globalisation has created a variety of traditions within a given community.

Turner sets up a very clear contrast between Islamic fundamentalism and the commercial processes of late capitalism. He argues that Islamic fundamentalism rejects modernist secularism because of its lack of coherent values and because of its gross inequalities of wealth and power (1994: 88). Fundamentalism has created an anti-consumerist ethic of moral purity based upon classical Islamic doctrine (ibid.: 92). The corruption of pristine faith is going to be brought about by Tina Turner, Coca-Cola and Ford (ibid.: 10). This erosion of faith 'has to be understood in terms of how the diversity of commodities and their global character transform in covert and indirect fashion the everyday beliefs of the mass of the population' (ibid.: 17).

Certainly, to the extent that Çatalhöyük has been threatened by antiquities dealing there are grounds for an opposition between commercialism and fundamentalist and nationalist concerns. The excavations in the early 1960s were closed by the Turkish state for a number of reasons, including problems with the conservation of wall paintings and sculpture. But at least some of the reasons for the closure concerned the purported disappearance of artefacts from the site and the involvement of James Mellaart in the 'Dorak Affair'. The latter involved the disappearance of a claimed 'treasure' of Bronze Age artefacts from northwest Anatolia. Recently the Turkish state has been successful in gaining the return of the Lydian treasure from the Metropolitan Museum in New York. Attempts are being made to return the Schliemann treasure to Troy (see Özdoğan, Chapter 5). All these instances foster a sense of national heritage and an assertion of Turkish identity in the face of the colonial encounter and in reaction against the pillaging of the extraordinarily rich and diverse antiquities of Turkey.

There are other ways in which commercialism might be thought to confront and erode Islamic fundamentalism. The site at Çatalhöyük is located in a traditionally conservative area, largely rural and with minimal technological development. More recently, massive irrigation schemes funded by international agencies have led to the rapid development of large-scale agro-industry. Yet the local population around the site tends to be traditional, conservative and strongly religious. The renewed work at the site and the project's plans for the future might be seen as opening up this local world to new commercial interests. The site guard, Sadettin, has applied for official permission to build a shop at the site to serve the increasing numbers of tourists. There are plans for T-shirts and a range of products. Several artists have asked to be given the right to make 'tasteful' objects derived from, but not replicating, the prehistoric finds for sale at the site, in Turkey, and in the USA. Travel agencies in Istanbul, Britain and USA vie with each other to organise special-interest tours. Plans are being developed for a museum and visitor centre at the site, and for international travelling exhibits of the art. Carpet dealers in Konya use designs from Çatalhöyük, or legitimated by books concerning Çatalhöyük (e.g. Mellaart et al. 1989), in order to enhance their sales. In Istanbul, a Turkish designer, Rifat Özbek, shows clothes modelled by Linda Evangelista and which incorporate the Çatalhöyük 'Mother Goddess' image. These clothes appear in *Hello* Magazine (January 1991) and demonstrate the ways in which the site can become involved in a global commercial market. These commercial opportunities are certainly taken up locally and nationally in Turkey and they have the potential to transform Islamic fundamentalist belief.

But other experiences suggest that such an opposition between a global commercialism and Islamic fundamentalism are overly simplistic. The relationships between the Çatalhöyük project and the local mayor (Çumra belediye başkanı), especially with regard to the 1996 local agricultural festival, illustrate the complexities well.

The mayor in Çumra is at present (since 1995) a member of the MHP party – Islamic but primarily nationalist. The rhetoric of the party is at times anti-Europe, anti-foreign involvement and anti-secular. At times it was difficult working with local officials who might be members of the MHP or the religious Refah party (banned in 1997). Some would very pointedly not shake hands with female members of the team, especially on Fridays, since such contact would mean washing again in preparation for the mosque. Our English-speaking Eurocentric friends in Istanbul were always surprised that we got on so well with the Mayor. In our early years at the site he helped us with accommodation in Çumra, with equipment and materials.

He always embraced me and showed the greatest of respect. In 1995 he asked us for some photographs, especially of the naked 'Mother Goddess' to put in the foyers of all the hotels in Çumra and in neighbouring districts. The belediye had its own hotel in Çumra. Inside it was full of Islamic religious references in its decor. Guests had to remove their shoes at the door. In such a context large images of the 'Mother Goddess' seemed so inappropriate, especially in a town in which all women always remained covered in public. Why did the Mayor want to do this?

The contradictions increased. In 1996 the Mayor made a formal proposal to the authorities in Ankara to set up a Çatalhöyük museum in Çumra itself. In the same year he announced to us that he wanted to call his annual agricultural festival the Çumra Çatalhöyük Festival. We were to provide a film and slide show, which we did, to a large and attentive audience. After the slide show the Mayor started handing out prizes for the best tomatoes and melons. I was embarrassed suddenly to be called on to the stage to be honoured and embraced in my turn, and presented with a plaque.

Why this public endorsement? What was the public advantage? After all, here is a foreign team digging a pre-Islamic site which confronts Islamic teaching both in its use of images and in its specific representations of women. Certainly the naked images are only acceptable because of their non-Islamic context. But the project clearly introduces commercialism and Western attitudes. Why should it be so overtly embraced by an Islamic nationalist from a political party on the far right? Part of the answer is simply that our work brings money into the region, it increases employment, and it encourages tourism. It contributes to economic development and helps to gain a popular vote. It was for these reasons that the Mayor wanted to build a museum in Çumra — so that tourists would come to the town as well as to the site, twelve kilometres away. But also, more personally, the Mayor finds himself, as a result of the project, the centre of media attention and the host to political figures who visit the site from Konya and Ankara. His wider political ambitions are served.

The Mayor's rhetoric at public occasions involving the site deals with the contradictions in subtle ways. Çatalhöyük, he says, is a site of great national significance. It is the source of Anatolian civilisation. And yet it belongs to the world. Its knowledge is for everyone, without boundaries. We wish to give it to the world. The international scientific interest shows the importance of Anatolian civilisation.

The Mayor continues, 'Çatalhöyük is for all humanity'. When I tell my Turkish friends in Istanbul about this they gasp, 'Did he really say that?' And in many ways his strategy is risky. There is all the reason in the world for him to be distrustful of us. There are many local people in the Çumra area who remember what happened in the 1960s, who blame the archaeologists, and who are suspicious of renewed foreign contacts. The site and its imagery might be seen as confronting Islamic traditionalists. And yet, overall, he has decided, at least for the moment, that it is in his interests to support, embrace and even promote the project.

In the above instance, rather than a simple opposition between Islamic groups and religion and the international and commercial components of the project, we see subtle ways in which adjustments are made in order to achieve specific aims, such as increased employment and political status. At least in Turkey some accommodation between the global and the Islamic is clearly possible. The same is true in the following example.

Women, their heads covered, their shoulders weighed from a long day's labour in the fields, are driven past the site at high speed in the backs of the trucks of their menfolk. Some of their sons and husbands are working as labourers on the new excavations. I asked for some women to work at the site but the menfolk refused to let them go. The younger women have been taught in school that Çatalhöyük is the origin of Anatolian civilisation, the origin of Cybele, the Earth Mother. The posters of the bare-breasted Mother Goddess seem very alien. 'The site is full of images, our menfolk say. It must be pre-Islamic'.

The women from the village confide in some of the women from the foreign team in their midst. In fact there is a remarkable and immediate rapport between the women – an embracing and incorporating of women, just because they are women. They confide that their men are very hard; they give the women little freedom, little money. It is a hard life. But in the end, after two years of negotiating, the men say the wives and daughters can work at the site after all. Perhaps they have grown to trust the foreigners. But, most likely, the men, the families, want the money. When the local people are paid, some of the women find it difficult even to sign their name, and they refuse to take the money – their husbands take it for them.

So, in this local case, men gradually accept the need to allow change in the actions of and attitudes towards the women in the community. Women and men locally turn a blind eye to the naked 'Mother Goddess'. If it brings tourists and jobs so much the better (say some men); if it brings us wages so much the better (say the women). Indeed, local attitudes seem to change in a number of ways.

Local attitudes to the past in the Çatalhöyük area are being studied by David

Shankland (1996). Folk knowledge sees the mounds as liminal. They are the landmarks that define the boundaries between communities. They are also the dwelling places of the spirits of the dead. At night the lights of the spirits can sometimes be seen as they travel from one mound to another. There is archaeological evidence that the Çatalhöyük mound was used as a cemetery from the Hellenistic period onwards. We excavated Byzantine graves on the East mound. And yet this tradition associating the mounds with the dead does not prevent the excavation by local communities of soil and clay from the mounds for building materials. Indeed the walls of the buildings in the local villages are full of sherds deriving from the mounds. Perhaps this practical use and the tradition of digging help to explain the acceptance of our own archaeological work at the mounds.

Shankland argues that this local folk knowledge is not matched by an in-depth historical understanding of the site. Although the site is mentioned in primary schools in connection with the origins of Anatolian civilisation, there is little knowledge of historical sequences beyond a simple pre-Islamic–Islamic opposition. He argues that it is for this reason that there has been little response to the Open Days organised for the local communities during our digging seasons.

On the other hand, I have been struck by the degree of fascination and interest when I have organised tours of the site for our workers. Their eyes wide at the images, and bubbling with questions, comments and parallels with their own lives, houses and artefacts, they are excited by ideas about interpretations of the site. Far from being alienated from their past by this engagement within a global system of universal scientific knowledge, their sense of local identity and community seems enlivened and strengthened.

> There are deep cuts across both East and West mounds at Çatalhöyük, paths worn by centuries of feet toiling from village to village in the Konya Plain. And there is a lone Islamic gravestone on the East mound, marking the burial place of a fallen woman, so the story goes. These mounds had a local meaning, a 'fork' (çatal) in their daily pathways. But now these routes and graves are cut off by a fence, locked gate and guards. The site has been taken over by the state and is being excavated by foreign teams with lasers and computers. Bus-loads of Goddess tourists from California engage in debates with the foreign archae-ologists about matriarchies.

But is it quite so confrontational? The notion of a simple opposition between local and global knowledge is undermined by the complexity of social and cultural currents at all levels in Turkish life. One such complexity derives from the division within Turkish politics between those who favour closer links with Europe and who welcome the recent Customs Union, and those who are suspicious of such links. The latter views are associated with fundamentalist and nationalist currents of thought. But the Turkish groups who have become most involved in the Çatalhöyük project tend to be very Eurocentric. The individuals involved tend to live in Istanbul, have often had an élite English-speaking education, and have often spent part of their lives in Europe or the USA. The Istanbul 'Friends of Çatalhöyük' organisation which has been successful in raising funds for the project comes largely from this group. Those people from Istanbul who come to the site include highly articulate, professional and well-to-do Turks, fascinated by our work and by its implications. They like the idea that in prehistory there were many cultural links between Anatolia and Europe. They are enthralled by the project's use of new scientific techniques and of the Web. Some organise and take part in the Goddess Tours. They are part of a global community.

> The first time it happened we were all very much taken aback. We did not know what was happening. A message had come to the dig house that the leader of the Istanbul Friends was bringing a group of people to the site, as part of a tour of Turkey. Would we meet them in the local restaurant in Çumra that evening?
>
> Most of the team went – about twenty of us at that time. We were ushered into a room with a long table around which about thirty middle-aged women, and a few men, were sitting. We were arranged amongst them. Alcohol is not allowed in public places in Çumra. But they provided a cocktail of cherry juice hiding vodka. The questions began. Why were we digging the site? Did we believe that men had been allowed into Çatalhöyük? Had we found evidence of the Goddess? Did we not realise that the bull's heads represented Her reproductive organs? What did the female members of the team think about my androcentric interpretations? How were their voices heard?
>
> The following day they came to the site. They were interested in our work, but they also stood in a circle and held hands and prayed. Afterwards they seemed genuinely moved. They said the presence of the Goddess was very strong. You could feel Her coming up through the earth.
>
> The Goddess Tours have become regular since then, although often occurring at times when we are not at the site. The participants are largely professional women from the USA, but they include women from Europe. And it is into this world that some of the Istanbul Friends easily fit. Indeed, some of the Friends from Istanbul were instrumental in tabling a motion at the Beijing UN Conference on Women which named Çatalhöyük as the spiritual centre of the Goddess Movement in Turkey and in the world.

The global character of these New Age Mother Goddess, Ecofeminist and Gaia Movements may confront traditional Islamic attitudes to women, but there are undoubtedly significant sections of élite Istanbul society that welcome such links outside Turkey and use them for their own purposes. Since Atatürk, the commitment to secularism has been a central, if recently diminishing, focus of political life in Turkey. Istanbul in particular is a social and cultural metropolis of enormous size and diversity. There are many shades of accommodation between secularism and fundamentalism. The old intellectual élite is global in perspective and contributes to a political debate which is complex and multi-stranded.

> When a group of the Istanbul 'Friends' association came to the site I could see they were angry, despite their politeness and support. They disliked the new dig house. It was unimaginative, dull, functional, not appropriate to such an important site. And worst of all, it was painted bright green! They decided they would not help fund the construction of the dig house. I was disappointed. I needed their help.
>
> The dig house, an ambitious version of an architectural genre found on many sites in the Near East, had been designed by an architect in the local museum service in Konya. Most of his previous work had dealt with the restoration of the wonderful Seljuk architecture in and around that city. The design was approved by the local ancient monuments board. I had contracted a builder from Konya who was strongly recommended by the local museums service. He turned out to be a great pleasure to work with. I respected and liked him enormously and trusted him completely. He chose green because the colour is identified with Islam. He and his family, like many in Konya, were strongly religious.
>
> It was anathema to some of the Istanbul visitors that the dig house should be painted green. It seemed inappropriate. But I decided not to bow to their demands that we repaint the building. It seemed important to respect local Islamic sensitivities in this case.

In other examples, too, it is possible to show local resistance to the global interests of Istanbul Turks or international commercial or New Age movements. For instance, the Istanbul Friends have started a clever and very successful campaign to 'Lend a Hand to Çatalhöyük' which involves giving handprint certificates (based on a Çatalhöyük wall painting) to donors. One proposal is that a long wall be built at the site on which donors can make their handprints. For the moment, this move has been resisted because of local concerns about site preservation. Perhaps the clearest example of the interaction between these different currents of interest in the site is the following:

> One of the commercial sponsors of the project is an international credit card company. With its Istanbul-based PR firm, this company is genuinely interested in supporting the project while at the same time making use of its commercial potential. For example, during press visits we all wear hats with the company logo, and a replica of the 'Mother Goddess' with the company

name is handed out to clients at receptions in Istanbul. The company sees a particular link to Çatalhöyük because I argued that obsidian could be seen as the first 'credit card'. Members of the team laughed when I told them and the obsidian specialist was embarrassed. Perhaps I was embarrassed, too, but I justified my compliance by arguing that obsidian was exchanged widely (like credit cards) and that ethnographically artefacts such as obsidian can come to act as media for exchange, and exchange involves setting up debt (and thus credit) between the giver and receiver.

In the end this global commercialising process would have an impact locally. The company wanted to set up an exhibit in the museum which showed the development of 'credit cards' from the first obsidian to the latest credit cards with micro-chips. I could not help but see the, probably unintended, outcome of this. Turkey is seeing a massively expanding market for credit cards, but the main take-up is in the urban centres. In rural areas there has been less impact. The exhibit and the message about prehistoric credit cards might not only legitimate the modern company's claim to be concerned with Turkish culture but also might encourage local interest and take-up.

Nevertheless, the support of the company was genuine and very much needed if the project was going to be able to continue and have any long-term benefit for local identity, tourism, employment and social change.

I wanted to hold a ceremony at the site to open the dig house. I invited the Minister of Culture as well as local and national politicians. The Minister of Culture had recently changed to be a member of Refah, the religious fundamentalist party. I wanted our sponsors to come to thank them. Indeed, the Minister of Culture would unveil a plaque listing their support. This 'photo-opportunity' was rejected by the credit card company which decided it did not want to be associated in this way with the Refah party. Here, commerce and Islam confronted each other and the former stood down.

In the end the Minister did not attend and sent his Director General of Monuments and Museums. The European Ambassador also came. West and East, secular and religious, met and talked at a podium decked out in a Turkish flag by the Mayor. The speeches described the importance of the project and I presented the buildings to the Turkish state. But the currents of differing meanings, strategies and interpretations were rife.

In all the political manoeuvring, the site and the local concerns seemed to play little role. They seemed overrun by global processes and oppositions. But on the other hand, the Mayor and other local officials made their speeches too and there was considerable coverage in the local press. Black Mercedes, flags flapping at high speed, swept in clouds of dust. Armed guards surrounded the mound, and out got the national officials. They came and went, involved in their own strategies. Local people had to be bussed in to create a crowd at the ceremony — a true 'rent-a-crowd'. The local people seemed to understand the motives behind the show for what it was. They tolerated the event as long as it meant they could continue to work, make money, and follow their own strategies. The ceremony, and the national, fundamentalist and global strategies in which it was enmeshed, was necessary if their own lives were to continue to change in ways they, from different points of view, wanted.

Thus, there is no simple opposition between global knowledge and interests and a local and fundamentalist Islam. New Age Women's Movements are received differently in different communities, national and local, in Turkey. In the local villages around Çatalhöyük and in Çumra people participate differentially and purposefully. They are not simply duped into being 'globalised'. People have to be bussed to the opening ceremony. A blind eye is turned to the naked Goddess in the visitor centre at the site. Locally, women may obtain their own wages and the Mayor follows his political ambitions. Locally, men and women use the past in their own ways. They may be drawn into a global process but they use that process locally in complex ways, rejecting some aspects and emphasising others. Change occurs, but in a complex and diverse way. It is no longer an issue of monolithic blocks, as in Europe versus the Orient, secular versus fundamentalist religion. Rather, there is a diversity of global and local experiences and responses within which Çatalhöyük is embroiled.

A reflexive moment

So far I have written in terms of an overall argument about the shift from East versus West to global versus local and I have made the point that local interests are not entirely taken over by global processes. All this, even my use of narrative 'thick descriptions', is situated within an academic discourse which might seem to be far removed from the events I am describing. I have constructed the events in a particular way because of my own interests. Indeed any analysis of heritage in the East Mediterranean is 'at a remove'; a past appropriated for intellectual gain. There are two points I wish to make about this process. The first deals with disjunction between the controlled and structured description or text and the contingent process. The second deals with the need to recognise that the archaeologist is not a disinterested observer but part of the process.

Our own emphasis on 'discourse' within the 'discipline' underlies the account I have given. I have written as if the processes I have been describing could be observed, channelled, controlled. Any attempt to write about how the Çatalhöyük past is used, and any attempt to write about how the past matters in the East Mediterranean cannot help but reduce historical processes to an organised scheme or flow. In the following account I want to demonstrate the limitations of this view.

> It ranks as one of the worst days in my life. I ended up stunned, bitter, angry and deeply depressed about whether the project would continue.
>
> The day had started so well. The credit card company had arranged an elaborate and expensive press trip to the site. In the morning between fifty and sixty newspaper and TV reporters turned up at the site. During the day the tours all went extremely well. Members of the team were dutifully wearing their promotional hats. The project was coming over as exciting and important. It was getting great coverage. The sponsors and the PR firm were happy. After all, this press day was to be the main return on their investment this year. There had to be a lot of good press coverage and it looked as if there would be.
>
> A few reporters had left and I was relaxing for a moment before the rest departed, when a member of the team came to say that a small bead had disappeared from one of our laboratories. It was one of the objects that had been on display and despite the continual presence of three team members the object had disappeared. The government representatives were told. They called the police. The reporters were searched and held at the site for three hours before being allowed to leave.
>
> Rumours started flying, but so many people could have taken it. There had been so many people there that day. I suddenly saw that in this one event, this one instant, the whole project could flounder. Despite all the planning, all the effort over five years could be undone in one brief act. After all, the site had been closed in the 1960s partly because of incidents in which artefacts disappeared. Would this event play into the hands of local or national groups who objected to the international or foreign character of the project? Even if a permit did continue to be granted, would we be able to gain sponsorship again? Indeed, in the following days the national press printed stories with headlines such as 'Scandal at dig of the century'. How could we ever get sponsorship again? I began to feel that, for one reason or another, the project might have difficulty continuing.

As it turned out, the press coverage during and after the event was very supportive. The papers started carrying positive accounts of the project which did not mention the theft of the bead. The sponsors continued their support and the central government authorities did their best to recover the bead. The damage seems to have been, at the time of writing, marginal. But in that moment and in the days immediately afterwards I feared the worst and I saw how fragile was the negotiated position for all players in the Çatalhöyük project. Everything happened so quickly and in such a variety of directions that the outcome was unpredictable.

Structure met conjuncture (Sahlins 1981) and no amount of discursive understanding of East/West, global/local, or even structure/conjuncture could determine or control the way in which things would go.

Such a critique of academic discourse in the context of archaeology and heritage in the East Mediterranean does not imply that the archaeologist should stand at a distance from the processes in which she or he is involved. Indeed this is the second point I wish to make about the need to be reflexive when gazing at, and encapsulating in theoretical discourse, the role of the past in the East Mediterranean. Since the writing and the discourse have effects, there is a need for positive engagement. In the events just described, I did write letters, get on the phone, make visits, increase security in the stores and laboratories and so on. While such activities could not control the way things went, they perhaps contributed, from a particular standpoint, to what was, is and will be an ongoing negotiation between different and changing interests.

As other examples of the need to move beyond the passive gaze to positive engagement, decisions had to be made, choices had to be taken, about whether to remove the green paint on the dig house. Equally, complex as the issues are, I felt it was important to push for the employment of women at the site. It was necessary, in these examples, to 'take sides'. The same has to be said even in the most 'open' and multivocal discourses. The results of the project are being placed on the Web and resources are being channelled into a variety of interactive and presentation media. These include hypertext (Thomas 1996; Tringham 1996). The aim here is to open the data from the site to multiple audiences, to allow different experiences of the site, to allow discovery in a range of different channels. But it is clear that there is no such thing as open multivocality. A certain level of knowledge is required to participate in hypertext presentations. And certainly the links and nodes are created by the producer of the hypertext. One has to make choices about what audiences are aimed at and what messages are to be given. As much as the Web and hypertext allow a greater diversity and openness of communication, the onus remains on the producer and writer to be reflexive about the impact of 'the text' in the world.

The same point can be extended to the writing of the present article. It could be argued that at least some of what I have written here might offend the groups involved in an ongoing archaeological and heritage project. I have taken the decision to say some things here because I believe that the issues are important and that our experience at Çatalhöyük might help to draw attention to the need for debate about the role of archaeology in a Near East which is involved in processes of globalisation. I have not said other things here because of the need to respect the perspectives of some of the groups and individuals involved. As noted above, I cannot predict the outcome of this intervention in what is a complex process. But

I do assert the need to monitor the results of statements and to engage actively from a particular standpoint.

Conclusion

Both in the academic debate about the prehistory of Anatolia and Çatalhöyük and in the practices of public engagement with the site, the old oppositions between Europe and the Orient or between secularism and religious fundamentalism are transcended by the processes of globalism and fragmentation. Çatalhöyük is caught in a maelstrom of perspectives and special interests. These are global in scale. But they are also highly diverse and fragmented, extending from carpet dealers in Konya and New York, to ecofeminists in San Francisco, to women in the local village near Çatalhöyük. Some of these engagements are highly commercial and disinterested – the past as play, the Orient as theme park. Others are motivated by specific highly charged interests. But passion and play are not opposed in some simple opposition. In the global process they interact and feed off each other in myriad ways, equally emboldening and undermining the other.

I have talked in this chapter of the 'team' working at Çatalhöyük. It may not be too much to say that I am no longer sure what the team is. The boundaries of those who do or do not work on the project are difficult to define. Certainly there are the named individuals who have permits to excavate at the site. But some specialists on the project do not visit the site. And many I have asked to contribute from around the world in order to, for example, help interpret the art have no close involvement with the core 'team'. And then what should I make of a psychoanalyst from California with a particular perspective on the art who publishes an article about the site in the 'New Scientist'? Or what should I make of an aboriginal artist from South Africa who wishes to come and work at the site to model her female sculptures? She also wants to contribute to our work. And since the site data are on the Web, what should I make of all those who write in and make their suggestions, or who write their own articles about the site based on our data, and contribute to 'our' understanding of the site? And what should I make of it if people take our data from the Web and change them and create a new alternative database of their own? Such things are at least potentially feasible. Rather than there being a well-bounded 'team' working on the project, Çatalhöyük is involved in a global process of interpretation. The 'team' is global. And I would argue it has to be if the divergent special interests are to be given access to the site. It is not possible to deny that contemporary information technologies allow an enormous dispersal of information so that numerous special interest groups can form and define themselves through an engagement. But so too there are many groups who do not have access to the technologies or to the knowledge necessary to use them. The fragmentation within and across the globalisation processes needs to be reflexively engaged with.

As much as those involved in the project may try to foster plurality and multivocality, the communication does not take place on a level playing-field. The techniques used on the site, from virtual reality to the sieving of micro-residues, promote a particular vision within the kaleidoscope. There is no solution to the paradoxes. Any attempt to 'make sense of it all', including the opposition between 'play' and 'passion', is itself a construct. It is for this reason that I have included so many 'thick descriptive' narratives in this chapter. It is only in the concrete moments of engagement that the socio-politics of Çatalhöyük take their form.

Bibliography

Childe, V. G. (1925) *The Dawn of European Civilisation*, London: Kegan Paul.

Duru, R. (1992) 'Höyücek Kazilari 1989', *Belleten* 61: 551–66.

Esin, U. (1991) 'Salvage excavations at the pre-pottery site of Asıklı Höyük in Central Anatolia', *Anatolica* 17: 123–74.

Hello Magazine, January 1991.

Mellaart, J., Hirsch, U. and Balpinar, B. (1989) *The Goddess from Anatolia*, Rome: Eskanazi.

Özdoğan, M. (1995) 'Neolithic in Turkey: the status of research', in *Readings in Prehistory. Studies Presented to Halet Çambel*, Istanbul: University of Istanbul, pp. 41–60.

Renfrew, A. C. (1973) *Before Civilization*, London: Jonathan Cape.

Sahlins, M. (1981) *Historical Metaphor and Mythical Reality*, Ann Arbor: University of Michigan Press.

Said, E. W. (1978) *Orientalism*, London: Routledge and Kegan Paul.

Shankland, D. (1996) 'Çatalhöyük: the anthropology of an archaeological presence', in I. Hodder (ed.) *On the Surface: Çatalhöyük 1993–95*, Cambridge: McDonald Institute for Archaeological Research and British Institute of Archaeology at Ankara, pp. 349–58.

Thomas, S. (1996) 'On-line hypertext in site interpretation', paper presented at TAG conference, Liverpool 1996.

Tringham, S. (1996) 'The use of hypertext in site interpretation', paper presented at TAG conference, Liverpool 1996.

Turner, B. S. (1994) *Orientalism, Postmodernism and Globalism*, London: Routledge.

Chapter 7

Beirut's memorycide
Hear no evil, see no evil

Albert Farid Henry Naccache

Introduction

Until November 1994, Beirut's archaeological site, the site of the oldest continuously inhabited city among the capitals of the world, and a repository to nearly five millennia of urban occupation, laid under its old Downtown. Then, in November 1994, with the participation of teams of European archaeologists under the international supervision of the UNESCO, bulldozers started destroying large sections of it. Today, the massive destruction of Beirut's archaeological site is an objective fact, easily ascertained by any observer. Similarly, an impartial look at what has happened shows beyond doubt that this destruction was needless and easily avoidable. These two points are reviewed briefly in the first part of this chapter. The second part of the chapter deals with a less tangible aspect of this disaster – that the loss of Beirut's archaeological site amounted to a Lebanese memorycide, a memorycide that might be of fateful consequences for the future of the Lebanese people. Finally, the third part of the chapter deals with some aspects of the association of the archaeological community in the destruction of Beirut's archaeological site. If archaeology is to matter, the international archaeological community, which has acted in the matter as a guild protecting its members, has to face up to its involvement in the destruction of Beirut's archaeological site, and hopefully draw some lessons from it.

The lobotomised phoenix

No one denies that there has been destruction of archaeological heritage on Beirut's site. What is argued by the spokespersons of the company ultimately responsible for the destruction, is that the damage was limited, and of a scale to be expected under the circumstances of reconstruction. Let us deal with these two points separately.

The following two maps illustrate the magnitude of the destruction that befell Beirut's archaeological site. In both cases the base map is the same, a street map of Beirut's old Downtown area. On the first map (see Figure 7.1) the areas are indicated where archaeologists worked alone as well as areas where they worked alongside bulldozers. On the second map (see Figure 7.2) are indicated the areas where bulldozers dug alone. By simply comparing the two maps it is evident that the areas where the bulldozers dug alone dwarf the areas where archaeologists were present. Somewhere around ninety to ninety five percent of the areas of the archaeological site where infrastructure and construction work had been done by the company have been simply bulldozed to the sea without any archaeological study. Clearly, the damage was not limited, and Beirut's archaeological site has suffered massive destruction on a scale at least an order of magnitude greater than what can be expected today in the case of construction work. Furthermore, this destruction was unnecessary and gratuitous. The specific context in Beirut could have enabled an exemplary dealing with the archaeological heritage, since the three basic ingredients needed to set up a proper program, namely *knowledge*, *time* and *money*, were available.

Knowledge

The rich archaeological site of Beirut had long been known to lie under most of present-day Downtown (Jidejian 1973; Salem 1970). The abandonment of the area due to the war, and the inevitability of reconstruction once the guns were silenced, offered an opportunity to do planned archaeological work on a multi-millennial urban site on a scale never available before, not only in Lebanon, but anywhere. Such war ravages had been seen in the cities of the Mediterranean and Europe in World War II, but in post-war Europe neither the awareness of the importance of urban archaeological heritage nor the modern means of urban archaeology existed. That Beirut's site should have been protected and thoroughly studied at the first opportunity was obvious. That the site should have been integrated in any plan for reconstruction of Downtown had been stated as early as 1978 (Barbier 1978), and forcefully reiterated in recent years (Naccache 1992, 1994a, 1994b; Schofield 1992).

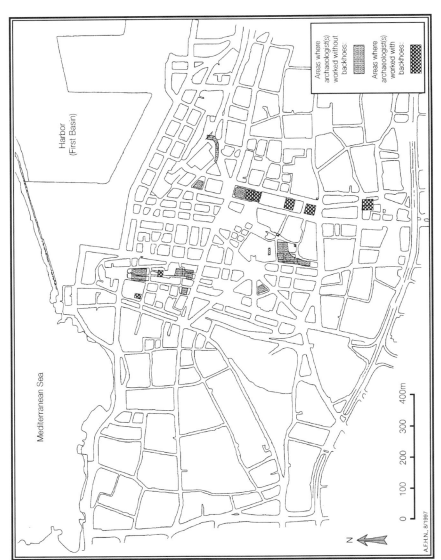

Mediterranean Sea

Harbor
(First Basin)

Areas where
archaeologist(s)
worked without
backhoes:

Areas where
archaeologist(s)
worked with
backhoes:

N

0   100   200   300   400m

A.F.H.N. 8/1997

Figure 7.1 Areas of Beirut's archaeological site where archaeologists went first
Source: Author's own drawing, 8/1997.

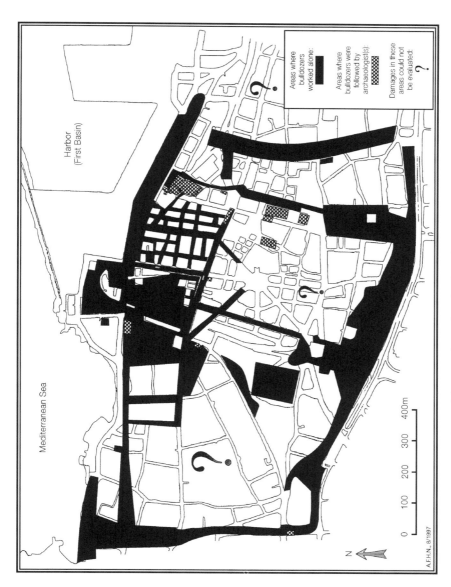

Figure 7.2 Some of the areas of Beirut's archaeological site where bulldozers went first
Source: Author's own drawing, 8/1997.

Time

Beirut's Downtown is a small and marginal part of modern Greater Beirut and all the economic and administrative functions it had performed prior to the war had long since been transferred elsewhere. Following the cessation of hostilities, the reconstruction of Lebanon's infrastructure and economy was an obvious priority. There was, however, no *economic* necessity, requirement or urgency to start the 'post-war reconstruction' of Lebanon by the reconstruction of Beirut's Down-town, as proven today by the fact that the reconstruction of Beirut's Downtown is only a marginal part of the overall Lebanese reconstruction plan. This does not mean that there was no need to revivify Beirut's Downtown, which had been the heart and symbol of unified Lebanon. However, to have Downtown play its role once again it was imperative that its rebirth would not obliterate the concrete repositories of its history, i.e. Beirut's archaeological and architectural heritage.

The pursuit of such a national aim should have been undertaken by the Leba-nese state. Instead, a private real-estate company was given the ownership of the entirety of Downtown, that is, the entirety of Beirut's archaeological site. I will refer here to that real-estate company as such, and not by its acronym "Solidere" – a word-play on "solidaire" (solidarity in French) – and I will not be concerned by the legal nature of the act that gave it title to the land. That is a matter which the previous landowners, now expropriated to the benefit of a private company, are still fighting in the courts. Be that as it may, since the real-estate company had been granted all the leeway it needed to plan its own policies, it was ideally placed to engage in large-scale and long-term planned archaeological work, and could have fully integrated archaeological work in its twenty years' planning process. Given what was already known of the site, advanced planning could have very easily allowed for extensive archaeological excavations without causing any overall delay to the project (Schofield 1992).

Money

In any rational planning, the archaeological wealth of Beirut would have been given proper consideration, and its major parts integrated into the overall urban planning in order to benefit from the "fortune in potential tourist dollars" (Eboch 1996) that it would have generated. As sole owner of Downtown, the real-estate company would have been the first and major beneficiary of all the "archaeological revenues" that would have been generated by a proper display of the historical wealth of the city. This is precisely why one of the basic principles of modern urban archaeology is that it falls to the developers to pay for the excavation of the archaeology that their projects threaten. The estimated overall cost of recon-struction of Downtown over twenty years being $5,000 million, a modest three percent of total development cost budgeted for the archaeological program would have amounted to a total of $150 million, or an average of $7.5 million annually. By any reckoning this sum would have been more than enough to mount a massive and efficient archaeological program, without being in any way a burden to the real-estate company, whose coffers were so overflowing that when the destruction started it had placed $300 million in bonds outside of Lebanon.

Beirut's archaeological program

Why this destruction happened is open to speculation. Yet there is no doubt of the result, nor that it was done by the real-estate company with the full backing of the Lebanese state and the participation of Lebanese and European archaeologists under UNESCO's supervision. Here, I cannot go into the grisly details of the destruction of well over 200,000 cubic meters of deposits of a nearly 5,000-year old city, including its successive harbours, acropoleis, fora etc. A description of the main points of the program that led ineluctably and predictably (Naccache 1994a, 1994b) to the systematic destruction of Beirut's archaeological site will have to suffice.

Beirut's heritage was not integrated to the urban plan, and the protection of the site, or its study and exploitation where it was unavoidable to excavate it, did not become parts of the planning policies. Worse, the adopted program ignored the existence of Beirut's archaeological site, and the whole 1,000,000 square meters of the site was designed as a salvage operation in unknown territory, with the archaeologists following the bulldozers everywhere – even, for example, in the "Ancient Tell" dating back to the Bronze Age, or in "Weygand" Street which, as it had long been established, overlaid the 2,000-year old "Decumanus" of Roman Berytus. After much fighting, the total funding for the archaeological program was brought up to around $4.5 million for a period of two years – and partly spent on the public relation campaign designed to present the archaeological work as a success. Less than a score of archaeologists were brought to work on the site, and for very short periods of time, averaging less than two months per team.

The verdict

If these facts are not enough by themselves to allow impartial readers to evaluate Beirut's archaeological program, let them compare it with the program mounted by Athens in the early 1990s. Here, for a 20,000 square meter section on the periphery of the archaeological site threatened by the planned construction of the Metro, archaeologists were given three years and $20 million. In addition, all the finds, even those dating from the period of the Turkish Ottoman, the Greeks' antagonist, were protected and integrated in the urban planning.

The cost of amnesia

The staggering economic losses that Beirut has sustained because, instead of being integrated into the reconstruction plan, large parts of its archaeological site were destroyed are, after all, only economic losses. And Lebanon has survived, in the last twenty years, mind-boggling economic losses. The more shattering and lasting loss for Lebanon will be that of a unique opportunity to elaborate a consensual national history.

A matter of life and death

Before returning to the issue of how archaeology interacts with the writing of history, a brief personal digression aimed at illustrating a concrete example of how the lack of consensual national history can affect the lives of people might be in order.

In March 1976, one year into the Lebanese war, my father was abducted and killed. Why? Because his identity card carried the mention 'Maronite' (an Oriental Catholic Church and community present mainly in Lebanon). In 1975, the Lebanese society, torn apart along the "Phoenician/Arab" rift, had imploded under the pressure of regional factors. The "Phoenician/Arab" rift, the Lebanese model of the "ethnic" doctrines that have ruined so many countries in the last part of the twentieth century, refers to the various ideologies according to which many "Muslims" consider that they are the only true "Arabs", and conversely many "Christians" consider themselves to be descendant of the "Phoenicians" and therefore as not being "Arabs."

Like many other Lebanese, my father took a stand for a multiconfessional and convivial Lebanon, and defied the militias that had set themselves to enforce the "ethnic separation" of the Lebanese people. He stayed in his neighbourhood. In his case it happened to be mainly Sunni Muslim, for others it was mainly Maronite, etc. During the mayhem of the first two years of the war, an estimated 150,000 Lebanese, or five percent of the population on both sides of the newly carved dividing line, lost their lives before the society could be rearranged along the "Phoenician/Arab" rift. The "Phoenician/Arab" affliction is not in an acute phase now, but is recognised as the main chronic ailment of the Lebanese body politic, so much so that the demand for a "Unified Lebanese History Book" is the only unanimously endorsed demand in Lebanon today. But no two Lebanese, historians or not, can agree on how to proceed from the available data to write such a history book and have it accepted by all parties.

In these circumstances, it should be obvious to anyone familiar with even the dictionary definition of archaeology that the loss of Beirut's archaeological site, a site that had been continuously occupied for all of Lebanon's history, and that has often been at the forefront of this history, would be a national disaster. However, some background information might be needed to show to those unfamiliar with the situation in Lebanon how the archaeological excavation of Beirut's site could have answered, in practice, the Lebanese historical needs.

A short history of Lebanon's histories

There has never been a "National History of Lebanon" accepted as such by all the Lebanese (for the latest and most interesting review of this situation see Corm, 1996). During the long slump experienced by the area under Ottoman rule, there was no amalgamated "National History," but only a concatenation of the traditional histories of the religious communities, an uneasy cohabitation of the traditional Sunni Islamic histories, elaborated a few centuries earlier, with the religious and folk histories of all the local minorities (all the fifteen non-Sunni religious communities). Because they were endorsed by the central power, the Sunni Islamic histories were dominant, but they were not accepted by the minorities as History, much less National History.

The first departure from the traditional fragmented historicising took place during the second half of the nineteenth century when, inspired by the national histories then being written in Europe, the first generation of local intellectuals – mainly Maronites – with a Western education attempted a bold gambit. In what has become known as the "Arab Awakening," they tried to put forward a non-religious "Arab" history that would be convivial to all the Arabic-speaking religious communities of Greater Syria. Even though this innovation was to have lasting effects, it never became official national history. These intellectuals did not have the power of a state to back them as happened, for example, in France (Dietler 1994). Moreover, the pattern they were following led them back to their starting point. Why this happened can best be grasped by looking at the process of the creation of modern Greek national identity that was taking place at the same time (Friedman 1992; Hamilakis and Yalouri 1996). This pattern required anchoring national history in a golden and prestigious Classical Age. The Classical Age for the Arabic-speaking people of the area had to be the Age of the Omayyad and Abbasid Empires. Which meant, given the state of historical knowledge then available, falling back under the sway of the traditional Islamic historians who had settled on a version favouring the "Islamic" Abbasid model over the "Arab" Omayyad. There was no breaking out of this conundrum within the confines of the traditionally available data, and archaeology was not then available, not even in its "youthful," "Orientalist" garb.

Such opportunity presented itself following World War I, when the power equation changed and the dominant Maronite élite of the new state of Greater

Lebanon went looking for a national identity. In the context of the bipolar confessional Lebanese society, the result of the Orientalists' invention of the "Phoenicians" was seized upon like manna from heaven. Here was a "scientific" way of shaking off the uncomfortable "Arabic cum Islamic" history. Was it not written in heavy and erudite tomes that the "Phoenicians" had lived in an area nearly coextensive with modern Lebanon, that they had undoubtedly preceded the "Arabs," that they had written a notable page in history and that, whatever it was they believed in, it was surely not Islam? No wonder that such "Phoenicians" held for some Lebanese the promise that the Pharaonic and Babylonian ages will later hold for the Egyptian and Iraqi states when these last tried to write specific, non-Arab histories for their respective countries.

In 1943, the power shifted again and, in order to agree on the independence of the state of Lebanon, the Maronite and Sunni leaders both compromised and reached the unwritten "National Pact," by which the former gave up French protection and the latter gave up unification with the Syrian state. However, as the journalist Georges Naccache then wrote, "Two negations do not make a Nation." This warning went unheeded and the political élite, busy apportioning among themselves the spoils of the administration of the state, did not engage in any serious nation-building program. Various committees came up with ineffectual histories of Lebanon pieced together by mutual concessions from the religious communities but, by and large, the Lebanese kept reading their history in imported books, with the disastrous results mentioned above.

Archaeology and history

Mass psychosis waxes and wanes, and the sobering effect of the rubble might not last long. This is why it was important to take advantage of the rubble of Beirut's Downtown to start a program of concerted archaeological research designed to uncover as much as possible about the history of this major Lebanese site. The proper archaeological study of Beirut would have been a first step towards the writing of the much sought-after "Unified Lebanese History Book." Unfortunately, the needed "research framework or set of objectives and priorities for the archaeological work" (Schofield 1992) was never elaborated. Instead, the minimalist archaeological program adopted had as its main goal the ahistorical aim "to collect data on the ancient use of space in the city of Beirut" (Curvers and Stuart 1995). Many interesting, if not vital, questions of Lebanese history that could have been addressed by an archaeological investigation of Beirut's site will now and forever remain unanswered. Here I will briefly outline three of these research objectives that would have been vital to the consensual rewriting of Lebanese history (Naccache 1991; 1992).

"Arabs" and "Phoenicians"

Establishing the continuity or discontinuity of the material culture of the first millennium BC inhabitants of Beirut might have helped answer the question of their "ethnic" identity. Were they "Phoenicians" or "Arabs," or, better, can we really differentiate between the two, and if so during what period? This is surely a vital question for Lebanese history. Although it might seem far-fetched within the outdated confines of the prevailing historical paradigm of the region, there was much available information that made of it a legitimate archaeological research objective (ibid.: 1996b).

Post-551 Beirut and the Islamic conquest

Very little was known of the fate of Beirut following the devastating earthquake of 551 AD. But Beirut must somehow have recuperated from the blow because Arab historians mention it as one of the main cities of the coast in the seventh and eighth centuries AD, and Muʿāwiyah used Beirut's naval workshops for the preparation of his maritime expeditions. The silence of the sources might be taken to imply that Beirut was peacefully integrated into the Arab Islamic administration, that is, that it was not conquered by force of arms. A confirmation of this deduction through well-controlled archaeological excavations would have been of the utmost value for Lebanese national history.

Beirut from the Mamluks to Fakhreddin

Lebanon acquired its modern confessional and linguistic physiognomy early in the second millennium AD, a period we know very little about. However, since Beirut had enjoyed a relative prosperity during the 350 years between the end of the Crusaders' occupation, in 1291, and 1635, the date of the crushing by the Ottomans of the emirate of Fakhreddin II el-Maani (the symbolic father of modern Lebanon), careful archaeological excavations of the thick strata of that period could have told us much about the daily life of Beirutis of all confessions. Thus, it would have allowed us to flesh out our deficient picture of the early stages of modern, specifically Lebanese, history.

It is a memorycide

Sadly, it is a well-known fact that very little of the period prior to the second century BC has been excavated, and that practically no archaeological remains of the period after the seventh century AD has been spared, much less studied. Thus, today, it has been confirmed that some of Beirut's urban layout is of hoary antiquity, but we are hardly in a better position than in 1975 to answer the pressing questions of relevance to national history.

The claim that a proper archaeological study of the site of Beirut could have helped in writing a consensual national Lebanese history is confirmed by the isolated find of a second century BC jar handle bearing in Greek letters the name "Abdoi," that of the local potter who produced it. Today, "Abdo" is a common name among all Lebanese, Christians and Muslims, and Lebanese from all confessions can identify with an ancestor named "Abdo." But for "Abdo" to become part of Lebanese history would require that we know about his/her life and time. The aborted archaeological program has denied the Lebanese an opportunity to acquire a common ancestor, i.e. to have a common history. Because the loss of the archaeological wealth of Beirut has been the result of conscious and obstinate policies, and since it amounted to a loss of a shared, albeit "forgotten" memory, we are entitled to describe it as a *memorycide*. And we can but fear the consequence of this *memorycide* on the future of Lebanon.

How could such a national catastrophe happen?

It is generally recognised that when the guns fell silent after sixteen years of war the Lebanese people, including the so-called *intelligencia*, were despondent and powerless and that, for the convenience of a regional settlement, Lebanon was deprived of its self-rule. As a result, Lebanese post-war governments have had very little say in determining Lebanese policies. Furthermore, inasmuch as Mr Rafic Hariri, the "father" of the real-estate company, has been Prime Minister since November 1992, the Lebanese conditions that allowed the memorycide to happen are relatively easy to understand, and of little interest for archaeologically-minded readers. What could be of more relevance to these readers is a reflection on the role played by archaeologists in this catastrophe.

The involvement of the archaeologists

Already in early 1993, the French critic Frédéric Edelman, commenting on the hullabaloo that accompanied the launching of the real-estate company, had foreseen the dire consequences of the Lebanese political set-up on the future of Beirut's Downtown. In a prescient article, Edelman (1993) reproached both UNESCO and the archaeologists for furnishing the real-estate company with the trappings of legitimacy, and noted that both were mistaken if they thought that they would benefit from what was planned for Beirut.

Three years later, Edelman has been proven right. As already mentioned, partici-pating archaeologists, Lebanese as well as non-Lebanese, accepted to take part in a program they knew to be flawed. They pretended to ignore the fact that Beirut's archaeological site extended underneath all modern Downtown, signed the legal papers that allowed the throwing to the sea of large sections of the site, and took an active role in promoting the public image of the real-estate company. The judgement about the quality of the archaeologist's work, on the small sections where they were given a few weeks access, will be made by the archaeological community when the final reports will be published. What can already be ascer-tained is that the archaeological teams had skeletal crews, minimal funding and primitive means at their disposal. It is highly unlikely that any of Lebanon's nearest neighbours, Syria, Jordan, Cyprus or Palestine/Israel, would have considered, in the last two decades, any such operation as adequate salvage excavation on even the most marginal site. Furthermore, apart from a British team which spent six months on a 1,100 square meter section, and a French team which spent an eighteen month stretch on a 560 square meter section, all the other teams submitted to a very tight schedule, being given only four to five weeks for their excavations under the fallacious pretext that reconstruction work had to proceed quickly. The pretext is fallacious as shown by the fact that more than a year after the archaeologists were stopped from working in the 'Old Souks' area, and the area bulldozed, there has still been no building activity there. Additionally, the ancient shoreline and harbour North of the "Old Souks," which were "investi-gated" in less than three weeks in early 1996, has been left as it is until early 1997 – the time of this writing. The new sewer system, for whose installation huge sections of the site were bulldozed, will not be connected to its purification plant for many years and will therefore be not operative until then. And finally, the boulevard that cut through the "Ancient Tell" will remain a dead-end for another decade; and the list could go on and on.

Not only did the archaeologists breach their professional code of ethics by accept-ing to participate in such a program, but they further reneged on their allegiance to the site by refusing to publicly state their misgivings about the program. If they had publicly denounced the well-known flaws of the program, and refused to continue their endorsement of the program, it would have had to be modified. There was a limit to how much the real-estate company could break the Antiquity law, and if but one archaeologist participating in the program had pointed out what was really happening to the site, measures would have had to be taken to redress the program. That this would have happened is illustrated by the following example of the causal chain that followed the first report of destruction.

To counteract the effects of the first reports in the local press of destruction of the "Ancient Tell" (Naccache 1994c), reports which were echoed by the international news agencies, in early 1995 the real-estate company mounted an international public relations blitz on the international press. Although these articles presented the archaeological work undertaken in Beirut as some kind of achievement, one of the journalists invited to Beirut reported the lone dissenting comments of the author of the present lines (de Roux 1995). These comments helped to persuade a group spearheaded by Dr Elie Wardini, a Lebanese residing in Norway, to voice its concerns in a letter addressed to Mr Federico Mayor, Secretary General of UNESCO. This letter was co-signed by many archaeologists from all over the world. Shortly after receiving this letter, Mr Mayor decided to visit Lebanon. This visit, although it may have appeared largely self-congratulatory (Lefèvre 1995a), helped nevertheless to save the small sections of the site that had been already excavated and that were deemed by Mr Mayor to belong to "World Heritage."

If Mr Mayor's visit turned out to be of little practical overall effect (ibid.: 1995b) it is because the participating archaeologists, Lebanese and European, defended what was happening in their particular sections, instead of speaking out against the program as a whole (personal communications by the heads of the Parliament's Public Work Commission in charge of investigating the matter, Mr Fouad Saad and Mr Mohammad Kabbani). Not only that but, once the ripples caused by Mr Mayor's visit had died down, some of the archaeologists involved, again Lebanese and European, actively participated in the promotional campaign financed by the real-estate company, presenting the whole program (through travelling exhibits, lectures and website pages) as a major achievement.

Unfortunately this disingenuous campaign has been successful and although, as we have seen, the scale of destruction is an indisputable fact, it has been extremely hard to get an airing of any critical views on Beirut's archaeological program in the archaeological press. This is particularly well illustrated by the reaction of the editor of a highly influential British archaeology magazine, who has consistently mobilised the archaeological community in defence of endangered worldwide heritage but who, even after reading the only published critical account of the program (Naccache 1996), refused to open the pages of his magazine to a further exploration of the subject, writing:

> I remain of the view that the destruction is not so very different, having regard to the special circumstances of post-war reconstruction, from those inflicted on cities across the Mediterranean and Europe. I come to that view without any first-hand knowledge, as you will be aware, but after extensive discussions

with colleagues with first-hand knowledge and large experience in urban archaeology.

(personal communication)

Such an attitude on the part of the participating archaeologists and the archaeological community begs an explanation which is attempted in the remainder of this chapter.

The archaeologists' predicament

As in all human groups, there are those moved by a combination of ignorance and/or the temptation of easy income. If placed in positions of responsibility, some of those, with little attachment to the site and "tempted beyond their ability to resist" by the "lure of a few moments of notoriety" (Keith 1995), might inflict large damage to the site, but they remain uninteresting as a phenomenon. One could point out the example of Dr Hares Boustany who supervised the archaeological program for the real-estate company and acted as its spokesperson on matters archaeological, and whose declarations are an anthology of misinformation (Naccache 1996c). Also Mr Hans Curvers who, with one assistant, assumed the responsibility for the whole of "Phase III," the "Salvage operation" in which archaeologists followed the bulldozers over the whole 1,000,000 square meter extent of Beirut's archaeological site, and who supervised 35 of the 60 so-called "chantiers archéologique de Beyrouth" (author unknown 1996).

The case of individuals with high moral standards who have nevertheless been gagged by their institutional position is much more interesting because it reveals not their trivial personal flaws but the constraints under which archaeologists have to work. On the lower rung of the power ladder we find some students who were, and still are, outraged at what they saw. However, because of their "inferior" status, and because they were only a minority among the large numbers of students who participated in the excavations, these students could not speak out and were reduced to keeping detailed files of all the crimes against Beirut's heritage which they had witnessed. At, or near, the top of the archaeological power ladder we find people such as Dr John Schofield from the Museum of London Archaeological Service, and Mr Philippe Marquis delegated to Lebanon from the Commission du Vieux Paris, two outstanding human beings who gave to Beirut "beyond the call of duty." If they had been listened to, Schofield and/or Marquis, both experts in urban archaeology, would have set up an exemplary archaeological program in Beirut. But they were not listened to and, moreover, they did not have the freedom to speak out. Both were civil servants having to account to their institutions and governments, that is, having the twin swords of redundancy and/ or dismissal continuously hanging over their heads. Keeping in mind that Marquis was an employee of the Mairie de Paris, and given that Mr Chirac, first as Mayor of Paris and then as French President, wanted France to benefit from Mr Hariri's largesse (Faton 1995), we can easily guess at Marquis' margin of manoeuvre.

Is pluridisciplinarity the solution?

The case of Schofield and Marquis is an illustration of one of the main problems with which archaeologists have to deal today. This problem is not specific to Beirut but is encountered worldwide. To put it succinctly, how do archaeologists harmonise the theoretical allegiance owed to the archaeological sites with the reality of the cultural, social and economic constraints under which they have to perform? To get a clearer perception of this problem we have to enlarge the scope of our analysis and look beyond the individuals to the archaeological community as a whole. With the drying-up of their traditional sources of funding, archaeologists have become "a test case for privatisation" (Dyson 1996), and the initiative for their work "has now decisively passed to the hands of the state, in commissioning work that it wants, and to powerful private companies" (Sherratt 1996).

Since Beirut's fiasco is the prototypical example of "post-academic archaeology" in which the "great bulk of archaeological activity . . . takes place either directly for the state, or within a national or international legal framework placing responsibility on a private firm" (ibid.), it can be used to test the validity of Sherratt's proposal for a solution. He proposes that academics "remove their internal barriers, between 'prehistory', 'ancient history' and 'modern history', and between history, anthropology and geography" as a way of reasserting archaeology's relevance.

To test that proposal, let us focus our attention on those archaeologists who had a patent vested academic interest in Beirut's multi-millennial archaeological site. One of those groups would be the classicists but we will not consider their case because Berytus is only one of a score of provincial Roman cities and the classicists might therefore argue that the fate of its site was of marginal academic importance. To illustrate these points, consider one elderly French classicist, who had worked on the site and published about it in the forties, put up a spirited fight for Berytus (Lauffray 1995), that is, till he was denied an entry visa to Lebanon even though he was a member of the Comité Scientifique International nominated by UNESCO to supervise Beirut's program. When he accepted to curtail his public declarations, as all members of the Comité Scientifique International were then asked to do, he was given his visa. We will consider instead what the Phoenicologists did while Beirut's archaeological site was being destroyed. Beirut, *en Phoinikè*, as it is referred to in Greek on one of its third-century AD mints, is one of the four main cities of the Phoenician heartland (the others being Gbeyl/Byblos, Saida/Sidon, and Tyr/Sour), and recent Phoenicology is very actively a multidisciplinary academic enterprise (Moscati 1995).

The Phoenicologists were busy in 1994–1995. 1995 saw the publication of two large and up-to-date, state-of-the-art volumes on 'Phoenicology'. The first has this to say about Beirut:

A ce moment même, une vaste (sic) campagne de fouilles se déroulant à Beyrouth Centre-Ville sous l'égide de l'Unesco et de la Direction Générale des Antiquités du Liban ressuscitée, a déjà engendré suffisamment de matériel pour qu'une étude parallèle puisse être entamée, celle-ci relative au profil régional de ce centre de la Phénicie centrale.

(Moscati (ed.) 1995: 508)

The second says: "A la suite des destructions récentes du centre-ville, l'IFAPO avait entrepris vers 1975 (sic) un programme archéologique, qui a été interrompu par la reprise des combats. Un nouveau programme pourrait être mis en route" (Krings (ed.) 1995: 100). And in October 1995, the community of Phoenicologists convened at Cadix, Spain, for its Fourth International Congress of Phoenician and Punic Studies, during which it honoured the Lebanese officials who had supervised Beirut's archaeological disaster. Meanwhile, one Phoenicologist, whose "project is to produce a detailed archaeological and historical analysis of the Phoenician homeland," chose Western Galilee in Palestine/Israel, "as a case study *because it is currently the only accessible part of the Phoenician homeland*" (emphasis my own) (Lehmann in Gitin 1996: 74).

The archaeologists versus Beirut's archaeological site

Let us now bring together all the strands of the argument that we have surveyed up to now. We have seen that of the archaeologists who participated in the Beirut archaeological rout some, quite humanly, did not care, and some who cared were prevented from acting by the constraints imposed on their jobs. We have also seen that for the wider archaeological community, even those who had vested academic interest in the proper archaeological study of Beirut's site did not do a thing to prevent the debâcle, and that some even went so far as to let themselves fall prey to the deceitful divisions of the modern political situation. This review, however brief, should be enough to establish that the archaeologists, be it those who participated in the program or those who had a direct interest in its results or the community at large, did not demonstrate any concrete allegiance to the archaeological site of Beirut, to its protection and its exploitation – academically or economically. It should also be enough to indicate that overcoming academic barriers within the archaeological discipline is not enough to overcome this professional failing, and that something else altogether is needed. Since the chances are high that such failing would occur again, and not only in Lebanon where, for instance, the archaeological site of Saida/Sidon will soon experience Beirut's fate, but all over the world, it is worth pondering on the lessons that can be learned from the events in Beirut.

World archaeology as a shared social construct

What happened in Beirut can partly be explained by the fact that its archaeological and historical heritage did not partake directly to that heritage that is of direct relevance to Western Archaeology, which happens at present to be the leading force in world archaeology. Unavoidably, such a situation is bound to repeat itself with the broadening of the definition of archaeological heritage to encompass all remains of human activities, wherever on the planet, and from all past times. Unavoidably, archaeologists will get tangled into the conflicts that archaeology as history writing creates between their own cultures and national histories and the cultures and histories of the peoples in whose land their sites are located. But this should not be viewed as a deterrent, or as a structural defect compromising the allegiance of the archaeological community to the world's archaeological heritage.

Even though the remains of human occupation and activity are material facts, to become part of shared human archaeological heritage this function has first to be assigned to them (see also Potts, Chapter 10; Hassan, Chapter 11). Since, however, "functions are never intrinsic, but always observer relative" (Searle 1995: 14), there has to be a collective agreement of the archaeological community to label archaeological remains from across the globe as part of the human heritage. This global assignment of "archaeological" function to all remains should not preclude the interest of particular individuals in particular remains, be they Greek, Roman, Jewish, Arabic, Chinese, Sinhalese etc., but is needed in order to ensure that to all remains are assigned the same functions, and that to all should be attached the same "rights and responsibilities, which can be performed only if there is collective acceptance of the function" (ibid.: 88).

If Beirut's example is any indication, it will require much soul searching and self-criticism on the part of the leaders of the archaeological community before global human archaeological heritage becomes part of our global social reality. This step, however, is required from the global archaeological community if it wishes to put itself in a position in which it can shoulder the social responsibilities that are raised by archaeological work on a worldwide basis.

Bibliography

Barbier, Y. (1978) *Sauvegarde du patrimoine et contribution à l'élaboration du plan d'aménagement du centre ville*, Paris: Unesco Publications.

Corm, G. (1996) *An Introduction to Lebanon and the Lebanese*, Beirut: Dar aj-Jadid (in Arabic).

Curvers, H. H. and Stuart, B. (1995) *Urban Archaeology in Beirut: a preliminary report*, http://almashriq.hiof.no/lebanon/900/930/930.1/beirut/reconstruction/curvers_unesco_april.html.

de Roux, E. (1995) "Beyrouth, plus grand chantier archéologique du monde," *Le Monde*, Friday 2 June.

Dietler, M. (1994) "Our Ancestors the Gauls: Archaeology, Ethnic Nationalism, and the Manipulation of Celtic Identity in Modern Europe," *American Anthropologist*, 96, 3: 584–605.

Dyson, S. L. (1996) "From the President," *Archaeology* 49, 6: 6.

Eboch, C. (1996) "The tragedy of Beirut," *Archaeology* 49, 6: 9.

Edelman, F. (1993) "Beyrouth à coeur ouvert," *Le Monde*, Thursday 11 February.

Faton, L. (1995) "Une doctrine abandonnée: La France et les coopérations françaises", *Archéologia* 316: 27.

Friedman, J. (1992) "The Past in the Future: History and the Politics of Identity," *American Anthropology* 94, 4: 837–59.

Girard, J. (1996) "Beyrouth: Les enjeux de la ruine. Le centre historique de Beyrouth est mort deux fois", *L'année du Patrimoine*, 4: 52–62.

Gitin, S. (ed.) (1996) "W. F. Albright Institute of Archaeological Research, Jerusalem: Project descriptions of Albright Appointees 1994–1995," *Bulletin for the American School of Oriental Research*, 298: 68–78.

Hamilakis, Y. and Yalouri, E. (1996) "Antiquities as symbolic capital in modern Greek society," *Antiquity* 70, 1: 117–29.

Jidejian, N. (1973) *Beirut through the Ages*, Beirut: Dar el-Machreq Publishers.

Keith, D. H. (1995) "A true adventure among pirates," *Antiquity* 69, 4: 402–3.

Krings, V. (1995) (ed.) *La Civilisation Phénicienne et Punique, Manuel de recherche*, Leiden: E. J. Brill.

Lauffray, J. (1995) "Beyrouth: Ce qui n'a pas été dit," *Archéologia* 317: 4–11.

Lefèvre, A.-C. (1995a) "Beyrouth: Le plus grand chantier d'archéologie urbaine au monde," *Archéologia* 316: 14–26.

—— (1995b) "Beyrouth: L'archéologie par le vide," *Archéologia* 318: 4–9.

Moscati, S. (1995) "L'Età della Sintesi," *RSF* 23, 2: 127–46.

—— (ed.) (1995) *I Fenici: Ieri Oggi Domani, Ricerche, scoperte, progetti*, Roma.

Naccache, A. (1991) "The present state of the archaeological sites in Lebanon, and how has the war affected them," in proceedings of the conference *In Defense of*

Lebanon's Antiquities, 28 June, Beirut: Lebanese Commission of Unesco (in Arabic), pp. 45–92.

—— (1992) "Beyrouth: Decouvrons son passé en construisant son futur," *L'Orient-Le Jour*, 9, 11, 12 May.

—— (1994a) "Archaeology and the rewriting of history," in H. Sadek (ed.) *In Defense of Archaeology and Architecture in Lebanon*, proceedings of the conference held on 28–29 January, Beirut: Cultural Center for South Lebanon (in Arabic), pp. 59–69.

—— (1994b) "Beyrouth: Will we search for her past, or will we destroy it?" *al-Nahar*, Literary Sup., Saturday 19 March, 4–9 (in Arabic).

—— (1994c) "Beyrouth's Heritage: The open massacre," *al-Nahar*, opinions, Friday 23 December, 13 (in Arabic).

—— (1996a) "The price of progress," *Archaeology*, 49, 4: 51–6.

—— (1996b) "The Empire of the Amorites Revisited," in Ismail F. (ed.) Proceedings of the International Symposium on *Syria and the Ancient Near East 3000–300 BC*, Aleppo: University of Aleppo Publications, pp. 29–50.

—— (1996c) "The cultural implications of development: The reconstruction of Beirut's Downtown, a historical viewpoint (Ancient History)," in proceedings of the conference *The cultural implications of development: The reconstruction of Beirut's Downtown,* 4 April, Beirut: Lebanese Commission of Unesco (in Arabic), pp. 72–105.

Salem, E. (1970) *Beirut, Crossroads of Cultures*, Beirut: Librairie du Liban.

Schofield, J. (1992) "Recommendations concerning the future management of the archaeology of Beirut," report submitted to the Lebanese Direction Générale des Antiquités.

Searle, J. R. (1995) *The construction of social reality*, New York: The Free Press.

Sherratt, A. (1996) "Editorial," *Antiquity* 70, 4: 491–9.

Author unknown (1996), "Les chantiers archéologiques du Centre-Ville de Beyrouth," *Archéologie et Patrimoine*, a joint publication of the Lebanese Direction Générale des Antiquités and Unesco, 4 April: 16–19.

Chapter 8

Conjuring Mesopotamia
Imaginative geography and a world past

Zainab Bahrani

Our familiarity, not merely with the languages of the peoples of the East but with their customs, their feelings, their traditions, their history and religion, our capacity to understand what may be called the genius of the East, is the sole basis upon which we are likely to be able to maintain in the future the position we have won, and no step that can be taken to strengthen that position can be considered undeserving of the attention of His majesty's Government or of a debate in the House of Lords.

Lord Curzon, address to House of Lords, September 27, 1909

Introduction

By 1909 the importance of the production of knowledge for the British colonial enterprise in the East was neither implicit in political rhetoric nor subtly expressed. In Lord Curzon's words it was "an imperial obligation . . . part of the necessary furniture of Empire" (Said 1978: 214). The need for this knowledge was stressed as an integral part of the process of colonisation, and one that would facilitate the continuation of European authority over the East. It is my contention that the development of the discipline of Mesopotamian archaeology and its discursive practices during this time cannot be isolated from this colonialist enterprise. Nor can it be divorced from the general Western historical narrative of the progress of civilisation which was necessary for the aims of a civilising imperial mission. I argue here that this narrative of civilisation was heavily dependent upon a discourse of Otherness which posited a "Mesopotamia" as the past of mankind, and furthermore that the presencing of Mesopotamia through this imperialist discourse constitutes the ground whence today archaeologists continue to unearth what counts as "historical fact," and to decide upon its acceptable mode of comprehension. First, in order to locate Mesopotamia's position in the Euro-American historical tradition I consider the historical dimensions of time and space as structuring horizons for the framework of "Mesopotamia." Second, I argue that this framework, which in Heidegger's words "serves as a criterion for separating the regions of Being" cannot be divorced from the cultural abstraction most commonly used to identify Mesopotamia: despotism.

Postcolonial critiques have pointed to how the process of imperialism was not limited to the overt economic and political activities of Western governments in colonised lands. An entire system of classification through the arts and sciences was necessary for the success of the imperial enterprise in the East and Africa.[1] Mesopotamian archaeological practices must be considered within this system, not only because this field concerns a region that was of geopolitical interest to the West, but because of its crucial place within the metanarrative of human culture. Archaeology, like other human sciences such as anthropology and history, allowed a European mapping of the subjugated terrain of the Other. While ethnography portrayed the colonised native as a savage requiring Western education and whose culture needed modernisation, archaeology and its practices provided a way of charting the past of colonised lands.

Mesopotamian archaeology is a discipline concerned with defining a particular past, and a particular culture within this past, and like in other archaeological or historical enterprises two of the basic constituents structuring the discursive practices of this discipline are space and time. These ontologically "obvious" measures are not neutral in archaeological practices. In fact, if we apply Heideggerian terms, it is within this structure of space and time that "Mesopotamia" was revealed as a Being-in-the-world. As an ontic phenomenon therefore, Mesopotamia is prefigured by the temporal structure of European metahistorical narrative. In other words, as I aim to show here, "Mesopotamia," as archaeologists generally think of this culture today, is a discursive formation.

The relationship of power to praxis in archaeological research has received some attention in recent years (Hodder *et al.* 1995; Shanks and Tilley 1987). Issues such as the promotion of one historical interpretation over another, or the focus on one sector of society at the expense of all others, have been confronted and discussed at great lengths by a number of scholars. In this chapter, it is not my intention to liberate a "true" Mesopotamian past from the power of Western representation. Rather, by analysing Mesopotamia as a phenomenon within Western archaeological discourse I hope to show how a particular Mesopotamian identity was required for the narrative of the progress of civilisation as an organic universal event. My intention then is to question the ontological or, rather, ontic concept of Mesopotamia as it has been determined by Western archaeological discourse, and to consider the ideological components of this phenomenon. In other words, I would like to open up the field of politicising inquiry in archaeology to consider Mesopotamia not as a factual historical and geographical entity waiting to be studied, excavated and interpreted according to one set of conventions or another, but as a product of the poetics of a Western historical narrative.

For Mesopotamian archaeology, scholarly considerations of the relationship between politics and archaeology has meant two things only: (a) interpreting the material and textual remains from ancient Iraq primarily as manifestations of political propaganda of Babylonian and Assyrian kings and, more recently, (b) pointing to the Iraqi Baathist regime's use of the pre-Islamic past for propagandist purposes. We, as Mesopotamian archaeologists, do not question the nature of our discipline, its parameters, and its interpretive strategies. I do not use the word "we" because I am a Middle Eastern scholar educated in the West. Eastern archaeologists work within the same parameters and according to the same interpretive models as Western archaeologists (see Özdoğan, Chapter 5), due to the fact that archaeology is a Western discipline that only became instituted in Middle Eastern countries while they were under European rule. As a "high cultural" activity and a humanist discipline we do not question its institutional character or presence. Mesopotamian scholarship assumes that the colonial context of its creation is irrelevant except as a distant, indirectly related, historical event. This attitude is not limited to archaeologists of Western origins. Therefore, Mesopotamian archaeologists, regardless of nationality, have been slow to reflect on the circumstances under which the constitution of the field of Mesopotamian archaeology occurred, and how its textual practices have formed ancient "Mesopotamia" as an area of modern knowledge.

On the level of the overtly political and ideological, ancient history and archaeology have certainly been areas of contestation as in, for example, Palestine/Israel (Silberman, Chapter 9) and Cyprus (Knapp and Antoniadou, Chapter 1). However, it is not only such geographical areas and histories that can be contested. In this chapter I would like to define and contest another terrain: the conceptual territory which functions in the production of Western culture as narration.

Space and despotic time

During the second half of the nineteenth century the myth of Mesopotamia as the origin of Western civilisation became institutionalised into the Western humanist tradition. This modern humanist field of knowledge is a "metatemporal" teleological discourse based upon the concept of culture as an organic natural whole; one that encompassed the entirety of the world. Time, in this cultural narrative, is visualised according to this organic structure and its potential evolution. The past was seen as a necessary part of the present Western identity and, its place in the serial development to the present, of paramount importance.

Michel de Certeau has defined the act of historical writing as a perpetual separation and suturing of the past and present (de Certeau 1975). In the case of Mesopotamia, the cut and suture are not limited to the separation and adhesion of past and present time as abstract phenomenological concepts. This reconstructive historical act has severed "Mesopotamia" from any geographical terrain in order to weave it into the Western historical narrative. In the standardised orthodox text book accounts of Middle Eastern history, Sumerian, Babylonian and Assyrian cultures can have absolutely no connection to the culture of Iraq after the seventh century AD. Instead, this past is grafted onto the tree of the progress of civilisation, a progress that by definition must exclude the East, as its very intelligibility is established by comparison with an Other. The Otherness of the Oriental past, however, plays a double role here. It is at once the earliest phase of a universal history of mankind in which man makes the giant step from savagery to civilisation, and it is an example of the unchanging nature of Oriental cultures.

In historical scripture, then, the Mesopotamian past is the place of world culture's first infantile steps: first writing, laws, architecture and all the other firsts that are quoted in every student handbook and in all the popular accounts of Mesopotamia. These "firsts" of culture are then described as being "passed" as a "torch of civilisation" to the Graeco-Roman world. If Mesopotamia is the cradle of civilisation, and civilisation is to be understood as an organic universal whole, then this Mesopotamia represents human culture's infancy. Already by the 1830s, even before the start of scientific excavations in the Near East, Hegel's lectures on the philosophy of history defined this area as the site of the infancy of human civilisation (Hegel 1956: 105). European historical writing had provided an interpretive framework in which the development of history was likened to the growth of the human organism, and in which the cradle of that organism was the East. When Mesopotamian material remains actually came to be unearthed in the decades following Hegel's lectures this evolutionary model was firmly in place. Therefore, Mesopotamian archaeological finds were interpreted according to a pre-established model. Conversely, architectural structures, visual and textual representations, as well as every other aspect of culture, were used to confirm a model of progress that had been established before these same cultural remains had been unearthed.

The temporal organisation of this evolution of human civilisation puts Mesopotamia into the distant primeval past of mankind, a time that is both "ours" (i.e. the West's) and that of a barbaric, not yet civilised, civilisation. Thus, the temporal placement of "Mesopotamia" also determines the spatial organisation required for this system to function. In terms of geographical land, Mesopotamia is not to be associated with Iraq as it can only inhabit a temporal, not a terrestrial, space. Thus, in this case, the will to power which is often turned to the production of history, has established as historical fact the development of culture as one Olympic relay with its starting point in a place that needs to remain in the realm of the West, although its savagery can never be totally overcome.

However, the Western historical narrative is not a coherent discourse which merely uses the East as the origins of civilisation for its own political ends, in the sense of appropriation of land, history, or the declaration of cultural and moral superiority; nor does the ancient Orient simply appear within this narrative as a representation of Otherness. The exercise of power may often work on the level of the consciously political. But at the same time, academic discourse as an apparatus of power, with its metaphoricity and rhetoric, is a matrix in which unconscious desire also manifests itself symptomatically. The representation of the ancient Near East within the Western historical narrative then is not limited to overt racial comparison and hierarchisation through linear time; it is also a form of control and fixing of that uncanny, terrifying and unaccountable time: at once "ours" and Other.[2]

In the simplest terms, if the earliest 'signs of civilisation' were unearthed in an Ottoman province inhabited primarily by Arabs and Kurds, how was this to be reconciled with the European notion of the progress of civilisation as one organic whole? Civilisation had to have been passed from ancient Mesopotamia and Egypt to Greece. Therefore, the contemporary inhabitants of this area had to be dissociated from this past, and this unruly ancient time was brought within the linear development of civilisation. However, as a sort of primeval European past it was also construed at the same time as an era of despotism and decadence and, paradoxically, Orientalist notions of nineteenth-century Eastern culture, systems of government and economy were projected backwards in time and applied also to Babylonia and Assyria. From within this matrix of control, the unruly despotic past continues to resurface in descriptive language and interpretive methods.

The structuring of historical time is not only a teleological device. It is my contention here that this temporal framework is necessary for the operations of taxonomy which were so crucial for the colonialist project. It has often been stated that in the evolutionary process of civilisation the telos is equivalent to the West. Countless texts from the Western historical tradition describe how civilisation was passed from the Near East through Greece and Rome to the modern West and this is hardly a point of contention any longer. However, it is my belief that this unilinear time also acts as an organising device for a taxonomy of political systems which are then aligned racially to particular past cultures that are, in turn, seen as the developmental steps of the human cultural organism.

According to Montesquieu, the so-called founder of political science, there are three species of government: the republic, the monarchy and despotism. The republic was the ideal government of Classical antiquity and monarchy that of the West. Despotism, according to Montesquieu, is the government of most Asian countries and, as Louis Althusser has pointed out, the first feature of despotism in Montesquieu's definition is the fact that it is a political regime which has no structure, no laws and lacks any social space. Montesquieu represents despotism as "the abdication of politics itself" hence its paradoxical character as a political regime which does not exist, as such, but is the constant temptation and peril of other regimes (Althusser 1972: 82). According to Althusser's description of Montesquieu's characterisation, despotism is "space without places, time without duration" (ibid.: 78).

Despotism's timeless quality then explains how latter day Middle Eastern despots can be converged with a primeval past world.[3] Mesopotamia therefore exists within despotic time as the mythical time of despotism or civilisation's unruly malformed past. I have discussed this abstraction in my previous work (Bahrani 1995) and will address it further below. However, first I would like to focus upon how the process of *naming* the historical region in question was so indispensable for its placement within the Western cultural narrative – because, as we have learned from the ancient Mesopotamians, a thing does not exist until it is named.

Name and being

The earliest European interest in the remains of the ancient cities of Babylon and Assyria stemmed from the desire for the validation of the Bible as an historically accurate document. As early as the twelfth century AD, Western travellers such as Benjamin of Tudela and Petahiah of Ratisbon attempted to identify remains of cities around the area of the city of Mosul in northern Iraq mentioned in the Old Testament. However, it was not until the seventeenth and eighteenth centuries that a number of European travellers began to record their attempts at the identification of ancient sites, sometimes with illustrations of those sites accompanying the written descriptions. The first organised archaeological expeditions or missions in Mesopotamia began in the mid-nineteenth century. This is also the time that a number of terms came to be applied to this geographical locale: Mesopotamia, the Near East, and the Middle East. While the latter two names were interchangeable originally, and encompassed a larger geographical terrain, Mesopotamia became instituted as the name of the pre-Islamic civilisation of the region that under Ottoman rule was known as Iraq. This name, Iraq, had already-long been in use by the local inhabitants of the region by the time of the writings of the geographer Yakut al Rumi (born 1179 AD/575 AH [Anno Hijra]) and the early tenth century AD (4th century AH) descriptions of the region by Ibn Hawkal.[4]

The terms "Middle East" and "Near East" came into use in Europe and North America in order to identify more clearly the vast geographical terrain that had previously been referred to simply as the Orient, an area that encompassed basically the whole of Asia and northern Africa. In order to distinguish what was nearer to Europe, in a time when European interest in this vast area was intensified, a closer definition of what Europe was dealing with became necessary. The term "Near East," which was first applied at the end of the nineteenth century, soon fell out of general usage. Nevertheless, it has survived until today primarily as a designation for the same geographical locus in the pre-Islamic period, for the place named the Middle East. This is especially true in academic literature produced in the United States. The name "Middle East" was coined in 1902 by the American naval historian, Alfred Thayer Mahan, for whom the center of this region for military strategic purposes was the Persian Gulf (Lewis 1994: 3). In this way a distinction came to be made between the region before and after the advent of Islam that implied the death of one civilisation and its replacement and eradication by another. Within this disciplinary organisation the term that came to be the acceptable name for Iraq in the Pre-Islamic period was "Mesopotamia." This revival of a name applied to the region in the European Classical tradition came to underscore the Babylonian/Assyrian position within the Western historical narrative of civilisation as the remoter, malformed, or partially formed, roots of European culture which has its telos in the flowering of Western culture and, ultimately, the autonomous modern Western man. Thus the term Mesopotamia refers to an atemporal rather than a geographical entity, which is , in the words of the renowned Mesopotamian scholar, A. Leo Oppenheim (1964), a "Dead Civilisation." This civilisation had to be entirely dissociated, by name, from the local inhabitants and contemporary culture in order to facilitate the portrayal of the history of human civilisation as a single evolutionary process with its natural and ideal outcome in the modern West.

The distinguished American scholar of Middle Eastern history, Bernard Lewis, tells us that only "two of the peoples active in the ancient Middle East had survived with a continuing identity and memory and with a large impact on the world. The Greeks and Jews were still Greeks and Jews and still knew Greek and Hebrew; in these ancient yet living languages, they had preserved the immortal works of religion and literature, which passed into the common inheritance of mankind" (Lewis 1994: 10). Therefore, according to this still commonly held view, the "torch of civilisation" was passed from Mesopotamia to Europe via the two "Eastern ethnicities" that are acceptable to the West: Greeks and Jews. Paradoxically, in the two main sources of the Western cultural narrative, Classical texts and the Bible, the Assyrians and Babylonians and their successors, the Persians, are the hostile Other, presenting a constant threat to the political freedom of democracy and the worship of the true God. The earliest archaeological expeditions to Mesopotamia then were unambiguous in defining the purposes of their mission. Since human civilisation was thought to originate in Mesopotamia, and this civilisation was transferred from the East to the West, the two justifications for the archaeological expeditions were repeatedly stated as being the search for the "roots" of Western culture and to locate the places referred to in the Old Testament.[5]

This obsessive desire to disassociate the past of the region from its present and to present it instead as a primitive stage in the evolution of mankind facilitated the concept of "Mesopotamia" as the rightful domain of the West, both in a historical and a geopolitical sense. A separation and division of (Sumerian, Babylonian, and Assyrian) cultures and an exclusion of the later history of the region was successfully articulated through the act of naming.

The acquisition of monuments and works of art that were shipped to London, Paris and Berlin in the mid-nineteenth century was thus not seen solely, or even primarily, as the appropriation of historical artefacts of Iraq but as the remains of a mythical pre-European past. Mesopotamian cultural remains unearthed in the first days of archaeological exploration then served to illustrate how the modern West had evolved from this stage of the evolution, and that Biblical accounts were true, thus that the Judeo-Christian God was the true God. Yet these were certainly not the only needs that dictated the archaeological endeavour in Mesopotamia. And, more importantly, the European concepts that formed "Mesopotamia" are not limited to the earliest days of archaeological work in the region. It is even more important to realise that the construction of a "Mesopotamia" within the discourse of nineteenth-century colonialism is not a thing of the past. The structure of this colonialist discipline continues virtually unchanged today, and remains all but unquestioned.

The most recent and comprehensive engagement of Mesopotamian scholarship with the issues of imperialism and Orientalism, with the "construction" of the field of Mesopotamian archaeology during the height of Western imperialism, was the 1990 conference "The Construction of the Ancient Near East" (Gunter 1992). The participants, however, confined themselves to the workings of the field of Ancient Near Eastern studies – whether publications, excavations, funding – to pre-World War II Europe and North America, and maintained that the field today is untainted by any political power interests. Mathew Stolper seems to be the exception when he says, "The European literary and intellectual history that shaped the study of the ancient Near East is not to be separated from political history" (Stolper 1992: 20). More significantly, however, although the contributors refer to the "construction" of the discipline during the period of Western imperialism, the major consensus seems to be that Near Eastern archaeology is the "stepchild of imperialism," thus having only an indirect relation to it, and that it was never used as a tool of imperial power (Cooper 1992: 133). A reading of the papers presented at this conference indicates that the silence in Mesopotamian studies regarding the colonial context of the field is not an oversight. The issue has indeed been brought up, but only so that it may be dismissed.

While conferences, such as the one organised at the Smithsonian, and articles written by a handful of scholars attempt to engage with issues of Orientalism and colonialism these endeavours, especially in the area of Mesopotamian archaeology, have been limited to positivist historical documentation of the origins of the discipline in the late nineteenth and early twentieth centuries. There has been no engagement with issues such as representation, cultural translation, or prevalent paradigms of discourse, which have been major areas of focus in related academic disciplines. Although there has been some concern with the recording of the events that occurred in the earliest days of Mesopotamian archaeology, there has been a decided lack of questioning of the (internalised) structure of the field and its practices. The rhetoric of objectivity and realism is today still operative in Mesopotamian archaeology. However, what I find equally disturbing is that now this objectivity is at times presented in the guise of politically correct "post-colonial" approaches that are alternatives to the hegemonic mainstream of the discourse.

The superficial incorporation of the vocabulary of dissent from the margins into the hegemonic discourse of the center without any reassessment or awareness of the epistemological boundaries of the discipline only serves to neutralise and deflect, thereby allowing the central system of practice to remain dominant and effective. In Gramsci's sense of the word, hegemony is not ideology and manipulation. Hegemony constitutes the limits of common sense for people, and even forms a sense of reality (Gramsci 1987; Williams 1973). Thus, the vague references to Orientalism and imperialism in the contemporary discourse of Mesopotamian archaeology have only served to further validate the status quo and preserve the conventional epistemological limits of the field. It seems that a principle of silent exclusion is in operation, barring any real oppositional views through the adoption of their vocabulary into the central dominant discourse.[6] Therefore, this mimicry and subsequent neutralisation of counter-hegemonic terms within the parameters of hegemony are decoys of sorts that lure the possible danger to the integrity of the discipline by deflecting any oppositional realities.[7]

Time of the Despots

Once identified and placed within a Western matrix of knowledge, "Mesopotamia" as the cradle of civilisation began to be reduced to characteristics that were identifiable by and recognisable to (scientifically) trained archaeological research. A number of powerful abstractions, not unlike those upon which ethnographers depended in order to get to the "heart" of a culture more rapidly, graphed a diagram for Mesopotamian archaeological practices. Components of this framework were a priori summaries of the East that discerning scholars could access through objective inquiry into every realm of culture. However, if we analyse this "value-neutral" research on the level of the mimetic description of the data we can see that the creative distortion inherent in all mimesis, as Aristotle describes it, forms a dominant mode of discourse. And, furthermore, this discursive mode is heavily dependent upon the prefiguration of the master tropes of metaphor, metonymy and synecdoche for its prosaic mimetic image of antiquity.[8] In metaphor, which is literally "transfer," a figure of speech is used in which a name or descriptive word is transferred to an object or action through analogy or simile. Metonymy, "name change," works through displacement. The part of a thing may be substituted for the whole, cause for effect or agent for act, whereas synecdoche (regarded by some as a form of metonymy) uses a part to symbolise a quality presumed to inhere to the whole (White 1973).

The main recurring tropical or hologramic abstraction in the textual practices of Mesopotamian archaeology is that of despotic rule. Working within the rhetorical boundaries and signifying processes of essentialising metonymy and synecdoche, scholarship has further identified a despotic Mesopotamia as a historical fact, and it is this abstraction of despotism that has allowed Mesopotamia to assume its position as a non-place. The abstract immediacy of Mesopotamia as a despotic entity is found in all manner of archaeological interpretation regarding this culture, from agricultural production to religion, and recurs repeatedly in descriptions of the arts and architecture (see Hodder, Chapter 6). Decay, violence, inertia and excess, all characteristics of despotic lands in Montesquieu's classification, are abstractions through which Mesopotamian culture is represented. Here, I focus on how despotism resurfaces in the form of metaphor, metonymy and synecdoche in the descriptions of aesthetic traditions and artistic genres of Mesopotamian culture. An early example can be seen in the writings of James Fergusson, the architect who worked with Austen Henry Layard in reconstructing the Assyrian palaces:

> Khorsabad formed a period of decay in Assyrian art . . . but this is even more
> striking when we again pass over eight centuries of time and reach Persepolis,
> which is as much inferior to Khorsabad as that is to Nimrud. In Persepolis, the

artists do not seem to have been equal to attempting portrayal of an action, and scarcely even of a group. There are nothing but long processions of formal bass reliefs of kingly state.

(Fergusson 1850: 363–4)

In this passage decay and repetitive inertia are characteristics of an architecture that is metaphorically defined for us, in Montesquieu's terms, as despotic. Such a viewpoint published in London in 1850, during the period of British colonial expansion in the East, should come as no surprise. However, abstractions of decay, repetition, inertia and despotism appear more often than not in descriptions of Mesopotamian material culture today. In a whole series of articles and books, Assyrian art – wall reliefs, free standing monuments and entire buildings – has been interpreted as despotic (e.g. Pittman 1996; Winter 1981). For instance, in a recent study of Sennacherib's palace, an entire building is interpreted as an oppressive propagandistic building (Russell 1991: 267). The architectural structure of the palace is described metaphorically as possessing the awesome magnificence of all oriental despots and the power to reduce troublemakers to submission, both in Assyria proper and in distant lands. Synecdochally here, consciously political propaganda is the part of Mesopotamian cultural practices taken to stand for the whole, integrating the entirety. The ideology of despots has clearly become a handy ethnographic abstraction through which archaeologists can get to "the heart" of Mesopotamian culture and describe its aesthetic practices more easily and quickly than if they were to accept the possibility of a certain amount of variation of purpose or means in the cultural production of this despotic non-place.

Political rhetoric and propaganda were certainly important components of Assyrian and Babylonian cultural production. In fact, I argue that no representation, regardless of its country of manufacture, can be entirely separated from politics and ideology. But all manifestations of Mesopotamian culture have been reduced through essentialising metaphors, synecdochally and metonymically, into one identity. While sculpture and architecture created under royal patronage were no doubt infused with some form of propaganda, many other factors went into their creation besides the consciously political. Reading all Mesopotamian cultural remains as nothing more nor less than the propagandist utterances of the king reduces this Mesopotamian identity to the epiphenomenon of articulate ideology and thus serves the rhetorical strategy of "Oriental despotism." In this way, current scholarship repeats and diffuses the prototypes of imperialism. Through the power of writing, abstractions that are colonial in principle are left intact.

This kind of essentialising metonymic and synecdochal representation does not take place solely in text. Since the mid-nineteenth century objects collected from Mesopotamian archaeological sites by Western travellers, adventurers or archaeologists have been displayed in Western museums as a metonymic visual presence of that culture. The categorisation of these objects, and their display in Berlin, Paris and London, in museums that were built or enlarged specifically for that purpose, was unquestionably part and parcel of the Western imperial project in the East in the nineteenth century. At the British Museum, the original installation of the Assyrian finds was advertised to the general public as both an antiquarian object of study and a national prize or trophy (Bohrer 1994; Jenkins 1992). Today, a metonymic method of display continues to be utilised in museums for Mesopotamian (and other Near Eastern) antiquities. A group of Mesopotamian royal monuments, including the famous Stele of Naramsin, formed the main focus of an exhibition entitled "The Royal City of Susa" at the Metropolitan Museum of Art in New York in 1992. These monuments had been mutilated and carried to Iran by the Elamites in the twelfth century BC. According to the established tradition in scholarship, the didactic material and the catalogue entries expressed horror at this act of theft and destruction. Oriental violence and cruelty was seen as a valid explanation for these actions (Bahrani 1995). "Stolen" works of art from Babylonia were placed directly in the central space of the galleries, as the main focus of the exhibition and as a prime example of, in this case, Elamite cultural practices.

Further, what is interesting for my purposes here is that neither the didactic material in the exhibit, nor the wall maps, made mention of the words Iraq or Iran. The reasoning behind this was, no doubt, that only the ancient names should be represented in a "high cultural" institution. However, I shall venture to say here that this is not common practice with exhibits representing ancient Western cultures within the same institution, nor others like it in this country. The museum and its representation of alien cultures is clearly not a value-neutral domain since this is the arena in which information and representations of other cultures are disseminated to the general public. The deliberate omission of the names Iran and Iraq from these maps and descriptions have only added to the general conception of this area as a non-place, and further strengthened the disassociation of the past and present of a particular geographical region (one which, whether relevantly or irrelevantly happened to be at the moment either at war, or without diplomatic relations to the United States), while paradoxically presenting these cultures as typically "Oriental."

My insistence on the political ramifications of this exhibition through its omission of names from the map may seem unwarranted or at best misguided; however, references to it in the popular press and leading newspapers in the United States indicate that its message was successfully deployed and understood. The following is an excerpt from an article published in *The Houston Chronicle*, after a US air attack on Iraq:

Before initiating his pre-inaugural raids on Iraq (Clinton) should have visited the exhibition at New York's Metropolitan Museum of Art called 'The Royal City of Susa.' Had he attended the exhibit, he would have seen that, like Saddam Hussein, the kings and queens of ancient Mesopotamia lived in mortal fear of losing face before their enemies.

(Makiya 1993)

The writer clearly associated an oppressive antique despotism with the dictatorship of Saddam Hussein, although confusing Iranian for Mesopotamian artefacts in his comparison. This is hardly surprising considering the exclusion of the names from the exhibition maps and descriptive texts. The omission of the names and the confluence of Iran and Iraq as one despotic entity is traceable to an established Western concept of the East which is still intact from the days of Montesquieu – namely, that everything East of the Mediterranean is one vast oppressive country. Because of the omission of the names and the nature of the display, the writer, Kanan Makiya, came away from this exhibition with a general vague notion of violence and oppression which he was able to apply generically and racially to Middle Eastern dictatorship – the contemporary oriental despotism.

The extraterrestrial Orient

The creation of a historical narrative in which space and time became transcendental horizons for the Being – Mesopotamia, was part of the larger discursive project through which Europe attempted its mastery of the colonised. The narrative of the progress of civilisation was an invention of European imperialism, a way of constructing history in its own image and claiming precedence for Western culture. But this narrative of world civilisation is a representation and one which necessarily requires what is described by Adorno and Horkheimer, as "the organised control of mimesis" (1944: 180). The economy of rhetorical structures in this mimetic organisation certainly depended upon prefigurative tropological languages. However, it also involved a metaphysical cartography that provided a conceptual terrain necessary for the narration. And the charting of an extraterrestrial Mesopotamia was essential for the success of this representational enterprise. Edward Said points out that "in the history of colonial invasion, maps are always first drawn by the victors, since maps are instruments of conquest. Geography is therefore the art of war" (Said 1996: 28). Historical cartography is also drawn according to the requirements of the victorious, and archaeology is instrumental in the mapping of that terrain.

Likewise, representation in archaeological writing is not a duplication of reality: it is a mimetic activity that cannot be neatly separated from questions of politics and ideology. The ancient Greeks were well aware that mimesis always involves distortion but by some transposition we have come to think of mimesis as an exact realistic copy.[9] In the *Poetics*, Aristotle defines representation as differing in three ways: in object, manner, and means of representation. The first is the thing or action which is represented, the second is the way in which it can be represented, and the last is the medium of representation. While the choices involved in the first and last aspect of representation are addressed in Mesopotamian archaeological theory, the second remains mostly disregarded, any mention of it construed as a radical subversive act. The image of Mesopotamia, upon which we still depend, was necessary for a march of progress from East to West, a concept of world cultural development that is explicitly Eurocentric and imperialist. Perhaps the time has come that we, Middle Eastern scholars and scholars of the ancient Middle East both, dissociate ourselves from this imperial triumphal procession and look toward a redefinition of the land in between.

Notes

1 The bibliography on this subject is vast but see Said (1993).
2 For the application of the Freudian concept of the uncanny to historiographic analysis see especially M. de Certeau (1975); H. K. Bhabha (1994).
3 As an example of this type of scholarship see Lewis (1996).
4 Encyclopaedia of Islam (1938), vol. 2, part 1 (H–J), Leiden: E. J. Brill, 515–19.
5 In 1898, for example, the Deutsche Orient Gessellschaft stated that these were the reasons for the newly established journal, *Orientalistische Literaturzeitung*, vol. 1(2), 36, 1898.
6 See Raymond Williams (1973: 3–16) for the concept of the deflection of oppositional "emergent" cultures by the hegemonic center. See also Edward Said, "Opponents, Audiences, Constituencies and Community" in *The Politics of Interpretation*, W. J. T. Mitchell (ed.), pp. 7–32.
7 Similar critiques have been made regarding the assimilation of postcolonial theory into what Stephen Slemon calls "an object of desire for critical practice: as a shimmering talisman that in itself has the power to confer political legitimacy onto specific forms of institutionalized labor" (Slemon 1994).
8 These are three of four master tropes defined and analysed by Hayden White in his *Metahistory* (1973). See also Paul Ricoeur (1984) for the function of mimesis in historical writing.
9 The current usage of the term in the English language according to *The Oxford English Dictionary* refers to very close, accurate, resemblance.

Bibliography

Adorno, T. and Horkheimer, M. (1944) *Dialectic of Enlightenment* (trans. J. Cumming 1972), New York: Herder & Herder.

Althusser, L. (1972) *Montesquieu, Rousseau, Marx* (trans. B. Brewster 1982), London: Verso.

Bahrani, Z. (1995) "Assault and Abduction: the fate of the royal image in the Ancient Near East," *Art History* 18, 3: 363–82.

Bhabha, H. K. (1994) *The Location of Culture*, London: Routledge.

Bohrer, F. N. (1994) "The Times and Spaces of History: Representation, Assyria, and the British Museum" in D. J. Sherman and I. Rogoff (eds) *Museum Culture*, Minneapolis: University of Minnesota Press.

Cooper, J. S. (1992) "From Mosul to Manila: Early Approaches to Funding Ancient Near Eastern Studies Research in the United States" in A. C. Gunter (ed.) *The Construction of the Ancient Near East, Special Issue of Culture and History* 11, Copenhagen: Academic Press, pp. 133–59.

de Certeau, M. (1975) *The Writing of History* (trans. T. Conley 1988), New York: Columbia University Press.

Fergusson, J. (1850) *The Palaces of Nineveh and Persepolis Restored: An Essay in Ancient Assyrian and Persian Architecture*, Delhi: Goyal Offset Printers (reprinted 1981).

Gramsci, A. (1987) *The Prison Notebooks* (Q. Hoare and G. Nowell Smith (eds and trans.), New York: International Publishers.

Gunter, A. C. (ed.) (1992) *The Construction of the Ancient Near East, Special Issue of Culture and History* 11, Copenhagen: Academic Press.

Hegel, G. W. F. (1956) *The Philosophy of History* (trans. J. Sibree), New York: Dover Publications.

Heidegger, M. (1962) *Being and Time* (trans. J. Macquarrie and E. Robinson), New York: HarperCollins.

Hodder, I. *et al.* (eds) (1995) *Interpreting Archaeology: Finding Meaning in the Past*, London: Routledge.

Jenkins, I. (1992) *Archaeologists and Aesthetes*, London: British Museum Publications.

Lewis, B. (1994) *The Shaping of the Modern Middle East*, New York: Oxford University Press.

—— (1996) *The Middle East: A Brief History of the Last 2000 Years*, New York: Scribner.

Mitchell, W. J. T. (1983) *The Politics of Interpretation*, Chicago: University of Chicago Press.

Oppenheim, A. L. (1964) *Mesopotamia, Portrait of a Dead Civilization*, Chicago: The University of Chicago Press.

Pittman, H. (1996) "The White Obelisk and the Problem of Historical Narrative in the Art of Assyria," *The Art Bulletin* LXXVIII, 2: 334–55.

Ricoeur, P. (1984) *Time and Narrative* (trans. K. McLaughlin and D. Pellauer), Chicago: The University of Chicago Press.

Russell, J. M. (1991) *Sennacherib's Palace Without Rival at Nineveh*, Chicago: The University of Chicago Press.

Said, E. W. (1978) *Orientalism*, New York: Vintage Books.

—— (1993) *Culture and Imperialism*, New York: Vintage Books.

—— (1996) *Peace and its Discontents*, New York: Vintage Books.

Shanks, M. and Tilley, C. (1987) *Re-Constructing Archaeology: Theory and Practice*, London: Routledge.

Slemon, S. (1994) "The Scramble for Post-colonialism" in C. Tiffin and A. Lawson (eds) *De-Scribing Empire: Post-Colonialism and Textuality*, London: Routledge.

Stolper, M. W. (1992) "On Why and How," in A. C. Gunter (ed.) *The Construction of the Ancient Near East, Special Issue of Culture and History* 11, Copenhagen: Academic Press, pp. 13–22.

White, H. (1973) *Metahistory*, Baltimore, MD: The Johns Hopkins University Press.

Williams, R. (1973) "Base and Superstructure in Marxist Cultural Theory," *New Left Review* 82: 3–16.

Winter, I. J. (1981) "Royal Rhetoric and the Development of Historical Narrative in Neo-Assyrian Reliefs," *Visual Communication* 7, 2: 2–38.

Chapter 9

Whose game is it anyway?

The political and social transformations of American Biblical Archaeology

Neil Asher Silberman

Is American Biblical Archaeology dying? By the final decade of the twentieth century, the signs of morbidity were unmistakable to some. Once dependable sources of government and private funding were increasingly difficult to come by. Job prospects for a new generation of scholars had turned steadily bleaker as many faculty positions in American universities formerly held by specialists in Biblical Archaeology were either being eliminated or filled by theologians and historians. To many worried observers a proud era of American overseas exploration seemed to be ending with a critical transformation of the character of American Biblical Archaeology's guiding institution, the academic consortium known as *The American Schools of Oriental Research* (ASOR). Since its establishment in 1900, ASOR had sponsored and supervised scores of American archaeological projects in what its members called the lands of the Bible – namely the area of modern Lebanon, Israel, and Jordan, with occasional forays into southern Syria, Yemen, and Iraq (King 1983). The archaeological achievements of its members were impressive, from historical geography, to refinement of excavation methodology, to biblical history and epigraphy (Meyers 1997). No less important was its modern religious function. Over the years, ASOR had forged an ecumenical coalition of American Protestant, Catholic, and Jewish scholars in a shared project of largely non-denominational biblical research (Silberman 1989: 244–8). Yet as ASOR prepared to celebrate its centennial, it seemed to be struggling for survival. The traditional unity of American archaeological efforts in the 'lands of the Bible' now had to contend with the political and economic realities of a patchwork of increasingly self-confident modern Middle Eastern nations, each with their own archaeological agendas and historical ideologies (ibid.: 1995).

While the ASOR research institutes in Nicosia (Harris 1989), Amman (Bikai 1993) and Jerusalem (Gitin 1997a) had each adapted to local conditions, gained enthusiastic local and international supporters, and were *individually* thriving, the umbrella organisation seemed to be drifting, searching for a coherent institutional identity. Throughout the post-World War II era, ASOR had been a dominant institutional force in the archaeology of the region. Yet with the rise of local departments of antiquities and large numbers of locally trained archaeologists, and with the growing influence of international organisations for archaeological preservation and tourist development (Killebrew 1997), ASOR was no longer quite so dominant. In most cases, its projects were now carried out in co-operation with local government agencies, universities or other foreign schools (Meyers 1997: 96–8). The focus of its members was no longer fixed only on biblical sites. Excavations, surveys and detailed studies of ancient technology, agriculture and environment were only occasionally used to illustrate or elucidate specific passages in the biblical text (a goal repeatedly emphasised as central to American Biblical Archaeology in Wright 1962). Indeed, the traditional biblical emphasis of ASOR seemed to be giving way to a more general anthropological and historical orientation. In 1997, ASOR separated its own annual meeting from the much larger annual conference of the Society of Biblical Literature (Jacobs 1997). And in 1998, ASOR's popular journal *Biblical Archaeologist*, long a staple of Sunday School libraries and generations of armchair archaeologists, voluntarily shed its scriptural associations, henceforth bearing the more general geographical designation *Near Eastern Archaeology* (Hopkins 1996).

To some, these changes represented a welcome expression of ASOR's widening horizons (Seger 1997). To others, they were symptoms of a wider and deeply disturbing cultural change. One particularly embittered observer was Professor William G. Dever of the University of Arizona, a long-time leader and officer of

ASOR, who surveyed the state of the discipline in a controversial public jeremiad entitled 'The Death of a Discipline' (1995). For years Dever had been a powerful voice within ASOR, calling for the abandonment of its traditional biblical orientation and for the adoption of processualist understandings of culture change and hypothesis-driven research designs characteristic of the New Archaeology (Dever 1980). Arguing that ASOR's biblical orientation had caused it to drift out of the archaeological mainstream during the 1960s and 1970s he had trained a new generation of American scholars in a more anthropologically-oriented brand of archaeology that he insistently called Syro-Palestinian archaeology in preference to what he considered the outmoded and theologically skewed name, Biblical Archaeology (ibid.: 1985). His efforts resulted in the creation of a significant new trend within the discipline, even if his students' scholarly output had not effected the sweeping epistemological revolution that he had hoped (ibid.: 1992: 364–6). Other, more traditional, biblically-oriented archaeological approaches had continued to exist within ASOR and the number of Israeli, Jordanian, Cypriot and Palestinian participants in ASOR conferences and field projects was growing – bringing with them a wide range of methodological, national, and cultural sensibilities. To Dever, the rising status of these non-American scholars within the discipline, combined with the steady erosion of financial support for American scholars and the loss of US university positions, endangered the leading role that Americans had always played in Biblical Archaeology. Writing about the current archaeological situation in the Middle East, Dever (1995: 52–3) bitterly noted that 'we are becoming increasingly marginalised, often reduced to the status of spectators at a game we invented.'

But whose game was it? What were its rules? In the months that followed Dever's open letter, a number of prominent scholars weighed in on the issue, publicly debating whether Dever's grim analysis was right (among many, Ben-Tor 1996; Levy 1996; Wiseman 1996). Some joined him in sadly draping black crepe on a long and noble enterprise now dying from a lack of support by American academia. Others proudly crowed that the discipline had never been more alive and well. The most biting rejoinder came from Professor C. C. Lamberg-Karlovsky of the Peabody Museum of Harvard who had long served as an honorary trustee of ASOR but who nevertheless came out of an entirely different archaeological world. In his pioneering excavations at Tepe Yahya in Iran (1986) and in his continuing explorations of the Bronze Age cultures of Central Asia (1994), Lamberg-Karlovsky's interest was in the emergence of complex society, completely unconnected with the goal of illuminating the biblical narrative. Thus, he cast scorn on Dever's appeals for support for American Biblical or 'Syro-Palestinian' archaeology, both of which he considered to be hopelessly parochial disciplines. Asserting that Dever had erred in equating 'a small and provincial aspect' of Middle Eastern archaeology with the whole, he wrote that 'if Biblical

Archaeology is dying, the reasons must be sought within that sector of research and not within the larger field of archaeology. Perhaps there is a biological law operating here: a narrow provincialism with a context of over-specialisation frequently leads to extinction' (Lamberg-Karlovsky 1996).

Professor Lamberg-Karlovsky's social Darwinist metaphor may have been effective as a stinging rhetorical device but it betrayed a profound blindness about the modern social function of all types of archaeology. The death or continued existence of American Biblical Archaeology was not a matter of the silent hand of evolution selecting what was intellectually the fittest and, therefore, worthiest to survive. It was the result of constantly changing political and economic priorities in twentieth-century global politics that indirectly determined *which* kinds of archaeology were most useful or effective or eloquent in addressing modern concerns. Whether Dever or any of his respondents grasped the situation the seeming rise and fall of American Biblical Archaeology was not due to a lack of enthusiasm by supporters or by the growth of competing archaeological institutions abroad. The day of unquestioned American predominance in Biblical Archaeology had given way to an age of intellectual and national diversity. Biblical Archaeology was not dying. It was changing. And the survival of ASOR would be entirely dependent on its ability to redefine its essential mission to reflect that emerging reality.

Errand to the wilderness: the genesis of American Biblical Archaeology

On one point Professor Dever was clearly correct: there is a distinct brand of American Near Eastern Archaeology that cannot be simply lumped together with other branches of the discipline, even those that happen to enjoy a current boom of opportunity and financial support in other areas of the modern Middle East. In contrast to the classical antiquarianism of the American Institute of Archaeology, the philological-epigraphic interests of the Oriental Institute of the University of Chicago or even the social-functionalist anthropology of the recent Harvard Peabody Museum expeditions, the ideological rationale of American Biblical Archaeology has always been primarily connected with the construction and elaboration of a modern ecumenical consciousness. With participants drawn from a wide range of American seminaries and university departments of religion its emphasis has long been on the study of civilisations and sites directly relevant to the shared appreciation of the Bible and the early history of Judaism and Christianity. The professionalism of the discipline and the increasing sophistication of its excavation methods have not affected this basic social function. Despite Dever's (1995: 51–2) assertions to the contrary it could be argued that with the exception of a brief boom period in the 1970s and 1980s, biblical archaeologists never held more than a handful of full-time university posts. Their primarily scholarly identity was as biblical scholars who went to the Middle East to dig during the summer and therefore had a vocational activity underlining the basic theological nature of their intellectual quest. Combining meticulous excavation with textual study, they sought to delineate the character of the civilisations that produced the unique historical events, personalities and scriptures that comprised the core of modern religious faith.

As I have argued at length elsewhere (Silberman 1982), Western archaeological exploration of Palestine must be viewed as a part of the larger Western penetration of the region yet, from its inception, American Biblical Archaeology filled a particular ideological niche. Throughout the nineteenth century, the most active and powerful participants in archaeological exploration were large, well-funded expeditions fielded by the main imperial powers with tangible imperial goals. Beginning with Napoleon's 1797 invasion of Egypt and continuing until the outbreak of World War I, British, German, Austrian and French scholars served as agents of direct political influence in the territorial heart of the vast, yet disintegrating Ottoman Empire. In marginal areas like Egypt and Mesopotamia where the remains of ancient civilisations offered monumental remains for the taking, great archaeological finds transported back to the national museums of Europe became symbols of imperialistic advancement and national prestige. Yet the government of the United States, fully occupied with civil war and expansion throughout the Western hemisphere, saw little political capital to be gained by a direct Middle Eastern rivalry with the European powers (for the embarrassing failure of the short-lived 'American Palestine Exploration Society' see Moulton 1928). As a result, the nineteenth-century archaeological explorations of Americans in the region were almost entirely unofficial, carried out as aspects of private pilgrimage and missionary work (Davis 1977).

American Biblical Archaeology was thus linked from its earliest days to the American missionary movement which was, before 1856, the sole organised American presence in the Levant (Tibawi 1963). As William Hutchinson (1987) has shown in his recent survey of the institutional development of the various American missionary organisations, the American goal, particularly in areas where territorial conquest was not an option, was always largely ideological. As elsewhere, American missionaries in the Middle East embarked upon a combined quest for technological and spiritual 'modernisation' that they hoped would result in the millennial transformation of the region (Field 1969). In Lebanon and Palestine, the representatives of the American Board of Commissioners for Foreign Missions (ABCFM) actively sought to expand their practical knowledge of local geography and language so that they could more effectively transform the lives of the region's inhabitants. American Biblical Archaeology was born in this context. In 1838 and again in 1852, Professor Edward Robinson of the Union

Theological Seminary travelled through Palestine accompanied by the Reverend Eli Smith of the ABCFM mission station in Beirut. In the course of just a few weeks the two men identified and mapped scores of biblical sites on the modern landscape thereby initiating the modern archaeological study of the land of the Bible and its historical geography (Hitchcock and Smith 1863). The Holy Land, long a theological concept, now became an archaeological and cartographic reality. Yet the ancient sites and buried artefacts of the land of the Bible did not possess a single, dogmatic meaning. They could, and would, be used to illustrate a wide range of theological, ideological – and ultimately political – themes (Vogel 1993).

Studied ambiguity of meaning and diversity of interests characterised the first generations of American Biblical archaeologists yet, by the 1890s, that kind of unofficial Biblical Archaeology of individual explorers and pilgrims, could hardly compete with a new corps of professionals. Embarking upon expeditions that were lavishly supported by great industrialists' fortunes or by the colonial departments of European empires, a growing caste of professional scholars and museum curators opened ancient tombs and laid bare ancient cities to harvest the artworks of Mesopotamia, Meso-America, Egypt, and Greece (Patterson 1995: 37–53). The informal methods of geographical exploration in the land of the Bible seemed hopelessly outmoded, and if Biblical Archaeology ever experienced a period of crisis in funding and opportunities for professional advancement, the 1890s and not the 1990s must be recognised as perhaps the deepest crisis of all. In his presidential address to the 1895 meeting of the Society of Biblical Literature, Professor J. Henry Thayer of Harvard forcefully called for more organised support for American scholarship in Palestine in particular (quoted in King 1983: 25). For except for occasional collecting forays by resident US consuls and monographs on biblical topography by visiting ministers, archaeology in the land of the Bible – though perhaps begun by Edward Robinson – had clearly become someone else's game.

Once again, the tactical course taken by American Biblical Archaeology was guided not by imperial models, but by the example of American missionaries. By the close of the nineteenth century, small denominational missionary groups like the Congregationalist-Presbyterian ABCFM faced crushing competition to their work posed by well-funded European government delegations, official church foundations and educational systems with transparently imperialist goals. As a result, the various denominational American missionary organisations decided temporarily to put aside differences of doctrine and ritual in service of a common American goal. The result was the creation of large ecumenical confederations, dispatching preachers, social workers and civil engineers in vast armies in the 'spiritual equivalent of imperialism', through the recruitment of eager (and 'amateur') missionaries from dozens of American colleges and seminaries

(Hutchinson 1987: 91–124). The archaeological response to the great power competition was almost identical. The establishment in 1900 of the American School of Oriental Research in Jerusalem, with its sponsorship by twenty one universities, colleges and seminaries (ranging from Harvard to the Union Theological Seminary to the Episcopal Divinity School to Auburn Theological Seminary to Hebrew Union College) represented an unprecedented act of ecumenical coalition building. And what made this enterprise so revolutionary was its unabashed intellectual diversity, even if it was restricted to a fairly conservative view of the historicity of the biblical text. The constitution of ASOR declared that 'the School shall be open to duly qualified applicants of all races and both sexes, and shall be kept wholly free from obligations or preferences with respect to any religious denomination or literary institution' (quoted in King 1983: 27). Thus, at a time when an old style Biblical Archaeology seemed to be dying, the rules of the 'game' were rewritten to accommodate a wide coalition of groups – each with their specific orientations – within a single, evolving intellectual enterprise.

Expanding the mission: Albright and his followers

The experiment took some time to bear fruit, for in the years immediately following the opening of the American School of Oriental Research in Jerusalem, the men and women who arrived as its early scholars-in-residence comprised a haphazardly assembled collection of experts in Bible, Islam and Classical studies. Without any substantial government support or even library facilities equal to those of the British-sponsored Palestine Exploration Fund, the Deutsche Orient-Gesellschaft, or the French Dominican Ecole Biblique, the Americans were left on their own to take field trips throughout the country and carry out small-scale digs wherever they could (for a general description of this period, see King 1983 and Silberman 1993). A brief but impressive excavation at Samaria sponsored by Harvard University (1908–1910), with only perfunctory connections to ASOR (King 1983: 39–40), was the only exception to the otherwise modest scale of American archaeological work. With the British assumption of rule over Palestine after World War I, ASOR projects paled even further in comparison to the British excavations at Ashkelon and Dor directed by John Garstang, the director of the newly created Palestine Department of Antiquities. There was also a new series of large-scale projects mounted by American institutions outside the framework of ASOR: the expedition of the University of Pennsylvania to Beth Shean (1921–1925) and the massive dig begun at the site of Megiddo by the Oriental Institute of the University of Chicago, funded by John D. Rockefeller Jr. (1925–1939). Yet spurred on by the imagination and energy of William Foxwell Albright, ASOR's young resident director in Jerusalem, ASOR pressed on with small projects. And some might say that like the proverbial, tiny mammal scurrying on the forest floor at the feet of the great dinosaurs, a novel and resilient evolutionary form emerged.

William Foxwell Albright is without question the godfather of American Biblical Archaeology, even though his reputation has recently been tarnished, in retrospect, for some of the specific archaeological and historical missteps he made (Dever 1993). Far more significant for the history of the discipline and for its future, however, was his creation of an entirely new way to do archaeology in the land of the Bible, as a self-consciously ecumenical ritual of religious scholarship (Albright 1964). In an earlier paper, I detailed the circumstances under which Albright became the director of ASOR in the 1920s and forged an unlikely partnership with an elderly seminary president from St Louis named Melvin Grove Kyle (Silberman 1993). It is important to stress that their colourful 1924 expedition to the Dead Sea, joined by scholarly representatives of virtually every ethnic community in Jerusalem (Kyle 1928: 24–6), helped transform archaeology from being the exclusive province of great museums, great powers and great fortunes, into a co-operative enterprise available to seminary students, ministers and religiously-minded amateurs of every faith. In strictly scholarly terms, the physical search for Sodom and Gomorrah – with expectations that the submerged remains of those sinful cities would be found precisely as described in Genesis – was a hopelessly naïve undertaking. Yet it proved far more viable as a model for future research designs than the impossibly ambitious excavation strategies of the great expeditions. Their intention was to dig the great tells down to bedrock, systematically shearing off their superimposed stratigraphic levels until nothing was left (King 1983: 77–8). The staffs of Megiddo and Beth Shean would eventually abandon their excavations long before reaching the bottom and disperse to other, shallower and richer archaeological hunting grounds in Egypt and Iraq. Yet the amateur adventurers and biblical scholars led by Albright would remain in the Holy Land for decades to search for other, smaller biblical cities and thereby to build a modern discipline.

Albright's subsequent excavations at the site of Tell Beit Mirsim (1926–32) are remembered primarily for his refinement of ancient pottery chronology – closely linked to events of biblical history (Greenberg 1997). Yet if there is an identifiable American 'game' of Biblical Archaeology it reached its recognisable form at Tell Beit Mirsim, not only as a certain excavation methodology but also as a social exercise of strenuous antiquarian exploration and pious religious devotion open to a wide spectrum of participants. At a time when the direction of the major British and American university excavations was entrusted to a small cadre of professional diggers and colonial functionaries, Albright and Kyle gathered together a staff of seminarians, graduate students and fellow biblical scholars from across the

United States (Running and Freedman 1975: 143–63). And although the relations with the local Arab workers were hardly less exploitative than those of the large excavations, even if on a much smaller scale (Silberman 1993: 13–14), the experience of archaeology was no longer quite so aristocratic or genteel. A participant in those early ASOR digs wrote about the once-in-a-lifetime experience available to ministers- and scholars-in-training through the fellowships and scholarships of the American School. He noted that 'a man who has the proper historical and philological preparation and interest can find no better opportunity to learn the methods and value of archaeology than to spend a summer thus in the bright sunshine and invigorating air of Palestine' (McCown 1943: 86). Slowly, under Albright's expansive vision, the circle of participation was widened far beyond the confines of American Christian manhood. In the 1920s he encouraged the work of a generation of Palestinian Arab scholars to further their research on local folkways and folklore in the hopes that it might provide insight into details of the biblical text (Silberman 1993: 10). Likewise, the American Jewish scholars, Cyrus Gordon and Nelson Glueck, became team members of the Tell Beit Mirsim excavations – as did, for a time, the Palestinian Jewish scholar, Benjamin Mazar.

The fact that Dr Nelson Glueck of the Hebrew Union College, an ordained rabbi, served as director of the American School in Jerusalem on and off for almost twelve years in the 1930s and 1940s (Gitin 1997b) is clear evidence of how great the ecumenical elasticity of ASOR had become. A 1929 *New York Times* account of the activities of ASOR found religious diversity to be its most noteworthy feature:

> To one who reads and hears constantly about the bitter strife between different religions and sects, and between conservative and liberal members of each sect, the very existence of such an institution may seem incredible. Yet such an American institution is now approaching its thirtieth anniversary, after a history unmarred by a single dispute of a religious nature.

(King 1983: 84)

The Golden Age was regrettably brief, for in 1948, the end of the British Mandate and the outbreak of war between the newly created State of Israel and its Arab neighbours, altered the ever-widening ecumenical direction that American Biblical Archaeology had taken over the years. The continuing hatreds of the Arab–Israeli War made co-operative work across the ceasefire lines impossible in the 1950s and 1960s. And while Albright continued to visit and cultivate scholarly contacts his archaeological protégés in Israel (Running and Freedman 1975: 275–84), the main focus of ASOR projects with its headquarters and library located in what had become the Jordanian sector of Jerusalem, shifted to Jordan and the West Bank (King 1983: 111–31).

Whatever attempts might have been made to maintain the old ecumenical coalition, the new political realities came to dominate. With most Jewish scholar members of ASOR sent on a special fellowship program to Israel, a new generation of ASOR leaders was in the meantime trained across the border in Jordan at the excavations of Tell el-Balata, biblical Shechem, near Nablus, from 1956 to 1968. Indeed, the staff list of the Shechem Expedition members reads like a Who's Who of modern American Biblical Archaeology: Paul and Nancy Lapp, Albert Glock, Lawrence Toombs, Edward Campbell, Robert Bull, Joe Seeger and William Dever, among others (King 1983; Wright 1965: 141–5). And although a distinctive 'American' method of excavation was perfected at this excavation, it could be argued that the relative isolation of the project and the homogeneity of its conservative Christian core staff members represented something of an aberration – not final refinement – of the traditional American game. In 1964, a major ASOR excavation was initiated in co-operation with the Hebrew Union College at Tell Gezer in Israel, but the politically-imposed separation between those ASOR members who worked in Jordan and those who worked in Israel remained intact.

The 1967 war and the Israeli conquest of the West Bank therefore constituted a major turning point in the history of ASOR. With the Jerusalem School and the West Bank excavation sites now suddenly in territory under Israeli occupation, important long-range decisions had to be made. The establishment of research centres in Amman (1968) and Nicosia (1968), in addition to the original American School in Jerusalem (now renamed the W. F. Albright Institute of Archaeological Research), ushered in an era of decentralisation rather than fragmentation for American Biblical Archaeology. Even if the conduct of archaeological work was still hindered by political tensions and unspoken restrictions on the free movement of scholars, there were at least the physical facilities for a vastly expanded American presence in the Levant. And the old tradition of coalition building was taken up with renewed energy as through the 1970s and 1980s, as the students and staffs of the various ASOR research institutes reached out to local scholars and governmental agencies. Professor Sy Gitin in Jerusalem delicately balanced the long-standing connections of the Albright Institute with both Israelis and Palestinians. Professor Stewart Swiny at the Cyprus-American Research Institute in Nicosia developed close working relationships with the staff of the Cyprus Department of Antiquities, especially under the tense atmosphere which followed the 1974 Turkish invasion. And in Jordan, Professor James Sauer and Dr David McCreery devoted themselves to the preservation and presentation of the heritage of the people of Jordan, a tradition that has been energetically followed up by Dr Pierre Bikai. The ecumenical coalition grew steadily larger as Israeli, Jordanian, Cypriot and eventually Palestinian students and scholars were encouraged to participate in ASOR projects. And despite the danger that the ongoing Arab–Israeli conflict could fatally splinter the membership of ASOR at moments of crisis or at the outbreak of hostilities, the ecumenical ideal survived.

The sheer diversity of ASOR's Middle Eastern and Eastern Mediterranean connections, both personal and professional, did not allow a single national, religious or ethnic chauvinism to prevail.

The continuing death and rebirth of Biblical Archaeology

Today, with its eclectic mixture of geographical locations, methodological and theoretical perspectives and close practical co-operation with Israeli, Palestinian, Jordanian and Cypriot officials and universities, the only element about ASOR that is dying is its strictly American character. It has become in fact – if not in formal constitution – an international consortium devoted to the archaeological excavation of the lands of the Bible without being committed, as an institution, to any particular religious understanding, national interest or historical ideology. The loss of American faculty positions and relative rise in influence of non-Americans in the field are symptomatic of that emerging reality, even if it has not yet been fully articulated or even acknowledged in official ASOR publications. The list of international participants at the 1997 annual meeting indicates the continually widening scope of the enterprise. While some may bemoan the end of strictly American leadership and the effect of Biblical Archaeology on American religious or cultural life (Dever 1995: 70), that is too sectarian a perspective. Although it has always been committed to a missionary-like vision of the modernisation of religious scholarship, American Biblical Archaeology has always been too diverse to be associated with one particular political or religious interest or goal.

This brand of archaeology certainly does not represent a side branch off the main line of evolutionary progress leading, as Professor Lamberg-Karlovsky suggested, to inevitable extinction. On the contrary, in an era when World Bank heritage projects and economic development plans are often transforming archaeology into an enterprise primarily aimed at attracting tourist dollars (Silberman 1995), or playing a role in the economic development of formerly outlying regions, the projects sponsored by ASOR offer a refreshingly vigorous clash of perspectives, intentions and outcomes. It may indeed be true that all modern archaeology is, by its very nature, a subtle didactic tool for the cultivation of industrial consciousness among all peoples by instilling a sense of sequential time, technological progress and increasing efficiency (Patterson 1987). But of all the archaeologies in the Middle East that produce evolutionary insights or patriotic symbols, the diversity of approaches encouraged by ASOR in its current, decentralised incarnation is unique.

Professor Dever and the others fatally misidentified the 'game' that they invented by confusing a process with a particular nationality. Over the decades, the unifying ideal of ASOR's region-wide scope has withstood the centrifugal force of the rising nationalisms and ethnic suspicions. It has even withstood the seductive appeal of the universalising scientism of New Archaeology. There is no question that an increasing number of ASOR excavation projects are carried out in co-operation (sometimes even as junior partners) with Israeli, Jordanian and Cypriot sponsors. There is no question that the employment prospects of American scholars are affected by the same brutal budgetary cutbacks that have affected all the humanities. But the present transformations of ASOR do not constitute omens of its imminent death. In its stubborn refusal to surrender itself entirely to the authority of the dominant archaeological paradigms and practices of each historical period, American Biblical Archaeology has always been dying. And its continuing survival is a testimony to the possibility that a certain brand of archaeology can survive by maintaining a coalition that attempts to bridge the particular interests of its members without homogenising them. It is impossible to know how long ASOR can survive without being pulled apart by its constituent interests or subsumed in the universalising whirlpool of 'global' archaeology. For in the brave new world of the twenty first century where transnational corporate development and the secular religion of industrial progress will increasingly dominate the archaeological agenda of every developing nation, archaeology itself may no longer be able to be claimed as *any* scholar's game.

Bibliography

Albright, W. F. (1964) *History, Archaeology, and Christian Humanism*, New York: McGraw-Hill.

Ben-Tor, A. (1996) 'Hebrew U's Ben-Tor responds to Dever', *Biblical Archaeology Review* 22, 2: 22.

Bikai, P. (ed.) (1993) *ACOR, The First Twenty-Five Years: The American Center of Oriental Research, 1968–1993*, Amman: American Center of Oriental Research.

Davis, M. (ed.) (1977) *With Eyes Toward Zion: Scholars Colloquium on American Holy Land Studies*, New York: Arno Press.

Dever, W. G. (1980) 'The impact of the New Archaeology on Syro-Palestinian Archaeology', *Bulletin of the American Schools of Oriental Research* 242: 15–29.

—— (1985) 'Syro-Palestinian and Biblical Archaeology', in D. A. Knight and G. M. Tucker (eds) *The Hebrew Bible and its Modern Interpreters*, Philadelphia: Fortress Press, pp. 31–74.

—— (1992) 'Syro-Palestinian and Biblical Archaeology', in D. N. Freedman (ed.) *The Anchor Bible Dictionary*, Vol. 1., New York: Doubleday, pp. 354–67.

—— (1993) 'What remains of the house that Albright built?', *Biblical Archaeologist* 56: 25–35.

—— (1995) 'The death of a discipline', *Biblical Archaeology Review* 21, 5: 50–5, 70.

—— (1997) 'Biblical Archaeology', in E. M. Meyers (ed.) *The Oxford Encyclopedia of Archaeology in the Near East*, Vol. 1, New York: Oxford University Press, pp. 315–19.

Field, J. A. (1969) *America and the Mediterranean World, 1776–1882*, Princeton: Princeton University Press.

Gitin, S. (1997a) 'Albright Institute of Archaeological Research', in E. M. Meyers (ed.) *The Oxford Encyclopedia of Archaeology in the Near East*, Vol. 1, New York: Oxford University Press, pp. 62–3.

—— (1997b) 'Nelson Glueck', in E. M. Meyers (ed.) *The Oxford Encyclopedia of Archaeology in the Near East*, Vol. 1, New York: Oxford University Press, pp. 415–16.

Greenberg, R. (1997) 'Tell Beit Mirsim', in E. M. Meyers (ed.) *The Oxford Encyclopedia of Archaeology in the Near East*, Vol. 1, New York: Oxford University Press, pp. 295–7.

Harris, C. U. (1989) 'The role of CAARI in Cyprus', *Biblical Archaeologist* 52: 157–62.

Hitchcock, R. D. and Smith, H. B. (1863) *The Life, Writings, and Character of Edward Robinson*, New York: A. D. F. Randolph.

Hopkins, D. (1996) 'Name change voted for BA', *American Schools of Oriental Research Newsletter* 46, 4: 7.

Hutchinson, W. R. (1987) *Errand to the World: American Protestant Thought and Foreign Missions*, Chicago: University of Chicago Press.

Jacobs, P. F. (1997) Napa, California: the 1997 Annual Meeting site, *American Schools of Oriental Research Newsletter*, 47, 1: 1.

Killebrew, A. (1997) 'Development and archaeology', in E. M. Meyers (ed.) *The Oxford Encyclopedia of Archaeology in the Near East*, Vol. 2, New York: Oxford University Press, pp. 151–215.

King, P. J. (1983) *American Archaeology in the Mideast*, Philadelphia: American Schools of Oriental Research.

Kyle, M. G. (1928) *Explorations at Sodom: The Story of Ancient Sodom in the Light of Modern Research*, London: The Religious Tract Society.

Lamberg-Karlovsky, C. C. (1986) *Excavations at Tepe Yahya, Iran, 1967–1975*, Cambridge, MA: Peabody Museum of Archaeology and Ethnology.

—— (1994) 'The Bronze Age Khanates of Central Asia', *Antiquity* 68: 398–405.

—— (1996) 'The sky is not falling', *Biblical Archaeology Review* 22, 1: 10.

Levy, T. E. (1996) 'Alive and well in San Diego', *Biblical Archaeology Review* 22, 2: 64–5.

McCown, C. C. (1943) *The Ladder of Progress in Palestine*, New York: Harper.

Meyers, E. M. (1997) 'American Schools of Oriental Research', in E. M. Meyers (ed.) *The Oxford Encyclopedia of Archaeology in the Near East*, Vol. 1, New York: Oxford University Press, pp. 94–8.

Moulton, W. J. (1928) 'The American Palestine Exploration Society', *Annual of the American Schools of Oriental Research* 8: 55–69.

Patterson, T. C. (1987) 'Development, Ecology, and Marginal Utility in Anthropology', *Dialectical Anthropology* 15: 15–31.

—— (1995) *Toward a Social History of Archaeology in the United States*, Fort Worth, TX: Harcourt-Brace.

Ra'anan, U. (1976) *The Frontiers of a Nation*, Westport, CT: Hyperion Press.

Robinson, E. (1841) *Biblical Researches in Palestine, Mount Sinai, and Arabia Petraea*, 3 vols, Boston: Crocker and Brewster.

Running, L. G. and Freedman, D. N. (1975) *William Foxwell Albright: A Twentieth-Century Genius*, New York: Two Continents Publishing Group.

Seger, J. D. (1997) 'Not the end for BA!', *American Schools of Oriental Research Newsletter* 47, 2: 5.

Silberman, N. A. (1982) *Digging for God and Country*, New York: Alfred A. Knopf.

—— (1989) *Between Past and Present*, New York: Henry Holt.

—— (1991) 'Desolation and restoration: the impact of a Biblical concept on Near Eastern Archaeology', *Biblical Archaeologist* 54, 2: 76–87.

—— (1993) 'Visions of the future: Albright in Jerusalem, 1919–1929', *Biblical Archaeologist* 56, 1: 8–16.

—— (1995) 'Promised lands and chosen peoples: the politics and poetics of archaeological narrative', in P. L. Kohl and C. Fawcett (eds) *Nationalism, Politics, and the Practice of Archaeology*, Cambridge: Cambridge University Press, pp. 249–62.

Tibawi, A. L. (1963) *American Interests in Syria 1800–1901*, Oxford: Oxford University Press.

Vogel, L. I. (1993) *To See a Promised Land: Americans and the Holy Land in the Nineteenth Century*, University Park, PA: Pennsylvania State University Press.

Wiseman, J. (1996) 'Crisis in Near Eastern studies?', *Archaeology* 49, 1: 14.

Wright, G. E. (1962) *Biblical Archaeology*, Philadelphia: Westminster Press.

—— (1965) *Shechem: The Biography of a Biblical City*, New York: McGraw-Hill.

Chapter 10

The Gulf Arab states and their archaeology

D. T. Potts

Introduction

In a region as politically volatile as Western Asia it might seem superfluous to begin this chapter by reminding readers that the sociopolitical context of archaeology in this area has been continuously evolving since the days of Loftus and Layard. What is perhaps less obvious to those who have never seriously considered the specific situation of the Gulf Arab states is the *political* basis for the different paths of development taken by archaeology there in contrast to the rest of the Middle East. While it is certainly true that economic factors, such as greater disposable wealth, have conditioned the recent trajectory of archaeology in the Gulf states, the underlying political and historical factor which set in motion divergent paths of development can be summed up in one word: colonialism.

In the nineteenth century, a vast swathe of Western Asia lay under the domination of the Ottoman Empire. Although it is not customary to consider the Ottomans a colonial power, there can be no denying that Iraq, Syria, Lebanon, Jordan, Israel and portions of northwest Saudi Arabia were occupied by what can only be considered a foreign, imperial power. Not so the Gulf coast of Arabia, however. The presence throughout this area of an Ottoman administration, however corrupt and inefficient, meant that in many cases foreign diplomats, adventurers and scholars had a responsible authority with which to deal, and one need only consult contemporary accounts of archaeological research in Iraq, for example, to see that by the late 1880s and early 1890s the Director General of the Imperial Museum in Constantinople, the Minister of Public Instruction, and indeed the Sultan himself took a serious interest in archaeology. Hermann Hilprecht, director of the American excavations at Nippur, readily acknowledged 'the powerful support of the Ottoman government'; and on the recommendation of Hamdy-Bey, Director General of the Imperial Museum, 'the government issued orders to the numerous officials of the provinces in Asia Minor and Mesopotamia to guard carefully all antiquities that may exist, to report to the Ministry of Public Instruction all new discoveries, and, when required, to transport them safely to Constantinople' (Hilprecht 1896: 56, 86; see Özdoğan, Chapter 5).

These developments created conditions which were very different from those prevailing along the Gulf coast. Although nominally under Ottoman authority, the areas of what are today Kuwait and eastern Saudi Arabia scarcely recognised the Sublime Porte. In 1920, Philby could still speak of 'the anarchy which reigned under Turkish suzerainty' in northeastern Arabia (Philby 1920a: 448), while a few years later J. K. Wright characterised the situation by saying, 'The normal state of affairs is one of virtual anarchy' (Wright 1927: 178). To this must be added the situation created by the fanaticism of the Saudi followers of Ibn 'Abd al-Wahhab (the so-called 'Wahhabi' movement), with their invocation of *jihad* or Holy War which was directed 'against those who did not observe Islamic duties . . . against the extremism of the Shi'ah in venerating the *imams*, and against the alien traditions of Sufi orders' (al-Rashid 1981: 30). In a part of the world known generally for its intrepid travellers and explorers, it is telling that no one attempted to initiate any sort of archaeological investigations in northeastern Arabia (apart from Bahrain which was more settled) during the nineteenth century. This explains why D. G. Hogarth, well-known chronicler of the history of Arabian exploration, made no less than five pages of comments on the report of Philby's discovery of ruins in central Arabia in 1917 (Philby 1920b: 185–9). Such was the rarity of archaeological knowledge deriving from this area, thanks to the generally anarchic and lawless conditions which prevailed there.

Further south, in what was known as the Pirate or Trucial Coast, the Qawasim family in the northern enclave of Ras al-Khaimah had begun, by the early nineteenth century, 'to involve themselves in more or less perpetual warfare between local competing powers in the area. They began to attack both Arab and non-Arab vessels passing through the Gulf waters' (al-Rashid 1981: 25; for a dissenting view see al-Qassimi 1986). This brought about punitive action by the Bombay Marine in 1809 and 1819 which culminated in a General Treaty of Peace signed in 1820 allowing the British to 'effectively mediate along the Arab littoral and frustrate the interests of outside powers' (Dubuisson 1978: 55). Until the end of the nineteenth century, however, the British government's aim in the Gulf was limited to 'the maintenance of peace and the suppression of piracy and the slave trade' (Tuson 1979: 129), and while successive Residency Agents became embroiled in the perpetual land disputes and inter-group rivalries which plagued the area, the

British 'presence' was committed to a policy of 'non-intervention in internal affairs' (Melamid 1953: 197) and to 'isolating the whole area from foreign contacts' (Abdullah 1975: 174). To the best of my knowledge, although various British officers made journeys to the Trucial Coast and into the interior of southeastern Arabia, the only antiquarian observations made were related to the presence of ancient copper mines (for full references see Potts 1990: 115–16) which, while certainly important, did not lead to the undertaking of any related archaeological fieldwork until the 1970s. Indeed, as late as the 1930s 'there was insecurity outside the towns, on account of Bedouin raids on the surrounding areas' (Abdullah 1975: 177).

To sum up, whereas much of the Near East in the nineteenth century had a government under the Ottoman Empire with which scholars interested in the pursuit of archaeology could deal, such was not the case in the Gulf. In the wake of World War I, when antiquities departments were established by the British and French in their respective mandate areas (Iraq and Palestine in the British case; Syria and Lebanon in the case of the French), no such developments took place in Kuwait, Saudi Arabia, Qatar or along the Trucial Coast. Untouched by the political forces which, in the nineteenth and early twentieth century had initially permitted archaeological exploration and eventually institutionalised it, the Gulf Arab states were not really touched by the forces of archaeological inquiry until the discovery of oil brought an influx of skilled foreign labourers into the area who were the first to see many of the region's most important sites.

Certainly this was the case in eastern Saudi Arabia, where the first sustained exploration of sites like Thaj, Ayn Jawan and the Dhahran burial mounds was conducted by Arabian American Oil Company employees (ARAMCO) and their families. Similarly, in Abu Dhabi, it was a BP oil company representative, Temple Hillyard, who first brought the settlement and graves of Umm an-Nar island to the attention of foreign archaeologists. And on Bahrain, where over 150,000 burial mounds which have made the island famous had been investigated intermittently between 1879 and the 1940s by a succession of mainly British officers and diplomats, it was an Iraq Petroleum employee, T. G. Bibby, who first conceived the idea of an archaeological investigation of the island's past (Bibby 1969).

The Danish expedition

In the early 1950s Bibby appealed to his wartime acquaintance, P. V. Glob, by then Professor of Prehistory at the University of Aarhus, and together they organised the first modern archaeological expedition to the Gulf region. In many ways, however, the expedition was anomalous. Although Danish archaeologists had been active at Hama in Syria before the war, there was little tradition of Near Eastern archaeology in Denmark, where Classical archaeology and Nordic prehistory dominated. Indeed, the staff of the Danish expedition was made up almost entirely of Danish prehistorians, more at home in the bogs and barrows of Jutland than on the tells of the Near East. Eventually, this was to have a devastating effect on the scholarly output of the project, for although much pioneering excavation was conducted by the Danish expedition, which eventually extended its field of operations to Qatar (1956), Kuwait (1958), Abu Dhabi (1958), Saudi Arabia (1962) and Dibba (1964) (Glob 1968: 16), the fact that most of the Danish team members had positions in museums throughout Denmark where their duties focused on Danish prehistory meant that, for many years, little of this important work was published except in brief notes in the Danish journal *Kuml*.

When Bibby and Glob first applied to the equivalent of the present Danish Humanities Research Council for funds to work on Bahrain they were turned down. Told that any future application of similar size would be likewise rejected, they wrote to Sir Charles Belgrave, the Ruler of Bahrain's adviser, asking whether His Highness Shaikh Sulman might make a financial contribution towards the cost of the expedition. As Bibby wrote in 1968, 'I should like to make it very clear just how completely unheard-of such a proposal was. Governments in the Middle East never contribute to foreign expeditions working in their country. On the contrary. It has been for many years the general rule that expeditions to the Middle East pay their own expenses' (Bibby 1969: 14). In fact, after receiving a positive response from Shaikh Sulman, the main oil company on Bahrain volunteered a contribution as well which, together with the reduced grant eventually awarded by the Danish research council, constituted the budget of the Danish expedition and 'set the pattern for our subsequent work' in the area where tripartite support – from the local government, from oil companies, and from the Danish scientific funding body – became the norm.

Funding foreign expeditions and sponsorship

To an ever increasing extent, the funding pattern established by the Danish expedition in the 1950s has continued to develop in many parts of the Gulf to this day. In the recent past, expeditions on Bahrain and teams in the United Arab Emirates (hereafter UAE) have been provided variously with accommodation, food, vehicles and workmen (some, or all, depending on the local authority) by the governments of their host countries. Air fares and other expenses (e.g. drafting and photographic material; salaries for specialists such as conservators, photographers, draftsmen) often come out of grants from national funding agencies as well as from local sponsors. While oil companies continue to be supportive, a wide range of other concerns such as car companies (e.g. General Motors), service companies (e.g. Dubai Duty Free), and tobacco companies (e.g. Rothmans) have given generously. Sponsorship by both local and multinational firms helps to 'green' the image of a firm, and supporting anything to do with archaeology and heritage in these rapidly modernising societies is almost invariably seen as a positive endeavour.

By supporting scholarly, scientific investigations into local history, Gulf State governments are invariably seen to be enlightened. Supporting archaeological teams is a sign of how forward thinking, and ecologically/politically correct a particular government is. While the level of serious interest on the part of the Gulf States' rulers varies from bemusement to serious concern to indifference, the high profile of archaeological research, reported upon consistently in the local and even international press, makes it imperative that the Gulf Arab governments be seen to be supportive. In some cases this has been costly as, for example, when a large block of prime real estate on the southern margins of Dubai was sacrificed by a local high-ranking shaikh who gave it to the Municipality for protection because it contained an archaeological site. Investments worth millions of dollars can be lost when the protection of archaeological sites and monuments requires calling a halt to a development project. On the other hand, doing so wins great *kudos* and increases the prestige of the individual making the sacrifice.

Engineers and slaves

In spite of the British presence in the Gulf, slavery was not abolished in the region until well into the twentieth century. The records of the Political Residency at Bushire on the Iranian coast contain, for the years 1935–1941, files on the 'kidnapping, purchase and export of slaves from the Trucial Coast', as well as documents detailing individual cases of the manumission of slaves at Muscat, the capital of Oman, between 1938 to 1942 (Tuson 1979: 16). The Political Agency on Bahrain has records of slave trading in Abu Dhabi between 1934 and 1938, and of slave trading in the Gulf generally during the period between 1931 and 1949 (ibid.: 54, 66). Cases of slavery in Qatar are reported as late as 1950, when slaves from Muscat and Saudi Arabia were still owned on Bahrain (ibid.: 99). The slave trade was active at Fujairah between 1941 and 1943 and slavery was still present in Kuwait as late as 1949 (ibid.: 146, 170).

If this digression on the subject of slavery seems out of place, I ask readers to think for a moment about a society thoroughly conditioned to the ownership of a portion of its labour force; to the statelessness that represents; and to the complete dependency of unfree labour on its masters which such a system creates. When Standard Oil of California secured the oil concession for Saudi Arabia on 29 May 1933, it created a demand for skilled labour in a wide variety of fields. Yet these labourers, whether petroleum engineers with PhDs or oil-rig hands from the Texas panhandle were, in all respects, dependent labourers, present thanks to the goodwill of the Saudi ruler, non-believers suffered only to tread on Saudi soil because of that particular expertise which was being bought for a very specific purpose. Slavery, as we have seen, was still very much an institution when these first imported labourers were brought into the region, and it is arguable that some of the Gulf Arab attitude towards slaves was extended to the skilled labourers of the oil industry and subsequent industries which have supplied the manpower (not a sexist term here since almost all the expatriate labour has been male) responsible for building the infrastructure of the modern Gulf states.

To some extent, that same attitude towards expatriate labour has been extended to archaeologists as well. Almost every Department of Antiquities in the region today employs skilled expatriate labour. In the 1970s and early 1980s, dozens of Egyptians were employed by the Saudi Arabian Department of Antiquities. In Qatar, during the 1980s, a Lebanese archaeologist was employed, while in Abu Dhabi, Dubai, Sharjah and Fujairah a variety of Iraqi, Sudanese, Indian and Jordanian archaeologists have been employed on short-term contract in recent years. While most of these archaeologists have degrees from the major universities in their respective countries, several have PhDs and have studied in Europe and Britain.

Western archaeologists have also been hired in some instances to perform specific tasks, just like their brethren in the oil industry. In 1976, the Saudi Arabian Department of Antiquities instituted a comprehensive survey of the entire country, employing on salary for short periods (generally several months) archaeologists from the United States and Britain. More recently, specific tasks like these have been executed elsewhere, for example, surveys of towers in Ras al-Khaimah; excavation and restoration of historic monuments on Bahrain and in Oman; and the co-ordination of museum exhibitions in a number of countries. All this work has in common the performance of contract work for a fee. In this regard, it differs radically from most 'traditional' archaeological work in the Middle East which has been research-driven. While data are certainly acquired through contract work of this sort, it is by no means a primary aim and publication is not necessarily one of its objectives. Interestingly, several of the museums in the Emirates, such as the Sharjah and Ras al-Khaimah Archaeology Museums, have employed archaeologists to steadily, if not systematically, help fill in the gaps in the archaeological record as displayed in the museum. In this sense, excavation for objects from a little known period becomes an end in itself which has no relation to traditional scholarly approaches to archaeological inquiry. While 'gaps in knowledge' may be seen in some Western quarters as a justifiable premise from which to launch new work, 'gaps on shelves' and the filling thereof would probably be scoffed at as a justification for undertaking an excavation. Yet in the context of providing the museum-going public with an unbroken sequence of cultural development in a local museum, filling in those gaps can assume a high priority.

Archaeological past vs. the Jahaliyya

Many a bureaucrat responsible for some aspect of archaeological research in the Gulf States has probably wondered at the periodisation of the pre-Islamic past as constructed by archaeologists. In a region which has yielded only a small number of inscribed objects, it is easy to see how traditionalists could dismiss the entirety of the pre-Islamic era as *Jahaliyya*, the 'age of ignorance'. Yet for archaeologists, the distinctions between early Dilmun and Umm an-Nar; mature Dilmun and Wadi Suq; Iron Age etc. have a life and vitality which is highly variegated and impossible to subsume under a single rubric. In an area which was so heavily influenced by the conservative Wahhabi movement in the nineteenth century, it is perhaps surprising that investigations into the pre-Islamic past have never been interdicted.

Yet how do the current inhabitants relate to their pre-Islamic predecessors? Do the modern inhabitants of the UAE and Oman identify themselves with the land known in cuneiform sources as Magan, or the archaeological culture known to archaeologists as Umm an-Nar? About the only overt sign of this is the decidedly uneconomical revival of the country's copper industry, so intimately associated with the ancient land of Magan in Mesopotamian sources. This helps to confirm what was once disputed, that Oman (and the UAE) comprise the region known in antiquity as Magan, but the quantity of copper available today in the Oman mountains, viewed in twentieth-century commercial terms, is so small that ore actually has to be imported in order to produce Omani copper. I leave that as an example for those interested in symbolic versus economically rational behaviour to muse upon.

Do modern Bahrainis see themselves as the descendants of the ancient Dilmunites? To be sure there is a Dilmun Hotel on Bahrain but, to date, there seems little evidence to suggest a conscious identification by the modern population with the remote past of the Bronze Age. Perhaps this is because most nationals, by whom I mean Arabs living in these states (as opposed to expatriate Indians, Pakistanis etc.), have some cognisance of the theory that they – the Arabs – did not arrive in the region until sometime late in the pre-Islamic era, perhaps as some traditionists contend, as a result of the repeated bursting of the Marib Dam in Yemen which allegedly sent waves of Arabs northward. Even if few modern nationals in the Gulf have ever studied this proposition carefully, most of them probably harbour a notion that the Arabs were not the original inhabitants of eastern Arabia, and in this they are surely correct. They are thus able to dispassionately contemplate the more distant past of the region without feeling any lineal attachment to its inhabitants. This no doubt explains why Arab nationals have no compunction in excavating pre-Islamic burials, or in letting Western archaeologists do the same – something they would not countenance if the burials were from the Islamic era.

Occasionally, however, more overt concerns are expressed over archaeological discoveries. One of the features of recent scholarship has been a fascination with the contacts which existed between Mesopotamia and the Indus Valley during the Bronze Age, contacts which were in some degree mediated by the peoples of the Gulf region. As more and more evidence of Harappan civilisation is discovered in the Oman peninsula, some worry has been expressed that local Indian and Pakistani expatriates – agitating quietly for more rights in countries where they and their parents may have, in fact, been born but of which they can never be citizens – will contend that the original, pre-Arab population of the area was 'Hindi'. This, they feel, would unleash a terrible situation in which claims of prior ownership would be made, something to be avoided at all costs. As for Christianity, it is recognised by most Arabs that Christians inhabited the Gulf region before the coming of Islam. In fact, few residents of the Gulf States probably realise how extensively Nestorian Christianity was practised in the area, even after the Islamic conquest. When a Nestorian church was discovered and quickly excavated by Saudi Arabian archaeologists at Jabal Berri in eastern Saudi Arabia (Langfeldt 1994) it did not take long before the site was seriously vandalised, but how much this had to do with serious anti-Christian sentiment is doubtful. By contrast, Shaikh Zayed, ruler of Abu Dhabi and President of the United Arab Emirates, was reported to be delighted at the discovery of a Nestorian monastery and church on the island of Sir Bani Yas in 1992 for it confirmed, in his view, what traditional Arab historians and oral tradition had always maintained.

Given the repeated efforts on the part of various Iranian governments to overthrow the Arab government of Bahrain and, more importantly, given that all eastern Arabia was under Persian/Sasanian control at the time of the Islamic conquest, what is the attitude of Arab nationals today to the Persian elements in their archaeological record? Has the Sunni–Shi'a split in Islam exacerbated hostility? It is difficult to find any overt rejection of what could broadly be termed 'Persian connections', be they in the painted pottery of the Bronze Age, or of the more recent Achaemenid, Parthian and Sasanian past. As with Christianity, few informed Arabs would ever deny that eastern Arabia was under the control of successive Persian empires, but the degree of inter-penetration has been so great – for example, with many Arab tribes settling after the Islamic conquest on the Persian coast of the Gulf; and with many Iranians from Bastak in Laristan settled in

Dubai for many years – that there seems little evidence to suggest any actively anti-Persian sentiments in reading the past of the region. Several islands in the Gulf, now occupied by Iran, are claimed by the UAE, causing a continual sense of strain in relations between the two countries, yet trade between the two is booming and, to date, rival readings of the past have not been invoked to legitimate territorial claims over land.

The future of archaeology in the region

Whereas from the 1930s and 1940s onwards a steady stream of young scholars from Lebanon, Syria, Turkey, Iraq and elsewhere began to study in the West, this has not been the case in the Gulf Arab states. It was not until the 1960s that students from the region began to go abroad for study in archaeology. A. R. Al-Ansary, recently retired professor of archaeology at King Saud University in Riyadh, was probably that country's first PhD in a subject related to the country's distant past (he studied at Leeds in the 1960s under the distinguished Semitist B. S. J. Isserlin). After A. H. Masry got his PhD at the University of Chicago in 1973, a steady stream of young Saudis went to Britain and the States to pursue graduate work in archaeology. In Kuwait, F. al-Wohaibi, presently Director of Antiquities, received his PhD at the University of Indiana, and in Oman the Director of Antiquities, A. al-Shanfari, obtained a doctorate from Naples. Apart from these scholars, and a few historians working in the universities of the region, the number of indigenous archaeologists is still very small. Finding bright students who are willing to forego lucrative careers in the public service and business sector for the pursuit of an academic or public archaeological career has proved frustratingly difficult, and in countries and emirates which would like to employ qualified nationals in positions of responsibility and activity, there are often very few candidates, if any, at hand.

Part of the reason for the difficulty in building up a pool of competent local archaeologists, and hence for the reliance on the importation of foreign, skilled labour in this field, is undoubtedly to be sought in the structure of university history curricula and the staffing of history departments where archaeology is most often housed. Here again we run into the problem of expatriate labour for in a region where nationals with PhDs or MAs are rare, recourse has been taken to the importation en masse of Arabic-speaking scholars from Egypt, the Sudan and most of the Arab countries of the Middle East. Unfortunately, these scholars arrive all too often with no knowledge of local history and archaeology, coupled with the common cultural prejudice of those who believe nothing existed in the Gulf in the days when ziggurats and pyramids loomed large in their native lands. As a result, they teach subjects like Umayyad, Abbasid, Fatimid and Ottoman architecture and ceramics, all of which is fine in Damascus or Cairo, but scarcely relevant in Al Ain or Kuwait.

If nothing else, today's archaeology museums in the region instil a sense of pride in the past and a belief in the worth of the culture of the area, regardless of how distant populations in the archaeological past are from those of today. In this respect, archaeology clearly plays a role in building national identities (cf. Blau 1995). It shows people a past which is not that of the Ottomans, Babylonians, Pharaohs or Abbasids. The task now is to follow up on this basis by revising school and university curricula so that local history and archaeology are given as much, if not more weight than that of Syria, Turkey, Egypt or Iraq (see Özdoğan, Chapter 5; Hassan, Chapter 11). In many ways the situation is reminiscent of that which existed until relatively recently in Australian schools and universities. It took many years before the history and literature taught in Australia was anything but British history and literature and yet now, when Australian history and literature are being given great emphasis (albeit not to the exclusion of British, European, Asian or, for that matter, American history and literature), it seems self-evident that Australians should obviously study Australia's past. The same is true of the Gulf States. Rather than focusing on the Fatimids and Ottomans, and denigrating their own past, the peoples of the Gulf States must look to their own histories and inculcate a spirit of inquiry into their past which will ultimately feed into the pursuit of archaeological and historical research in the universities and museums of the region.

Will this make it irrelevant for non-Arab archaeologists, like myself, to think of continuing to work in the area? The goal of bringing up generations of Arab archaeologists is not to exclude non-Arab ones from working in the area. Knowledge and its pursuit is today global, impelled by e-mail, fax, international conferences and multi-national co-operative projects. When British and European scholars undertook archaeological excavations in the era of empires and colonies, one could say that some of the work done was imposed on the region in which it was carried out, yet another arm of colonialism. I argue that nowadays the same charge cannot be laid at the door of a non-Arab archaeologist wishing to work in an Arab country. The planet is now the field of inquiry, and many of the same human issues are being investigated simultaneously in many countries by scholars who are not native to those countries. Knowledge is not the monopoly of any one body of scholars, and the 'right' or 'privilege' of studying a given topic is not something to which one must be born. Black or white, Arab or not, these are no grounds for determining what is sound archaeological research in an area and, while I think it is imperative for the good of the Gulf Arab States that they each have a competent body of national archaeologists and a lively public debate on the meaning and uses of archaeology in their country, these individuals should have no claim to an exclusive right to conduct archaeological investigations. There are many points of view, many agendas, many voices in archaeology, and room for still more. The more work that is conducted in this region, the deeper will be our understanding of its past. How we wish to manipulate the data and use the knowledge gained may be very different from how a Bahraini or a Saudi wishes to, and our constructs should by no means pre-empt those of another researcher. Even if regional identities were already clear in the Bronze and Iron Ages, passports had not been invented when many of the people whom we investigate lived and the sites we excavate were inhabited. Let us hope that research in the area in the years ahead remains something which will not come to be determined by the colour of one's passport.

Bibliography

Abdullah, M. M. (1975) 'Changes in the economy and political attitudes, and the development of culture on the coast of Oman between 1900 and 1940', *Arabian Studies* 2: 167–78.

al-Qasimi, S. M. (1986) *The myth of Arab piracy in the Gulf*, London: Croom Helm.

al-Rashid, Z. M. (1981) *Su'udi relations with eastern Arabia and 'Uman (1800–1870),* London: Luzac.

Bibby, T. G. (1969) *Looking for Dilmun*, New York: Alfred A. Knopf.

Blau, S. (1995) 'Observing the present – reflecting the past: attitudes towards archaeology in the United Arab Emirates', *Arabian Archaeology and Epigraphy* 6: 116–28.

Dubuisson, P. R. (1978) 'Qasimi piracy and the General Treaty of Peace (1820)', *Arabian Studies* 4: 47–57.

Glob, P. V. (1968) *Al-Bahrain*, Copenhagen: Gyldendal.

Hilprecht, H. V. (1896) 'Explorations in Babylonia' in Hilprecht, H. V. (ed.) *Recent Research in Bible Lands: Its Progress and Results*, Philadelphia: Wattles, pp. 45–93.

Langfeldt, J. A. (1994) 'Recently discovered early Christian monuments in north-eastern Arabia', *Arabian Archaeology and Epigraphy* 5: 32–60.

Melamid, A. (1953) 'Political geography of Trucial 'Oman and Qatar', *Geographical Review* 43: 194–206.

Philby, H. St. J. B. (1920a) 'Across Arabia: From the Persian Gulf to the Red Sea', *Geographical Journal* 56: 446–68.

—— (1920b) 'Southern Najd', *Geographical Journal* 55: 161–91.

Potts, D. T. (1990) *The Arabian Gulf in Antiquity Vol. I*, Oxford: Clarendon Press.

Tuson, P. (1979) *The records of the British Residency and Agencies in the Persian Gulf*, London: India Office Records.

Wright, J. K. (1927) 'Northern Arabia: The explorations of Alois Musil', *Geographical Review* 17: 177–206.

Chapter 11

Memorabilia

Archaeological
materiality and
national identity
in Egypt

Fekri A. Hassan

Introduction

Among the great threats that face humanity today is the eruption of violent
chauvinistic sentiments by political factions, religious sects, or so-called ethnic
groups. Although patriotic nationalism that once sparked many wars in Europe is
politically distinct from current overzealous chauvinistic movements, both are
linked with notions of group-identity. It seems that the rise of Western-styled
nationalism in the context of modern imperialism and industrialisation in the past
has led to a rippling effect that has now reached all the corners of the globe and is
refracting back causing unfathomable backlash (Pagden 1995). Nationalism among
colonials was a force of resistance, but with the recession of overt imperialism and
the retreat of nationalism in the face of multinational corporations and global
economics, chauvinistic separatist movements threaten the viability and political
stability of many ex-colonial states (Prakash 1995). The need for "nations" as
administrative blocks is perhaps unavoidable in a world of global economic
transactions. At the same time, uncritical celebration of diversity and blind
chauvinism can be counterproductive. Powerful (mostly Western) nations are
creating economic cartels shaping a political landscape of a unified ruling élite and

a disorganised mass of poor nations with internal and inter-national ethnic, religious and economic conflicts. It is accordingly imperative to re-examine our notions of nationalism and the role archaeology plays in fostering nationalist ideals. It is heartening that archaeologists have begun recently to engage archaeology in such urgent matters as attested to by the recent publication of Kohl and Fawcett (1995), Díaz-Andreu and Champion (1996) and Atkinson, Banks and O'Sullivan (1996). These publications have been the subject of an insightful review by Hamilakis (1996). I am particularly in agreement with Hamilakis (ibid.: 977) that "nationalism" defines identity within a specific socio-political context. In this chapter I provide a context for the search of national ideologies in modern Egypt and its implications for an "Egyptian" sense of identity. I also concur with Hamilakis (ibid.: 976, see also Hamilakis and Yalouri 1996) that it is rewarding to examine the role of past images and symbols in the nationalist narrative. This not only falls well within the archaeological domain of inquiry, but is also an essential component of identity formation processes.

In my treatment of the subject, I stress the role of objects of the past as icons of social memory that through performances and daily presentations contribute to a social memory (see also Kotsakis, Chapter 2; Brown, Chapter 3). The rise of Western nationalism was closely linked with the emergence of "national" memories (Fentress and Wickham 1988: 127–37). This national memory is shaped and guided by the upper middle classes and the intelligentsia through rhetorical discourses directed at other members of society or at external opponents. Certain episodes, themes and events become the subject of social memory and remembrances. Examples cited by Fentress and Wickman (ibid.: 127) include the English obsession with the nation-state and the Industrial Revolution; the Italian with the city-state, the Renaissance and the Risorgimento; and the US obsession with the frontier. Invoking the past is a matter of common political discourse. In 1981, François Mitterrand, at his presidential inauguration, instituted a "cérémonie à la mémoire" at the Pantheon. He laid red roses on the tombs of Jean Moulin, the Resistance hero, among others (ibid.: 137).

According to Fentress and Wickham (ibid.: 128) "almost all political rhetoric depends on the past as a legitimation device." Although this may seem a strong statement, it finds support from Smith (1986) in his extensive treatment of *The Ethnic Origins of Nations*. The past, according to Smith, is used to appeal for precedent. However, the past legitimates because of the aura of sanctity and power it is given by some deep psychological processes, especially, as Smith notes, at times of rapid change or major ruptures or junctions, as in the rise of nationalism or the establishment of new political regimes, when the past acquires a special relevance. This may explain the current fascination with archaeology and monuments, and the use of the past by ethnic, religious and political groups in their competition for power.

Aware of the dispersive and centrifugal forces of postmodern thought, I am alarmed by the spread of an intellectual milieu that works against the creation of corporate, co-operative human groups and the attack on the project of establishing common human goals based on shared human experiences (see, for example, Young 1990: 121–32). I think it is erroneous to discontinue the search for universals and transcultural commonalties because it allegedly spreads within an intellectual scheme that subverted it for the glorification of a hegemonic West. The Enlightenment provided the basis of a global intellectual revolution celebrating the fraternity of human societies to the extent of placing "savages" on equal, if not superior, footing to Frenchmen by no less than a French savant. The inception of this cultural "relativism" sustained an ethos of anthropological inquiry that provided an antidote to judging others with one's own criteria. However, cultural relativism does not imply a rejection of transcultural commonalties and a shared human biological and cultural heritage (see Hill 1992 for a discussion of moral relativism).

Claims advocated to enhance certain political or religious causes may be judged against scholarly knowledge. Although the theoretical and methodological foundations of science may not answer ethical questions, and they may even serve criminal and evil causes, scholarly knowledge (science in the broad sense of the word), as a mode of inquiry that in principle rejects dogmatism and endorses critical thinking, eschews pre-judicial claims in favour of collective, reflective judgement, subjects individual observations and statements to cross-examination and scrutiny, and offers a guarantee against fascist regimes, religious fanatics, intellectual tyranny and solipsistic nihilism. Attracted to archaeology because of a belief that an examination of our deep past can contribute to an understanding of our contemporary human predicament, I welcome the current concern for an archaeology for the future, and hope that the following reflections, based on my personal experience and an insider's knowledge of Egyptian history, will serve as a reminder that archaeology is a major force in contemporary world affairs, and that as archaeologists we may consider the greater implications of our practice and our role in shaping a new world that will drastically alter the course of human civilisation. As Ucko (1990: xx) has remarked in his foreword to *Politics of the Past* (Gathercole and Lowenthal 1990), "the problem confronting archaeology today is an acutely moral one. Access and presentation of the past in everyday life, not just in museums and at archaeological sites, is crucial in shaping our future."

As humanity undergoes a transition toward transcultural affiliations and multicultural nations, the presentation and interpretation of the past will play a major role as a source of identity and outlook (cf. ibid.: xviii). Accordingly, I propose here that it may be useful to consider the remains of the past as objects of recollection and remembrance serving as signposts marking the path to the future.

Memory lane

Until the explosive growth of Cairo in the last three decades which consisted of the development of new neighbourhoods such as Madient Nasr, the majority of Egyptians lived in the midst of a historical landscape marked by mosques, inns, mansions and tombs clinging onto existence from the Islamic past of Cairo. The neighbourhoods include the core of Ottoman–Memeluk–Fatimid Cairo, celebrated in Naguib Mahfouz's trilogy *Bein Al-Qasreen*. This core still serves as the heart-throb of the Al-Qahira in the minds of Egyptians who flock to this quarter during the *Mawlid of Sidna Al-Hussein* (the anniversary of the martyrdom of the grandson of the prophet). It is also the site of celebrations throughout the month of Ramadan (a month of fasting from dawn to sunset followed by a sumptuous meal and an evening of partying and recreation). This ancient quarter with its prominent Al-Hussein Mosque, Al-Azhar and the Memeluk alleyways of the Khan Al-Khali Bazaar is the Mecca of Egyptians. It confirms and reaffirms the religious Islamic heritage of Egypt and its role in learning, particularly Islamic learning. Medieval book stores with yellow books, cheap as well as lavish editions of Islamic texts, surround Al-Azhar – the oldest university in existence dating to AD 972. The religious ambience of the quarter infused with the distinct smell of spices, incense, oriental perfumes, grilled kebabs and the hum of crowds, street peddlers, children and radios is intermixed with popular Sufi practices, which has become an integral element of folk Islamic thought and practice since Memeluk and Ottoman times.

Gone and forgotten

There is no place in Egypt where intellectuals congregate in the embrace of Pharaonic monuments as they do in the Hussein quarter. However, it seems from archaeological excavations that such a place existed in front of the sphinx in Greek times where celebration and festivities were commonplace. Today, the Pharaonic past is hardly the focus of Egyptian celebrations or festivities, and hardly the theme of intellectual inspiration. Even Naguib Mahfouz who began his career by translating a short history of ancient Egypt and a couple of novels inspired by Egypt's Pharaonic past, moved quickly to situate his novels in the context of the Hussein quarter. His early novels were largely forgotten. The celebration of the inundation of the Nile (*Eid Wafa En-Nil*) regarded as a continuation of a Pharaonic custom is also no longer the focus of public festivities after the construction of the Aswan High Dam (*El-Sadd Al-Ali*). It is also remarkable that the pyramids are rarely visited except during the compulsory school excursion or an occasional escape from Cairo by amorous couples. They are also visited for recreation during festive occasions. Surprisingly, many who reside in Cairo have also rarely visited the pyramids or the Egyptian Museum. In Egypt, schools, not the home, are in general the center of disseminating a knowledge of the Pharaonic past of Egypt. By contrast, Islamic heritage is an integral part of growing up at home.

The reawakening of memory

The eyes of Britain were closely focused on Egypt following the showdown at Abu Qir, the naval battle that ended with the abortion of the Napoleonic campaign to Egypt. In part to check the commercial expansion of the French in the Middle East, and primarily to secure the link with India, Britain manoeuvred to occupy Egypt in 1882 (see Marsot 1985 for a short history of modern Egypt). A vigorous movement for independence followed. Among the first nationalists was Moustafa Kamil, a young lawyer and the son of an engineer who founded the National Party (*Al-Hizb al-watani*) in 1890. His call for independence was passionate and eloquent. More than anyone, he was perhaps the most influential in promoting the idea of *Al-Wattan* (homeland) and *Al-wattanyia* (nationalism). Moustafa Kamil (see Figure 11.1) awakened a sense of Egyptian nationalism grounded in the Pharaonic history of Egypt. In a moving speech in 1907, he declared:

> We do not work for ourselves, but for our homeland, which remains after we depart. What is the significance of years and days in the life of Egypt, the country which witnessed the birth of all nations, and invented civilisation for all humankind?

> (Tawfik 1981)

On 18 March 1919, Saad Zaghloul, the leader of the Egyptian delegation who were refused permission to travel to England to present the case for Independence, was arrested together with three of the delegates. The whole country was galvanised. Demonstrations and strikes erupted everywhere. The "revolution" (thawra) was met with brutal force. In what became a pattern afterwards, students led the demonstrations and were the first to shed their blood for independence.

The revolution of 1919 was a turning point in the history of Egypt. The national alliance in 1919 was remarkable and long-lasting. Everywhere the crescent embraced the Cross. Women also demonstrated in a show of camaraderie with men. Students, government employees, lawyers, Coptic priests, the Sheiks of Al-Azhar, peasants, workers and shopkeepers banded together. The national spirit was inflamed when on 11 December 1919, British soldiers pursued demonstrators inside the Al-Azhar Mosque, an act of sacrilege recalling the defilement of Al-Azhar by French cavalry in 1798.

The unification of Copts and Moslems, of men and women, of workers,

Figure 11.1 The statue of Moustafa Kamil in downtown Cairo

peasants and bourgeoisie was legitimated by an appeal to "eternal Egypt," "young Egypt" and, above all, Pharaonic Egypt. Poets such as Ahmed Shawki, Hafez Ibrahim, Ismail Sabry and Al-Baroudi began to invoke the pyramids in a genre of nationalistic poetry comparing Egypt's past glory with its impoverished present and extolling the Egyptians to restore and revive Egypt's ancient splendour and hegemony. Historical plays by Ahmed Shawki, the prince of poets, also invoked the Pharaonic heritage of Egypt as in his renowned work, *Cleopatra*, which became a favourite as a school play.

Writing of the 1919 revolution Al-Mueilhi, in *Hadith 'Isa ibn Hisham*, remarks that it was the spirit of Egypt that was behind the revolution:

> That magical spirit that alone built the Pyramids, and it alone understands the Pyramids. The masses [during the revolution] sang of the glory of the Pyramid builders and were proud to be related to them. One often heard the phrases, 'Sons of the Pharaohs', 'Our ancestors built the Pyramids', 'Egypt is the mother of Pyramids', etc. Saad Zaghloul addressed the masses saying, 'You are the inheritors of the oldest civilisation. The link between the past and the present is complete. I remind modern Egyptians with the Independence of Egypt in Pharaonic times, Glorious Egypt, because the sentiment of Independence ties us to them. The noble memories inspire us and breathe the spirit of struggle.'

There was also the translation of James Beiki's *Ancient Egypt* by Naguib Mahfouz in 1932 and three subsequent novels on Pharaonic Egypt (*'bath Al 'aqdar*, Fate's Folly, 1939; Radobis, 1943; *Kifah Tieba*, The Struggle of Thebes, 1944). It was also at that time that Tawfik Al-Hakim, Egypt's best playwright (educated like Taha Hussein in France), produced *'awdat Al-Rouh* (The Return of Soul) referring to the rebirth of Egypt. He began writing this pioneering novel in 1937 while in France (it may be noteworthy that the first version was in French). Gamal Abdel-Nasser, the young army officer who led the revolution in 1952 ending the reign of Mohamed Ali's dynasty, was greatly influenced by the nationalistic plea expressed by Al-Hakim in *'awdat Al-Rouh*.

In this novel, a French Egyptologist explains to an English irrigation engineer the roots of the 1919 revolution as follows:

> This people, whom you consider ignorant, knows a lot. The Egyptian knows by his heart, not by his mind. The wisdom is in his blood and he does not know that; and the strength is in himself, but he does not know. This is an ancient people. If you get one of the peasants and open his heart you will find sediments of 10,000 years of experience and knowledge, deposited one on top of the other without his knowledge. However, in critical moments these experiences come out to his aid. This may explain to us [Europeans] this moment of history as we witness an astonishing mutation underway . . . The strength of Egypt is in its fathomless heart. He who appeals to the heart of Egypt, gives it back its soul.

The theme of rebirth not only inspired poets, novelists and playwrights but also painters and sculptors. The artistic legacy of this moment of birthing is undoubtedly the statue of "The Renaissance of Egypt" (*Nahdet Misr*) by Mahmoud Moukhtar (see Figure 11.2) unveiled in 1928 (first exhibited in Paris 1920). Trained in Paris, Moukhtar produced the first national monument since Pharaonic times inspired by the principles of the art of those distant times (Abu Ghazi 1994).

The Pharaonic style, curiously absent from the architectural landscape of Cairo which is either "Oriental" or Western, was adopted for the sepulchre of Saad Zaghloul. Hidden in *Al-Mouneira*, a neighbourhood close to the seat of government near Abdine Palace since the time of Khedive Ismail, I came upon it once by chance (see Figure 11.3). However, I clearly remember another monument also of Saad Zaghloul at *Mahtet el-Raml* in Alexandria. As a boy visiting the beaches of the Mediterranean city with its distinct Greek and Italian character, I was fond of climbing the pedestal of the statue, sitting in the lap of young Egypt in the figure of a seated Pharaonic woman (see Figure 11.4).

Figure 11.2 Statue of the "Renaissance of Egypt" (Nahdet Misr)

The denial of memory: the fashioning of political identity

In 1952, young army officers, led by Gamal Abdel-Nasser, forced the resignation of King Farouk and within two years sent the British troops packing back to Britain. Distrustful of political parties, the young officers dissolved all of them. Egypt was launched on the road of military authoritarianism. The policy of Gamal Abdel-Nasser (Mansfield 1969) was based on creating a block of nations to counteract the colonial policy of "Divide and Rule." He saw Egypt at the heart of an Arab circle. A common language (Arabic), religion (Islam), culture and close historical ties were conducive to the consolidation of Egypt's ties with the Arab world.

Gamal Abdel-Nasser (1918–1970), however, went too far. In his rush to secure political ties he purposely underplayed Egypt's Pharaonic heritage. Following a political union with Syria which was quickly dissolved, Egypt was officially deprived of its historical name "*Misr*" and renamed as the southern province of the United Arab Republic (1958–1961). Nasser brandished pre-revolutionary Egypt as a dark age of corruption (*Fassad*). In banning all political parties in the hope of

Figure 11.3 Mausoleum of Saad Zaghloul, Cairo

rallying the nation around his revolutionary regime he broke all ties with the nationalist leaders of modern Egypt. The memories of Saad Zaghloul and Moustafa Kamil were overlooked. The political discourse that centered on Pharaonic Egypt was replaced with a discourse that placed Egypt within the folds of Arab nationalism.

In attempting to annihilate all potential opposition, Abdel-Nasser also began to liquidate the Moslem Brothers, a religious "party" that had wide support among the peasants and poor urban workers (mostly migrants from rural areas). Capital-ising on the religiosity of Egyptian peasants (with a rudimentary knowledge of Islamic teachings), the Brotherhood, with sophisticated secret (underground) organisational cells and a paramilitary wing, was a real threat. Abdel-Nasser's confrontations with them proved to be disastrous for Egypt in the long run. They were jailed, tortured and harassed. Their leaders were tried in revolutionary (military) courts and many were executed. One of their leading programmatic writers, Sayed Qutb (1906–1966), became, upon his execution, one of their martyrs. Qutb (1993), in challenging Abdel-Nasser, opposed "Arab nationalism" in favour of "Islamism." He denounced Arab nationalism in favour of an alliance of Islamic nations. He was, in fact, influenced by the writings of the Pakistani Islami-cist Abu "Ala" Al-Maodoudi (1903–1979). An alliance with the Moslem world ensured for Pakistan a base of support in its struggle to establish an identity *vis-à-vis* India of which it was once a part (Omara 1987).

Figure 11.4 "Mother Egypt", the pedestal of the statue of Saad Zaghloul in Alexandria, Mahtet el-Raml

Many Egyptians were swept up by the rhetoric of Arabism. For the young generations of Egyptians born after the revolution (1952) in the late 1950s and early 1960s, Egypt as Pharaonic Egypt was plotted out. However, identification with Arabism has never really penetrated the Egyptian "soul" remaining an official line especially because: (1) the Egyptians rarely trusted governments; (2) Abdel-Nasser's popularity was a result of his image as an antagonist of imperialism and corruption and not as a head of a government; (3) his policy of repression created a sense of fear and mistrust; (4) his denial of Egypt's nationalist history was disdained by the older generation (then in their forties to sixties, who were children or youths at the time of the 1919 revolt); (5) Egyptians use the word "Arab" to refer to Bedouin nomads or the inhabitants of the Arabian Peninsula; and (6) because Arab unity has never materialised due to rivalries, feuds, disputes and conflicts among "Arab" leaders, who were constantly creating barrages of verbal abuse on the air waves. Egypt under Nasser was also embroiled in a war in Yemen opposed by Saudi Arabia.

Fekri A. Hassan

Sadat's Egypt: the search for identity

Badly defeated in 1967 in a devastating six day war with Israel, the hopes of those who followed Nasser were no longer entranced by the slogans of Arab nationalism. Anwar Al-Sadat (1918–1981), who followed Nasser, realised that the US would never allow Israel to be defeated and opted for peace after a limited victory in 1973 (see Waterbury 1983). He reconciled with Saudi Arabia (antagonised by Nasser), engineering an oil boycott that hurt the West and greatly benefited Saudi Arabia. In the meantime, the Saudis began to support Islamic movements abroad to bolster their political base. They financed religious groups in Egypt and thus fermented political instability between the secular regime and the followers and descendants of the Moslem Brothers. Many of them worked in Saudi Arabia and supplied funds to their associates in Egypt.

Sadat also reawakened an *Egyptian* identity that reached beyond Gamal Abdel-Nasser's Arab Nationalism to the Egyptian nationalism of the pre-revolutionary era. Diplomatically, Egypt became officially the Arab Republic of Egypt (ARE), restoring, to the delight of many Egyptians, the name of "Egypt" of which it was deprived under Nasser. For the generation of the revolution (*Geel Al-Thawra*) in their teens or early twenties, who drank Arab nationalism with their mother's milk, the transformation was perplexing.

Peace with Israel and a new economic policy encouraging foreign investments, as well as international loans and development aid, contributed to a widening gap between poor and rich. Open display of Western goods in a sea of poverty with no sense of affiliation with the government, a Pharaonic past, or an Arab nation left a vacuum that was soon exploited by the extremist descendants of the Moslem Brotherhood. Sadat was felled by the bullets of one of them. He was assassinated as he stood to salute the procession of an army parade marking the anniversary of the 1973 victory. His tomb now lies below one of the scant reminders of Egypt's Pharaonic past: a monument, with a pyramidal design, for those who died in the 1973 war. In a perceptive analysis of the murder of Sadaat, Lewis (1993) captures the paradox of the historical construction of Egyptian identity. According to reports, the assassin of Sadat cried out "I have killed Pharaoh." As Lewis remarks (1993: 376) "Pharaoh," as used by the assassin means "tyrant" following its usage in the Old Testament and the Koran. Lewis also takes account of the thesis presented here:

the European science of Egyptology made the language of Egypt known for the first time to the Muslim Egyptians, a new sense of identity began to transform their perceptions of themselves, their country, and their place in the world. Their sense of themselves became patriotic and national rather than religious and communal, and they formulated new and different views of the past and hopes for the future.

The use of the term "Pharaoh" by the assassin, according to Lewis (ibid.) encapsulates a central dilemma of modern Egyptian identity. This "dilemma" has led to attempts of pseudo-historical scholarship that assert that Arab civilisation is Pharaonic and that Egyptian civilisation is Arabic (see for example Al-Hakim 1994), or at least maintain that Egyptians can be descendants from both the Pharaohs and the Arabs. Foad (1978), for example, asserted in her book *The Personality of Egypt*:

> It is an honour and a blessing to be Egyptians and Pharaohs . . . We carry a name known to the world before religion, languages and nationalism. We are Egyptians first, and we are Christians and Moslems, and we are also Arabs by tongue and destiny.

> (1978: 263)

However, some Egyptian intellectuals turned their back on the Arabs and looked across the Mediterranean to Europe, claiming the links that were established over more than 900 years from the time of Alexander to the Arab conquest when Egypt was well within the sphere of Greek, Hellenistic and Roman cultures (see, for example, the discussion of the thought of Hussein Fawzi in Gibrael 1995: 86–112, and of Taha Hussein's *The Future of Culture in Egypt* by Al-Katib 1981). However, Hussein Fawzi, like Yehia Haqqi, were advocates of an Egyptian nationalism that finds its thematic foundation in the character and personality of Egyptian peasants and simple folk.

In his essays on Egyptian life compiled in *An Egyptian Sindbad* (first published in 1938), Hussein Fawzi proclaims his faith in "the people of my land, who consist of millions deprived of good health, education, and both physical and psychological well-being." He regards the monuments and cultural achievements in Egypt not as a product of the rulers, but as the legacy of the Egyptian people, "the pyramids, the monuments, the Pyramid Texts, the churches, the mosques and Memeluk mausoleums . . . all these archaeological relics evoke the names of kings, khalifs, and sultans, but they truly belong to those who build them, the Egyptian people" (cited in Gibrael 1995: 96). Published two years before *Egyptian Sindbad*, Taha Hussein's (1993, orig. 1936) *Mustaqbal al-Thaqafa fi-Misr* (The Future of Culture in Egypt), was widely debated because of his claim that Egypt belongs to the Mediterranean world. However, Taha Hussein was also aware that "the elements of Egyptian culture belong to an ancient Egyptian heritage, an Islamic–Arabic heritage, and of what Egypt has gained and gains everyday from the best fruits of modern European civilisation" (cited in Al-Katib 1981: 140). Taha Hussein (1993: 212) specifically takes notice of the needs of the Egyptian Antiquities Organisation. He suggests that the organisation (then in the hands of foreigners) must one day be in the charge of Egyptians, who not only should learn the language of Ancient Egypt but also Greek and Latin in order to be on equal footing with European scholars.

Fekri A. Hassan

Egyptian pastiche

The British journalist, D. Stewart (1965), remarked in his small book on Cairo that "Cairo is not a Pharaonic City. Only the women with their eyes lined with kohl recalled the Pharaonic past!" Dressed in a colourful and diverse array of attires, men and woman walk in the streets of Cairo surrounded by a pastiche of memorabilia. The most prominent aspects of the materiality of the past as it surrounds, embraces, and engages Egyptians consists of the European-styled building from the times of Ismail that are showing at present signs of dilapidation and decay. In many parts of Cairo, mansions, villas, and elaborate apartment buildings are torn down to make room for nondescript houses to accommodate the burgeoning population of the city. Minarets from all periods protrude from corners to proclaim and underscore the predominance of Egypt's Islamic heritage. The "Arabisation" of Egypt following the influx of petrodollars from the Gulf emirates and Saudi Arabia led to a proliferation of scrawny mosques lodged in small crannies between buildings. It also promoted a race to build the tallest minarets possible.

The plurality of Egyptian pasts is perhaps nowhere as clear as in Tahrir Square (Liberation Square), formerly, Midan Al-Ismailiyia (after Khedive Ismail, the grandparent of King Farouk, the last of the Alawi kings of Egypt). Barracks of the colonial British army were located in that square. As one crosses the bridge toward Al-Gizeria, the statue of Saad Zaghloul (with Pharaonic panels in granite) looms in front of the new Opera House, constructed by the Japanese following an Islamic style.

Egypt's effective past is materially that of its Islamic heritage and the more recent European inlay. The Pharaonic past is a political card. It can arouse passionate responses among certain intellectuals, but it has not effectively become an integral or a predominant element of the materiality of Egyptian life. Perhaps the only vibrant continuity with Egypt's Pharaonic past is the Nile River. But it no longer floods and is imprisoned within its bounded channel. Lined with high-rise Western hotels, it belongs to the European and Arab tourists who can afford them. The tower of Cairo, a prominent feature by the Nile, epitomises Egypt's lost architectural identity. No one knows for certain what it is. Built by CIA money, reported to have been a bribe to Abdel-Nasser that he didn't accept, it rises meaninglessly in Cairo's skyline.

A stable political future of Egypt depends upon an ability to integrate its pasts and recognise its Pharaonic, Hellenistic, and Islamic heritage, and to place that variegated heritage within the course of a global civilisation. Egypt's links with the West are not limited to the recent history of confrontation, colonisation, and decolonisation. An active cultural and educational program to engage the public and schoolchildren in archaeological activities that show Egypt's long multicultural and rich past is essential to combat what I perceive to be a loss of affiliation, which is exploited by subversive extreme religious parties. Islam promotes diversity and amity among nations, "*Inna khalaknaqum sho'oban wa-qbala l'ta'arafo*" (We have created you as nations and tribes so that you may get to be acquainted with each other). Islam's contributions to the West, and the cosmopolitan character of Islamic civilisation, bringing peoples and knowledge together from China to Spain, ought to be the subject of a new arrangement of the Islamic Museum and teaching kits. Pharaonic Egypt must also be presented in a manner that highlights its contributions to humanity and in order to dispel popular misconceptions about ancient Egypt. The government should also sponsor architectural projects that encourage an Egyptian architecture inspired by its rich and varied past. Postmodern architecture with its penchant for cultural pastiche may offer a grammar for integrating Egypt's architectural elements in a striking form.

Summary

The past is a contested ground. It is also a word that denotes among other things events that have already happened. Some of these events contribute to the shaping of our lives. The advent of writing or the invention of vaccines are but two recent examples. The development of emergence of upright posture, and language, are two prehistoric examples. We may know or not know the origin, causes or consequences of such influential events. They may persist as latent history. They contribute to "what" we are, but may not be significant in what we think "who" we are. Our sense of "identity" in modern times has been largely influenced by a "nationalist" ideology. It is an ideology manifest both in discourse, practice and materiality. It has become embedded in a nexus of commercial, industrial, financial and military activities permeating and materialising many facets of our lives. Material icons of heroism, ancestral glory and cultural achievements are objects of national[ist] pride and identity.

The rise of European nationalism was linked to an expansion of commerce, industrial development, and imperialism. The rise of industry was also closely linked with the advent of a political ideology and discourse that highlighted and reified "freedom," "equality" and "democracy." In the intellectual altercations that ensued between Europe and its colonised subjects, "nationalism" and "independence" were not only issues of common discourse, but they were also ideologies legitimated by invoking the achievements of the ancestors and a glorious past (see Bahrani, Chapter 8). The search for a legitimating past assumed the same range of strategies employed by Europeans to give credence to their claims of territorial homeland and national unity.

The Egyptians, who have been estranged from their own Pharaonic past for more than approximately fourteen centuries, were under the rule of Memeluk and Ottoman rulers (the Memeluks were warlords descended from foreign slaves who began to rule Egypt in AD 1250). With the conversion of Egypt to Christianity and later Islam, the Pharaonic past slipped into the subterranean domain of latent culture, and disappeared from the master discourse of identity. However, an Islamic "identity" was not an element of a "nationalist" ideology. Egyptians recognise that they belong to "*Al Umma Al-Islamia*" (often translated as Islamic Nation), but they neither regard themselves as Arabs nor Ottomans. If anything, they distance themselves from any such nationalist identification (and use them only for character assassination). The Egyptians view the "Arabs" as nomads "*Badow*" (Bedouins), and disdained "*Al-Atrak*" or "*Tarakwa*" (Ottomans or Turks) who regarded the Egyptians as a serf. The Turks, in fact, created a deep awareness of a class hierarchy in Egypt which still informs the cultural manifestations of social identity. Under the Turks, a chasm separated the Egyptians, mostly designated as "peasants" (*Fellahin*) and *Pashas* (Lords), who were often Turkish viceroys and functionaries. The Turkish ranks, *Pasha* and *Bey*, once banned by the revolutionary officers of 1952, are still commonly used.

The discourse and practice of Islam became for the Egyptians, under the oppressive rule of the Memeluks and Ottomans, a source of cultural affiliation and a "refuge." It was not until 1919, in response to British colonialism, that Egyptian nationalism in the modern European sense became a key element in the political rhetoric of liberation and independence. Egyptian nationalism (*Al-Qawmiya Al-Misryia*) was legitimated by an appeal to the common people as the source of political power, and by invoking the glory of Pharaonic achievements, which were the focus of scholarly learning and broad publicity in Europe since the 1860s– 1880s, when the political leaders were youths.

A common Pharaonic past bypassed issues of creed (*milla*) and was a source of nationalist pride, an antidote to the humiliation of the Egyptians by foreign invaders, from the Persians in the sixth century AD to the British, who occupied Egypt in 1882. Poets, writers and journalists recalled the grandeur of Ancient Egypt (often with the Pyramids as its paramount icon) and exhorted the Egyptians to emulate their great ancestors. However, the revival of the past remained on an abstract, "intellectual" level and has scarcely penetrated the core of cultural practice and materiality. The attempt to "racinate" the people of Egypt in a Pharaonic past after 1919 was deeply shaken by the dominance of the rhetoric of Arab nationalism in the 1960s. The revolutionary regime's attack on the political religious [Islamic] party (*Al-Ikhwan Al-Muslimeen*) under Gamal Abdel-Nasser, and subsequently and paradoxically the support for an Islamic movement by grants from other countries under Anwar Al-Sadat (to undermine Nasserite socialists), coupled with the reinstatement of "Egyptian nationalism," added a volatile ingredient to Egyptian political life. Religious messages have invaded secular media and are penetrating civic life. "Islamic" garb is commonly displayed by some men and women. Mosques with exceptionally tall minarets have appeared in two of the major squares (Al-Abbassia and Bab el-Hadid). Little corner mosques nestle on the first floors of many apartment buildings. Plaques with Koranic messages are hung in living rooms (overlooking French style furniture) and shops.

In a world where many countries have a similar experience to that of Egypt, an understanding of the role of materiality in recent history (the role of objects in cultural memory), and specifically the role of archaeological objects (monuments, ruins, relics and other traces) in the dynamics of self-identity, "nationalism," "ethnicity" and group affiliation is of the utmost importance if archaeology is to participate in the current transition to globality.

> The land of Egypt embraces all previous civilisations. Its sky is where humanity first perceived the presence of a creator god. History has not known any other nation that reached as much power and glory as Egypt achieved. It dyed all other elements by its own colour, and remained at first glance in possession of itself throughout history. Foreigners ruled Egypt, but Egypt always got rid of its foreign rulers. That Egypt always regains itself is now a historical norm. Egypt, as anyone can judge, will forever remain Egypt.
>
> (Mme Juliette Adam on the occasion of her return from a visit to Moustafa Kamil in Egypt in 1904, ten years after the British Occupation)

Bibliography

Abu Ghazi , Dia (1994) (in Arabic) *Al Mathal Moukhtar* (The Sculptor Moukhtar), Cairo: All-Hiya Al-Misryia lil-Kitab.

Al-Hakim, S. (1994) (in Arabic) *Misr Al-Pharo-Araobia* (Pharo-Arabian Egypt), Cairo: Marz Al-Hadara Al-Arabia lil-Ilam wal-Nashr.

Al-Katib, A. H. (1981) (in Arabic) *Misr wal-Misreen* (Egypt and the Egyptians), Cairo: Kitab el-Youm.

Atkinson, J. A., Banks, I. and O'Sullivan, J. (eds) (1996) *Nationalism and Archaeology: Scottish Archaeological Forum*, Glasgow: Cruithne Press.

Díaz Andreu, M. and Champion, T. (eds) (1996) *Nationalism and Archaeology in Europe*, London: University College London Press.

Fentress, J. and Wickham, C. (1988) *Social Memory*, Oxford: Blackwell.

Foad, N. A. (1978) (in Arabic) *Shakhsiat Misr* (The Personality of Egypt), Cairo: Al-Hiya Al-Misryia Al-Ama lil-Kitab.

Gathercole, P. and Lowenthal, D. (1990) 'The Politics of the Past', *One World Archaeology* 12, London: Routledge.

Gibrael, M. (1995) (in Arabic) *Qira'a fi Shakhsiayat Misryia* (A reading of Egyptian personalities), Cairo: General Authority of Cultural Centers.

Hamilakis, Y. (1996) "Through the looking glass: nationalism, archaeology and the politics of identity," *Antiquity* 70: 975–8.

Hamilakis, Y. and Yalouri, E. (1996) "Antiquities as symbolic capital in modern Greek society," *Antiquity* 70: 117–29.

Hill, J. D. (1992) "Contested pasts and the practice of anthropology," *American Anthropologist* 94, 4: 809–15.

Hussein, T. (1993) (orig. 1936) (in Arabic) *Mustaqbal Al-Thaqafa fi-Misr* (The Future of Culture in Egypt), Cairo: Al-Hiya Al-Misryia Al-Ama lil-Kitab.

Kohl, P. L. and Fawcett, C. (eds) (1995) *Nationalism, Politics, and the Practice of Archaeology*, Cambridge: Cambridge University Press.

Lewis, B. (1993) *Islam in History. Ideas, People, and Events in the Middle East*, Chicago: Open Court.

Mansfield, P. (1969) *Nasser's Egypt*, Harmondsworth: Penguin.

Marsot, A. L. A. (1985) *A Short History of Egypt*, Cambridge: Cambridge University Press.

Omara, M. (1987) (in Arabic) *Abu Ala Al-Maododi wa Al-Sahwa Al-Islamia* (Abu Ala Al-Maododi and the Islamic Awakening), Cairo: Dar El-Shorouk.

Pagden, A. (1995) "The effacement of difference: colonialism and the origins of Nationalism in Diderot and Herder," in G. Prakash (ed.) *After Colonialism: Imperial Histories and Postcolonial Displacements*, Princeton, NJ: Princeton University Press, pp. 129–52.

Prakash, G. (ed.) (1995) *After Colonialism: Imperial Histories and Postcolonial Displacements*, Princeton, NJ: Princeton University Press.

Qutb, S. (1993) (16th edn) (in Arabic) *Ma'lem 'ala Al-Tarik* (Signposts on the Road), Cairo: Dar el-Shrouq.

Raymond, A. (1993) *Le Caire*, Paris: Librairie Arthème Fayard.

Smith, A. D. (1986) *The Ethnic Origins of Nations*, Oxford: Blackwell.

Stewart, D. (1965) *Cairo*, S. Brunswick, NJ: A. S. Barnes and Co.

Tawfik, N. (1981) (in Arabic) *Moustafa Kamel*, Cairo: Kitab Al-Hillal.

Ucko, P. (1990) "Foreword," in P. Gathercole and D. Lowenthal (eds) *The Politics of the Past*, One World Archaeology 12, London: Routledge, pp. ix–xxi.

Waterbury, J. (1983) *The Egypt of Nasser and Sadaat*, Princeton, NJ: Princeton University Press.

Young, R. (1990) *White Mythologies: Writing History and the West*, London: Routledge.

Chapter 12

Ancient Egypt
in America
Claiming the
riches

Ann Macy Roth

From the decipherment of hieroglyphs down to the present day, Egyptologists have frequently been in the peculiar position of having to explain that their subject is *less* interesting than people think it is.

Antonio Loprieno 1996

Introduction

For more than three thousand years before the birth of Christ, on the banks of the Nile river in northeastern Africa there flourished a great civilisation. Its people composed love poetry, medical treatises, books of wise sayings, and instructions for the interpretation of dreams. They built monuments of stupendous size, great beauty and, more rarely, both. They developed complex conceptions of the divine and sophisticated answers to the eternal human questions about life and death. Their government revelled in red tape and bureaucratic tangles, while ordinary people complained about dishonest officials and excessive taxes. They traded extensively with foreigners, sometimes fought with them, and often ridiculed their peculiar appearance and odd customs.

This great civilisation has been claimed as an ancestor by many constituencies, in the past and in the present (see Hassan, Chapter 11). Greek authors cited it as the origin of many of their customs and beliefs. The Romans decorated their imperial city with its transplanted monuments. During the Renaissance, Europeans became fascinated with what they saw as its lost mystical knowledge. At the end of the eighteenth century, the Napoleonic expedition to Egypt resulted in a renewal of interest in Egyptian civilisation in France, and then in the rest of Europe. This interest soon spread to North America, which was eventually to become the site of one of the most complex and contested set of claims to the Egyptian past.

In the early nineteenth century, just as the first successful steps were being taken towards understand the Egyptian hieroglyphic writing system, the government of the newly independent United States of America was busy incorporating the mystical symbolism then associated with Egypt into its civic identity. The unfinished pyramid on the Great Seal (now to be seen on the back of every dollar bill) and, later, the obelisk chosen to honour President Washington were the most prominent of the Egyptian-inspired motifs that were used to express the pretensions and aspirations of the new state to the mystical wisdom of ancient Egypt. Unfortunately, at the same time that this symbolism was being invoked, the texts left by the Egyptians were proving not to contain the mystical wisdom and philosophical arguments that Classical authors had led the world to expect. The traditions preserved by the Masonic order and the Rosicrucians may have had roots in Egyptian culture (the enigmatic hieroglyphic writing of later periods, initiation traditions preserved in mortuary texts, and specialised taxonomic knowledge that supported religious authority); but the larger culture of ancient Egypt revealed itself to be far more accessible and prosaic than its popular reputation would have predicted.

The American spirit is tenacious of its myths, however, and the less fantastical reconstruction of Egyptian culture has, for over a century, fought an uphill battle against a plethora of competing visions. In architecture, fashion and home decoration Americans are exposed to Egyptian-inspired motifs, intended to conjure up exotic associations with luxury, sex, mystery and death. The figure of the bemused archaeologist discovering an Egyptian tomb or attacked by a vengeful mummy is a staple of the comic pages, and products from cigarettes to computers to pretzels are advertised using Pharaonic images. An Egyptian-themed gambling casino has recently opened in Las Vegas, Nevada, and civic celebrations, such as the annual spring festival in Memphis, Tennessee, have adopted Egyptian themes for their parade floats. Such claims upon the Egyptian past are largely harmless. But other American constituencies advocate reconstructions of ancient Egypt in the service of their own goals that seriously distort the Egyptian past.

American Egyptologists are probably the smallest of three segments of the American population with an interest in propagating a vision of Egypt's past. The adherents of the mystical, symbolic beliefs of the Masons and Rosicrucians, which date back to the seventeenth century and perhaps further, have been joined by the more numerous disciples of various New Age religions, heavily steeped in pseudo-Egyptian mysticism. A third American claimant for the Egyptian past is the Afro-centric movement which has almost as many variants as the New Age religions, but which in most cases finds cause for African-American pride in the achievements of early Egyptian culture.

Mystical claims

The most evocative and exotic claims upon the Egyptian past are the popular excursions into imagined Egyptian mystical religions, which rarely have much relation to the beliefs of the ancient Egyptians themselves. The traditions of the Masons and the Rosicrucians are, at the very least, greatly modified from whatever ancient Egyptian antecedents they once had. But many newer traditions have developed with even less dependence on authenticity or evidence. These newer reconstructions tend to be far removed from anything the ancient Egyptians would have believed. That ancient Egyptians, dead for thousands of years, could put effective and horrible curses on anyone who disturbed their mummies or tomb equipment is implicitly believed by a surprising number of people, many of whom are extremely sceptical about other forms of supernatural intervention in human affairs. Seemingly hundreds of Americans claim to have been Egyptian royalty (usually famous Egyptian royalty) in their previous lives – few ancient Egyptian peasants seem to have been resurrected as Americans. Curiously, the ancient Egyptians themselves did not believe in earthly resurrection and their posthumous curses tended to be legalistic rather than melodramatic; but adherents of these Egypto-mystic beliefs have no reason (or desire) to be aware of these historical facts. They prefer to impose their beliefs or wishes upon the Egyptian past, thereby associating this evocative and ancient tradition with their own goals.

Pyramids are the focus of many such impositions. Some Americans claim that the Egyptians built the pyramids by a lost science of levitation. Many theories surrounding these monuments are based upon the claims of the British pyramid-fancier C. Piazzi Smyth (1864), whose theories about the predictive power of the Great Pyramid were intended to prove that English units of measurement were divinely ordained and to prevent England from adopting the metric system. During the 1970s, the pyramid shape was believed by many people to be magically effective in attaining everything from more effective meditation to sharper razor blades and longer-lasting fresh fruit. Although this particular fad seems to have been superseded by others, Americans continued to be fascinated by things Egyptian, and to attribute to the Egyptians still undiscovered and unequalled powers and abilities.

Another type of misinformation about Egypt that has captured the American imagination is the claim that the pyramids and other icons of Egyptian culture were not built by the ancient Egyptians at all, but by "ancient astronauts," as Däniken (1970) argued or, as Hancock (1995) has recently proposed, by refugees from a lost, highly technological civilisation that once flourished in Antarctica. As Feder (1990: 158–9) has pointed out, such theories of extra-terrestrial intervention are inherently racist, since they are almost always used to explain constructions found in Third World countries, and are built on the unspoken assumption that the indigenous inhabitants would be incapable of having produced such things themselves. Extraordinary migrations are never thought necessary to explain Greek temples, monumental Neolithic tombs in Europe or the medieval European cathedrals. Only the achievements of darker skinned non-Europeans need to be attributed to extraterrestrial assistance. Nonetheless, these claims continue to attract the American imagination, as testified by the recent film *Stargate*, in which a race of immortal "gods" from another planet are said to have forced the primitive Egyptians to build the pyramids as part of a giant teleporter.

Mystical alternate versions of ancient Egypt are hardly limited to American culture, of course, and many of the most popular of these fantasies were first conceived in other countries. However, the American situation is exacerbated by the way that these theories reinforce American cultural assumptions, and the consequent commercial value to the media in propagating them. The American fascination with imagined Egypts that cannot be defended on the surviving evidence has not been lost on the American entertainment industry. The various cinematic lives of Cleopatra, Biblical epics, multitudinous films recording *The Mummy* and his various family members, adventure movies of the "Indiana Jones" ilk, and the more arcane dramas of *The Awakening* and *Stargate*: with all these Hollywood has demonstrated a voracious appetite for Egyptian themes, generally the further from the accepted scholarly reconstruction, the better.

More dangerous still, because allegedly educational, is the increasing number of television programs about Egypt made to fill the ever-expanding number of cable channels, part of a new commodity often referred to as 'info-tainment.' Although such programs are in many cases produced by well-intentioned organisations, their sources are rarely Egyptologists. It is difficult, with so many people who claim to speak authoritatively about ancient Egypt, for people outside the academy to know whom to believe. This is even more true of audiences, who tend to assume that anything they see on television is well supported by the evidence. An example is J. A. West, whose guidebook to Egypt (1985: 482) identifies him as "an independent Egyptologist" who has "spent fifteen years studying and writing about ancient Egypt." West is a follower of the symbolic and mathematical interpretations of R. A. Schwaller de Lubicz and Lucy Lamy, and apparently has no academic training in Egyptology; yet he claims, backed by a scientist from Boston

University, that the Sphinx has been damaged by water erosion, and thus was built before the Sahara became a desert (ignoring 4,500 years of occasional rainstorms and the effects of the ensuing flash floods on a monument that is built in a hole at the foot of the Giza plateau). This claim was the basis of an adulatory television program, which was narrated by Charlton Heston (implying the higher authority of Moses himself), and which won an Emmy award as a documentary.

Such television programs often depict professional Egyptologists as rigid conservatives, blind to the wonders of simple, non-scholarly "common sense" logic. They are consulted only to act as a foil to the iconoclasm and irreverence of the insightful amateur and his exciting contention that everything we think we know is wrong. They defend traditional (therefore boring) interpretations and object impotently to the selected bits of evidence cited that distort the overall picture. But to refute such theories, one must give listeners the true context for each misleading bit of evidence cited, so that they can see either that it is exceptional, violating a far more prevalent pattern, or that it can be explained more simply in terms of the other evidence. This sort of extensive background can only be presented properly when one has the attention of an audience and it is not well suited to the minute-long sound-bites that scholars are expected to produce in such circumstances. Simple ideas, based on just a few facts, are easier to communicate, however unjustified they may prove to be.

In addition to the logistical difficulties of explaining complicated circumstances within a televised format, there is a further difficulty in that television thrives on conflict. Arguments make for good television, and the audience is often less interested in the difference between the pictures of the past being presented than it is in the conflict between the proponents of each version. The advocates come to personify their positions, and these personifications take on an archetypal character. The moderator of the discussion, or the editor of the documentary, tends to enhance this conflict and the audience's sympathy by presenting the combatants as equals in terms of scholarship. The renegade self-taught Egyptologist, it is stressed, has spent many years studying this problem and made many trips to Egypt to verify his findings, while the professional's training is not mentioned: only his institutional affiliation is given, to demonstrate his attachment to the status quo. The difference between the combatants in knowledge or training is ignored in the name of "fairness," so that the only evident contrast is in their open-mindedness: the stubborn "traditional" scholar appears to ignore the possibility that the ideas of someone outside the closed guild of his or her academic field could be correct. The sympathy of the audience is, of course, with the challenger.

This emphasis on conflict is not limited to superficial presentations of Egyptology. It can also be seen in programs that present understandings of the evidence soundly based upon academic theories. The program *This Old Pyramid*, part of the Nova series funded by the American Public Broadcasting Service, was an investigation into various theories about pyramid construction that filmed a useful exercise in experimental archaeology: an attempt to build a small pyramid using ancient methods. Nonetheless, it was felt necessary to bring in untenable theories and their proponents (for example, the proposal that the pyramids were constructed of a concrete-like substance, poured in place, based on a misinterpretation of the nummulitic shells and other inclusions in the limestone.) Apparently it was thought worthwhile to present such ideas because the conflict of opinions about them created a dramatic interest.

In addition to their predilection for conflict and for simplistic theories that explain many disparate phenomena, these television programs have a third, more subtle bias: they play upon the anti-intellectual tendencies of American society. Americans have always favoured "simple, common sense" ideas, associated with the hardy frontiersmen and women. By contrast, the views of "pointy-headed" intellectuals connected with scholarly institutions are associated with the élitism of the European class system, with their consequent moral decadence and their sheltered "ivory tower" oblivion to the realities of life. To hold a doctorate in an arcane subject such as Egyptology predisposes an American audience to expect a close-minded, élitist viewpoint. When Egyptologists are asked to comment on wildly imaginative or blatantly wrong reconstructions of the Egyptian past, they fulfil this audience's expectations by finding fault with it. There is no need to discuss the evidence; the dramatic necessities of the form are satisfied simply by the presentation of an obstruction that creates a conflict and converts the theorist into the valiant independent-minded underdog.

The result of these factors is a very favourable climate for the publication and broadcasting of other claims to Egypt. As more and more of these flawed or fictionalised programs are produced, broadcast, and re-broadcast repeatedly, the public scepticism about the validity of unspectacular reconstructions based on a full understanding of the evidence, and their hostility to the academic field that produces them, can only increase. Ironically, the academic field of Egyptology is increasingly being marginalised by the very popularity of its subject matter.

Afrocentric claims

An interesting commonality of methods can be seen between the iconoclastic mystical claims about ancient Egypt and the public manifestations of the movement known generally as "Afrocentrism." As with the adherents of Egypto-mysticism, this movement benefits from the public's – and hence the media's – attraction to simple "everything-you-know-is-wrong" hypotheses supported by minimal evidence, and to a conflict between tradition and "innovative" ideas. However, the motivations and goals of the Afrocentric movement are different;

and although the two groups of Egypt-enthusiasts are sometime allied, ultimately their views are incompatible.

The American manifestation of the Afrocentric movement is closely based on the association of African-Americans with Egypt's Pharaonic past. (There are other kinds of Afrocentrism, as Adams (1993) has pointed out, but what he calls "Nile Valley Afrocentrism" seems to be the most popular.) It combines a traditional African-American identification with the glories of Egypt that dates back to the early twentieth century writings of Marcus Garvey and the arguments of the late Senegalese scholar, Cheik Anta Diop. More recently, it has incorporated the conclusions of Martin Bernal to support the earlier assertions of James that ancient Greek culture, and particularly its philosophy, originated in Egypt.

American Afrocentrists vary in their claims, but five general principles can be identified that figure in most of their formulations. These principles, which I have discussed in detail elsewhere (Roth 1995), are (1) that the ancient Egyptians were black; (2) that ancient Egyptian civilisation achieved greater things than is generally believed; (3) that ancient Egyptian civilisation had a greater influence on Greek and Roman civilisation than is generally believed; (4) that ancient Egyptian civilisation originated south of its Pharaonic territory and maintained and extended those contacts so that all African cultures are related to it; and (5) that Egyptologists, as participants in a Eurocentric field, have conspired to hide all this from public knowledge.

The movement's underlying claims are inarguably correct: Egypt is located on the African continent, and its people are therefore, by definition, Africans and the Pharaonic culture was, by definition, an African culture. Whether Egyptians (ancient or modern) can be called "black" depends on modern social definitions; but given the large range of skin colours and physical features of self-identified black Americans, it is not unreasonable to say that many, though not all, ancient Egyptians would have been categorised as black by modern Americans, compared with the modern American population. On the other hand, in the modern Egyptian view, compared with the modern Egyptian population, far fewer ancient Egyptians would have been categorised as black, simply because modern Egyptians have a different frame of reference. And in their own culture, of course, the ancient Egyptians would not have been categorised at all, since we have no evidence that they made such "racial" discriminations. Whether or not the Egyptians were "black" is thus a social judgement and varies from society to society.

Even the category of "African" is inappropriate within the indigenous ancient Egyptian framework, since the ancient Egyptians were unaware of the geographical divisions that seem so "natural" to us: various barriers, ranging from sea to desert to rapids, separated them from surrounding peoples and we have no evidence that they felt closer to any one group of foreigners than to the others. These claims of an African-American affinity with ancient Egyptians based on their similar ranges of skin colour (and to some extent features) are well justified only in the context of a modern political statement countering the racist claim that "black" people or "African" people have never achieved a great civilisation.

The next three claims, in contrast, would greatly affect our conception of the history and interrelations of cultures in the ancient world if they could be proven. The attribution to the Egyptians of greater technological and intellectual achievements, of a greater influence on Greek civilisation, and of closer connections with other early African societies would radically alter the way not only African-Americans, but Europeans and Americans of European descent view their cultural heritage. These questions, unlike those of race, are interesting scholarly questions, and are being investigated by traditional scholars and Afrocentrists alike. The questions asked by the Afrocentric movement have, to a certain extent, stimulated Egyptologists and other scholars studying the ancient world to take a wider view and to back down from the extreme anti-diffusionist positions of the middle twentieth century (which were in turn a reaction to the extreme diffusionist views of the early twentieth century, which are often quoted by Afrocentrists).

It is in the area of Egyptian achievements that the Afrocentrists come closest to the Egypto-mystics. Both groups tend to glorify Egyptian achievements, in both the technological and intellectual spheres, and hope to show that the Egyptians had greater knowledge and skills than has been acknowledged by Egyptologists. The arguments of both groups for such achievements generally come from misunderstandings of the evidence, or from the hyperbolic accounts of Greek and Roman writers, or from selective citation of scholarly or popular sources (usually dating to the earliest decades of Egyptology or even before) that are not generally accepted by the Egyptological community.

Many Egypto-mystics and the Afrocentrists will ultimately come to a parting of the ways, of course, because the mystics so often attribute Egyptian achievements to non-Africans (e.g. men from Mars or Atlantis). Those claiming an extra-terrestrial origin for Egyptian civilisation are, of course, more racist even than Afrocentrists claim Egyptologists are, since their theories clearly imply their assumption that such a civilisation could not have come into being among the indigenous Egyptian people without outside help.

One difference between the two groups is that the Afrocentrists usually support their ideas by citing scholarly authorities, whereas the Egypto-mystics tend to support their claims with imaginative and usually culture-bound interpretations of primary sources. While primary sources are, of course, more authoritative than the opinions of scholars, they are also more ambiguous, and are liable to misunderstanding or misrepresentation by people without a more general knowledge of the patterns in the evidence. Because scholarly sources usually lead back to the primary evidence, Afrocentrists are often better grounded than the mystics in the culture as a whole, as the mystics tend to focus on only a few types of evidence.

Unfortunately, most Afrocentric claims about Egyptian achievements are based not on recent Egyptological research, but on the work of far earlier scholars. Because the more recent sources are not easily available, or have not been translated, Afrocentrists tend to use the outdated reprint editions of popular works written in the early parts of this century, particularly the works of E. A. Wallis Budge. These sources often present speculative conclusions that are no longer tenable, and professional Egyptologists tend to dismiss contentions that are based upon the assertions of these authors. At the same time, the use of older sources allows Afrocentrists to claim that Egyptologists are predominantly racist (since many of these earlier authors unthinkingly express the racist assumptions of their time.) Their lack of understanding about the present directions of the field also leads them to make general statements about the field that Egyptologists know not to be true, for example the repeated assertion that most Egyptologists believe that Egyptian civilisation was brought into Egypt by a Dynastic Race, a long discarded theory (Yurco 1996: 65–8).

This leads to the final claim of many Afrocentrists, that Egyptologists of European ancestry have purposely misrepresented Egypt's past out of racial chauvinism and a determination to belittle the heritage of people of African ancestry. While this claim is highly exaggerated, it is not without a certain truth, at least historically. Most Egyptologists have been Europeans or Americans of European descent, and as such have in many cases unconsciously imbibed a low opinion of non-Europeans as part of their cultural background. Only in recent decades has the racism of this assumption been widely acknowledged and condemned and it is quite likely that many of the unquestioned conclusions of earlier scholars have been to some extent distorted by these assumptions. Egyptologists would do well to identify such conclusions and revise them accordingly.

Nonetheless, many of the claims made by Afrocentrists about racism in the field are not true. Perhaps the most prevalent, the claim that Napoleon's troops shot the nose off the Sphinx at Giza in order to hide the African appearance of the face, is simply not tenable. There is clear textual evidence that the damage to the face of the Sphinx was done in 1378 AD, by a religious Muslim who feared that it was the object of improper worship (Haarmann 1980). In addition to the discussion of this incident by several medieval historians such as Makrizi, representations of the Sphinx before the arrival of Napoleon show that the damage was already done. Moreover, Napoleon's alleged motive makes no sense. There are many pieces of statuary in Egypt with 'African' noses; surely knocking off one of them would be futile. Since the Napoleonic expedition was in many ways the impetus for the beginning of the modern scholarly field of Egyptology, the story symbolically serves to indicate the distrust Afrocentrists feel for Egyptological research.

Another problem between Egyptologists and Afrocentrists arises in the area of Egyptian morality. Afrocentrists attribute to the ancient Egyptians a more highly developed moral system than other early cultures and many later ones as well. These claims are based on texts such as wisdom instructions, and the "negative confession" of Chapter 125 of the Book of the Dead. However, such claims are often broader than the evidence will bear. Even a scholar so well versed in Egyptology as Maulana Karenga (1996) can be misled by these assumptions, as when he claims that the ancient Egyptians saw capital punishment as morally wrong. He cites as evidence the papyrus Westcar story, in which the magician Djedi objects to the king's order that a condemned prisoner be used to test Djedi's ability to reattach a severed head. In fact, Djedi is not objecting to capital punishment *per se*, but only to the use of the prisoner's death as an occasion for magical entertainment. Moreover, the executions that accompany a "happy ending" elsewhere in the same text make it very clear that the story's author did not oppose the death sentence. Because we may find capital punishment immoral, many Afrocentrists would like to show that the ancient Egyptians did too. Attempting to fit ancient Egyptian morality into a modern, liberal Western mould distorts the picture, and prevents us from finding out what ancient Egyptians really believed.

Such attempts to make the Egyptians moral (according to modern Western standards) can also be seen in the distaste that is expressed by some Afrocentrists when Egyptian sources reveal behaviours that we would not approve today. In archaeology classes, I have had students object vociferously to the presentation of evidence for human sacrifice surrounding royal and élite burials of the First Dynasty. They have no evidence for this objection, other than the suspicion that it is a plot to make the ancient Egyptians look bad, and their conviction that "the Egyptians could not have done such a thing." Similar objections are made to the episode in the "Contendings of Horus and Seth" in which Seth attempts to sodomise Horus. I was in one case asked whether I was claiming that the ancient Egyptians were "gay" and, when I referred the student back to the text itself, he expressed grave doubts about the accuracy of the translation. Such firmly held assumptions that the moral structures of ancient Egyptian civilisation are in all ways admirable and worthy of emulation show a lack of the critical adherence to the evidence that is necessary for an accurate reconstruction of the past. If Afrocentrism is to succeed as a scholarly approach, it must take a critical, scholarly view of its conclusions, rather than assuming them at the outset.

Egyptological claims

There is a third group of Americans that claims some authority for its reconstruction of the ancient Egyptian past. The United States has an active community of professional Egyptologists who work in its major museum collections of Egyptian antiquities and who teach in its nine graduate programs in Egyptology (at Berkeley, Brown, Chicago, Johns Hopkins, Memphis State, New York University, UCLA, University of Pennsylvania and Yale.) This is a small number of programs, compared to the proportionate number supported by smaller European countries, and it is notable that several major universities have no Egyptologists at all. While courses on Egypt are taught by Egyptologists (and, more often, non-Egyptologists) at other colleges and universities, it is remarkable that the field in which there is so much popular interest is so little represented by programs of study. The rather marginal role played by Egyptology in American academia is perhaps not unrelated to the direction that the public fascination with the subject has taken.

How do American Egyptologists react to the competing claims of non-professionals to have "more interesting" truths to communicate about ancient Egypt? Most would say that they ignore such claims and, to some extent, that is true. Books and films by non-professionals are rarely reviewed in professional journals, and their proponents only rarely attend professional conferences. Afro-centric and mystical views are rarely introduced in academic courses on Egypt, unless they are raised as questions by the students, and in such cases professors usually dismiss them as quickly as possible. The academic field of Egyptology sees itself as above the fray of the popular claims about ancient Egypt, patiently conducting its research without reference to them.

In fact, some recent trends in American Egyptology can be seen in part as a reaction to the adherents of a mystic vision and the increasingly vocal claims of Afrocentrists. There has been, since the middle of the century, an increasing retreat into the arcane in American Egyptology. No longer are overarching, synthetic histories written for popular audiences by the best and most senior scholars in the field. Instead, the field as a whole has encouraged specialisation, and specialisation in the areas of least general interest to the general public, such as the nuances of Egyptian grammar, particularly in the late and non-monumental phases of the language, such as Late Egyptian, Demotic and Coptic. Such specialisation is commonplace in other fields as well, of course, but in Egyptology there seems to be a special incentive to focus on areas that are inaccessible to amateurs.

Archaeology, as compared to the philological specialties, necessarily remains somewhat more accessible and interesting to the non-specialist because field research can only be funded by appealing to the larger community, either in applications for grants or appeals for private sponsorship. Nonetheless, the increasing movement away from mortuary sites and towards detailed scientific analysis of settlement materials, and particularly the claim that Egypt is simply being used as a test case to test more general anthropological hypotheses (a holdover from the New Archaeology that has only comparatively recently reached Egyptology) shows that here, also, Egyptologists are attempting to differentiate themselves from non-professionals, cutting themselves off from the need to deal with the adherents of mystical or Afrocentric approaches to the subject of Egypt's past. This preference for narrow specialisations may hide us from the eyes of Afrocentrists and Egypto-mystics, but it also hides the value of our work from those in other academic fields and disciplines (linguistics, anthropology, and the like) and prevents us from playing the larger roles in the academic dialogues of our day that our subject matter should justify.

In fact, what truly differentiates most professional Egyptologists from Egypto-mystics and Afrocentrists is not our special technical skills, which can be duplicated by amateurs, but our attempts to be critical in outlook. Even our knowledge of the evidence is less important than our ability to put it into perspective and see patterns in it. This difference is particularly apparent when one looks at the work of Martin Bernal (1987, 1991). Bernal is a scholar, and presumably adopts a scholarly, critical attitude within his professional research; he clearly also has a great deal of detailed knowledge of ancient Egypt and other ancient cultures. But myriad footnotes do not in themselves constitute scholarship. Bernal focuses only on the isolated facts and pieces of evidence that support his predetermined hypotheses, rather than drawing hypotheses from the broad universe of all the data by finding consistent patterns in it. He does not consider alternative explanations for his data that might disprove his hypotheses; he does not honestly confront the possibility that his hypothesis might be wrong and look for evidence that would disprove it. In this, he resembles the adherents of a mystical Egyptian past and also many Afrocentrists. Such a procedure privileges the preconceived conclusions over the evidence left us by the ancient Egyptians themselves, and shows a great disrespect for the past it pretends to reconstruct. The ancient Egyptians deserve more than to serve as pawns in a modern chess game – they deserve the respect of a genuine inquiry into their history and culture for its own sake, as free from prejudice and predetermined notions as possible.

The task of Egyptologists, if we want to show that sort of respect to the past and to defend the validity of our field, is two-fold. First, we must attempt in our own research to be as "objective" as possible, to recognise and excise the distortions caused by our Eurocentric history, and to be open to alternate interpretations if they seem to fit the pattern of the evidence. Second, we must stop avoiding the alternative versions of the Egyptian past that are being propagated, and begin to engage them. We must learn to explain not only where the errors lie but also how we arrive at our conclusions, making the process of historical scholarship clearer. We must learn to communicate the excitement of our own engagement with the evidence to others, and justify the areas where we believe research needs to be done. We and our professional organisations must object to falsehoods and distortions of the Egyptian evidence. The results of such a program would be a better Egyptology, one that is a responsible reconstruction of the past and one that is more vital and engaged with the larger culture that supports it.

Bibliography

Adams, R. (1993) "African-American Studies and the State of the Art," in M. Azevdo (ed.) *Africana Studies: A Survey of Africa and the African Diaspora*, Durham, NC: Carolina Academic Press, 25–45.

Bernal, M. (1987) *Black Athena: The Afroasiatic Roots of Classical Civilization*, volume 1, New Brunswick, NJ: Rutgers.

—— (1991) *Black Athena: The Afroasiatic Roots of Classical Civilization*, volume 2, New Brunswick, NJ: Rutgers.

Däniken, E. von (1970) *Chariots of the Gods*, New York: Bantam.

Feder, K. L. (1990) *Frauds, Myths, and Mysteries: Science and Pseudoscience in Archaeology*, London: Mayfield.

Haarmann, U. (1980) "Regional Sentiment in Medieval Islamic Egypt," *Bulletin of the School of Oriental and African Studies* 43: 55–66.

Hancock, G. (1995) *Fingerprints of the Gods: A Quest for the Beginning and the End*, London: Heinemann.

Karenga, M. (1996) "The Maatian Concept of Human Dignity: A Passage from the Narrative of Djedi," paper delivered at the St Louis meetings of the American Research Center in Egypt, St Louis, MO (*Abstracts*, p. 5).

Loprieno, A. (1996) Talk presented at Debating Afrocentrism in the Academy, a conference held at Johns Hopkins University, 2 November.

Roth, A. (1995) "Building Bridges to Afrocentrism: A Letter to my Egyptological Colleagues," *Newsletter of the American Research Center in Egypt* 167–8 (September and December), and republished (1996) in "The Flight from Science and Reason" in P. R. Gross *et al.* (eds), *Annals of the New York Academy of Sciences* 775: 313–26.

Smyth, C. Piazzi (1864) *Our Inheritance in the Great Pyramid*, London: A. Strahan.

West, J. A. (1985) *The Traveler's Key to Ancient Egypt: A Guide to the Sacred Places of Ancient Egypt*, New York: Knopf.

Yurco, F. (1996) "Black Athena: an Egyptological Review," in M. R. Lefkowitz and G. Rogers (eds) *Black Athena Revisited*, Chapel Hill: University of North Carolina Press, pp. 62–100.

Index

continuing death and rebirth of 185–6; the genesis of 178–81

American Board of Commissioners for Foreign Missions (ABCFM) 179, 180

'American Palestine Exploration Society' 179

American Public Broadcasting Service 221

American School of Oriental Research, Jerusalem 181, 183, 184

American Schools of Oriental Research (ASOR) 175–6, 177, 178, 181–6

Amman 176, 184

Ammathus 15

Anagnostou, I. 60n

Anatolia 19, 112, 116, 117, 120, 138

Anatomically Modern Humans 87, 100

'ancient astronauts' 220

Andah, B. W. 17

Anderson, Benedict 3, 8, 45, 50, 51, 57, 72

Anderson, Perry 71

Andreou, S. 47, 61n

Andronikos, Manolis 53

Ani, Turkey 120

Ankara 129

Annales school 71

Al-Ansary, A. R. 197

Antarctica 220

anthropology 5, 6, 7, 57, 58, 154, 160, 176; social-functionalist 178

anti-consumerism 127

antiquarianism 29, 178

antiquities: Byzantine 115; destruction and illicit trade in 13, 16, 18, 24–9; Egyptian 115; Hellenistic-Roman 115; Mesopotamian 170; Near Eastern 115; Ottoman prohibitions on exports 115; Turkey accused of 'selective destruction' 119; Turkey's rich and diverse antiquities 128

Antiquities Law (Cyprus) (1935) 30

Antoniadou, Sophia 2, 5, 7, 161

Appadurai, Arjun 8, 72

Arab conquest 211

Arab Republic of Egypt (ARE) 210

Arab-Israeli War (1967) 183, 184

Arabia 190, 191, 196

Arabian American Oil Company (ARAMCO) 191

Arabian Peninsula 209

Arabism 209

'Arabs' 146, 148, 149

Arabs: in the Gulf Arab states 195; at the Tell Beit Mirsim site 183; and Turks 112, 121

ARAMCO *see* Arabian American Oil Company

Archaeological Institute and Museum (AIM) 93, 96, 104n

Archaeological Institute, Sofia 96, 102, 105n

archaeological record: deliberate distortion of 17; misinterpretation for political ends 17

archaeological sites: presentation as cultural attractions 33

archaeological theorising: focus on Europe and the Americas 2; stemming from Anglo-American institutions 2

archaeological theory, developments in 7

archaeology: Aegean 51; American biblical *see* American biblical archaeology; anthropological 59; biblical 15; birth as a discipline 2; boycotting of South African archaeology 7; Bulgarian *see* Bulgarian archaeology; Byzantine 48, 52; classical 15, 46, 47, 52, 58, 59, 192; colonial 30–1; current fascination with 201; as defence 53–5; defined 111; effective and politicised stance 7; emotional power 9; European evolutionary 15; experimental 222; feminist 6; global 5, 186; Greek 44, 48, 51, 52; as history of art 46; as history writing 156; increasing involvement with national politics 74; Kurdish 120; of landscape 58; Mesopotamian 160, 166, 167, 168; Middle Eastern 177; military origins of modern archaeology 27; and nationalism 9, 13, 58, 59, 201; nationalistic 9, 17; Near Eastern 167, 191–2; political role 13; the politics of 15, 16–18, 29–32; and politics *see under* individual countries; postcolonial 6, 31–2; postprocessual 6–7, 10, 17; processualist 98; Southeastern